THE FINANCIAL BEHAVIOR OF JAPANESE CORPORATIONS

THE FINANCIAL BEHAVIOR OF JAPANESE CORPORATIONS

Robert J. Ballon & Iwao Tomita

KODANSHA INTERNATIONAL
Tokyo and New York

Book design: Polly Christensen
Composition: G & S Typesetters, Inc.

Distributed in the United States by Kodansha International/USA Ltd.,
through Harper & Row, Publishers, Inc., 10 East 53rd Street, New
York, New York 10022. Published by Kodansha International Ltd.,
2–2 Otowa 1-chome, Bunkyo-ku, Tokyo 112 and Kodansha Interna-
tional/USA Ltd., 10 East 53rd Street, New York, New York 10022.

Library of Congress Cataloging-in-Publication Data

Ballon, Robert J.
    The financial behavior of Japanese corporations.

    Bibliography: p.
    Includes index.
    1. Corporations—Japan—Finance.   I. Tomita, Iwao,
1924–   . II. Title.
HG4245.B35   1988   658.1′5   88-80135
ISBN 0-87011-901-X (Kodansha International/USA)
ISBN 4-7700-1401-5 (in Japan)

CONTENTS

TABLES

INTRODUCTION

THE TRADITIONAL PICTURE of Japanese corporate finance is
one in which leverage and large interest payments reduce earnings and
banks are relied on excessively for operating as well as investment capital.
Such was the case as long as growth was outpacing capital accumulation.
With slower economic growth following the first oil crisis (1973), the
business environment changed drastically in many areas, including financial management. The sharp appreciation of the yen in the mid-1980s
added considerable pressure to the changes that steady deregulation of
capital markets was already forcing on financial and industrial institutions. In the process of adjusting to economic change, the financial behavior of Japanese corporations matured. They are ready to face the
future—however uncertain it may be—with a stronger will than ever to
assure corporate survival in the context of a restructuring of the economy
and of business. Thus, the timid are encouraged and the bold confident
that the means are available to finance both innovation and adaptation.

The challenge of Japanese business to Western corporations has grown
in intensity. More than ever corporate presence on the homeground of
Japanese competitors requires careful planning and expensive investment. A marketing presence is required to face the fierce competition
prevailing in the Japanese domestic market. A manufacturing presence is
required to match the local demand for quality and adaptation. A research and development presence is required to participate in the technological drive of Japanese competitors. Today, a financial presence is
required as well to tap local opportunities and further demonstrate corporate commitment. All this is demanded of the expatriate executive or
his Japanese counterpart in terms and conditions that change by the day,
if not by the hour.

Western views of business in and with Japan are not without merit, but
Japanese views are equally legitimate. "Foreign" business in Japan may

enjoy some owner-specific advantages; nonetheless it must operate in an industrial environment that is often unfamiliar and to which non-Japanese assumptions must not be applied hastily. Just as current Western assumptions about the ways to do business are the result of the elaboration over time of values and practices, Japanese corporate values and practices are also evolving. Experiences of the past, for better or for worse, guide and support actions in the present.

For non-Japanese corporations operating in Japan, the challenge is to perceive Japan in "Japanese" terms. The words found in English-Japanese and Japanese-English dictionaries must be understood in terms of the actions expressed by these words, if the words are to be of practical relevance. Rather than simply to cloak a Japanese experience in a term expressing a foreign experience, it is necessary to trace the origin and evolution of the terms, even English terms, used by the Japanese. The term "corporation" itself results from Western experience and has been applied without further ado to the Japanese experience. In a remarkable recent analysis of the Japanese corporation, the authors preferred the Japanese term *kaisha* to the term "corporation" because it forced a contrast of the Japanese entity with the Western "corporation" (Abegglen and Stalk 1985). In the same vein, financial and accounting terminology is of Western origin, the product of a specific historical evolution. From the late nineteenth century on and today more than ever, this terminology has been a Western import into Japan, where it soon starts to reflect in actual usage the historical behavior of Japanese companies themselves. Western terminology has not "Westernized" Japanese financial behavior, but it certainly has "modernized" it.

What is "Japanese" about Japan's financial behavior? It is universal business behavior, for sure, but with an explicit twist: a keen awareness of the imperative of *survival* in a constantly changing environment. The Japanese concern about survival often puzzles Westerners, who tend to speak of survival only when circumstances indicate a definite danger of death for the individual concerned. The Western interpretation implies a bad omen, and thus it is shunned in the business context, except for stating that "the company did *not* survive." To the Japanese, the only way to survive is to have been alive yesterday and stay alive today. Survival is not a matter for tomorrow; it is the result of the past and the problem of the present. And, by the way, the Japanese appear to be good at survival, as Japan, its society and economy, has been working at it for many more centuries than its Western counterparts!

Corporate survival takes on the immediacy of the present and becomes the basic pattern of behavior. It determines how the Japanese look at their corporations and how they act in the corporate context. Practically, it means corporate growth or, as forcefully stated by Abegglen: "Be better, not behind. If not better, be different." Thus, any concern about the future is inevitably overwhelmed by the imperatives of the present. In this volume, an attempt is made to learn from the past to better understand and handle the present.

Such was also the purpose of our previous book, *Financial Reporting in Japan* (1976), in which we looked at Japanese corporate financing in the light of the high growth of the 1950s and 1960s that came to a halt in 1973. The 1970s and 1980s have witnessed no less drastic changes. If Japanese corporations were good at handling fast growth, they are apparently no less adept at handling slow growth—and not because the latter is less traumatic! We believe that the framework of the previous book still holds, but the contents have to be brought forward into the present. Our intention is to describe the Japanese corporation's financial behavior in a "hands-on" fashion by looking at how management perceives and handles the financial dimension of corporate activities.

Part 1 describes the peculiar environment in which Japanese enterprises operate. Corporate interdependence is a deep-rooted value that finds its expression in social, and no less in economic, behavior. It determines how the institutional participants in Japan's industrial society interact at the macro and micro levels. It is the fabric of industrial Japan and is manifest in the constant interaction between government authorities and business organizations, among companies, and within companies themselves. A major instance of this interaction has been stable shareholding. Corporate interdependence, however, does not preclude business failure.

Part 2 focuses on corporate financing. Slower economic growth, access to international financial markets, and deepening exposure of domestic financial markets to foreign influence are making obsolete the traditional postwar view that high debt was the price to be paid for rapid growth. Japanese corporations are fast gaining financial sophistication, and indirect financing (bank loans) is being replaced by direct financing (shares and bonds).

Part 3 is concerned with accountants and auditors. The corporate financial function is an abstraction; the employees involved are the reality, and they remain Japanese in their behavior. The so-called internationalization of the financial markets appears to have outpaced that of the corporate financial officers and their subordinates. Independent auditing of corporate books would help bring the Japanese financial function into line with international practice, but certified public accountants (CPAs) number no more than a few thousand.

Part 4 addresses the foreign reader of Japanese financial statements. It reviews financial reporting in its major forms, as elaborated by legislation and practice, and describes the major peculiarities to be kept in mind.

The authors remain painfully aware throughout this volume that numerical data are out of date the very moment they are formulated and become more so by the time they are used. Such is the price we pay for an ever changing present. Our hope, nonetheless, is that our analysis will benefit two audiences, communications with whom are all too often at cross purposes. One is the expatriate executive who put his career on the line when he accepted a transfer to Japan and who may have become terribly frustrated by discovering every day some other aspect of Japanese business he had not been aware of or to which his attention has not been drawn by his Japanese colleagues. The other audience is the Japanese executive who, not without diffidence, tries to explain his own behavior and thus improve the climate of international business where it has been perturbed by Japanese inroads. He may also have become frustrated when what he says apparently has been misunderstood (due to ignorance) or misinterpreted (due to prejudice) by his non-Japanese interlocutors. Our analysis assumes that in order to know where Japanese companies are going, it is more enlightening to know where they come from than merely to use a foreign standard!

Our work has greatly benefited from the generous help of Koji Tajika and the staff of the Tohmatsu Awoki & Sanwa Audit Corporation (Tokyo), who provided much of the technical input. Jeff Char helped greatly in surveying the background for Part 2. Our very special thanks go to Dr. James C. Abegglen, who read the manuscript and provided insightful comments, although our views did not always converge.

This book is dedicated to the memory of a coauthor of our previous book, Hajime Usami.

ONE

CORPORATE INTERDEPENDENCE

1

CORPORATIONS IN JAPAN

MORE THAN A CENTURY AGO, when the Meiji government (1868–1912) set a new national and international course for Japan, no one could have expected a quick rise of either military or economic power. Yet "the spirit of the samurai and the ability of the merchant" (*shikon shōsai*), each sponsored in its own way by the new central government, combined to originate a dynamic industrial state. Contrary to Western experience where it had been largely the result of private initiative, in Japan the new style of life required by a modern state based on capital was initiated at the public level. Profits were not to be only a private affair; prosperity and national strength were to be pursued. Although the Meiji Restoration had brought hardship to the merchants when many lost family businesses and resources, it was not long before they participated in new but risky ventures.

In the early 1880s, one of the largest government investments, the Kamaishi Mines, failed and was put up for sale. After some hesitation, the operations were bought by a private entrepreneur, Chobei Tanaka, who was convinced to purchase by his head clerk who argued that

> a few million yen in government investments and eight years of effort must not be permitted to go to waste. Somebody must continue the operation of the mines or all the machines will rot and enormous amounts of ore would be lost to Japan. He further stressed that a defeat at this stage would discourage for a long time any further attempts in iron mining. His final argument was that the government would certainly not fail to lend assistance to someone who undertook to continue its own frustrated efforts. (Hirschmeier and Yui 1975: 193)

Such a lofty mixture of idealism and realism served Japan well at the macro as well as the micro level. In the eyes of the Japanese people, an

TABLE I.

Household Saving Rates as Percentage of Disposable Income:
International Comparison (1975–1985)

Year	Japan	U.S.	West Germany
1975	22.8	8.8	15.1
1976	23.2	7.1	13.3
1977	21.8	6.1	12.2
1978	20.8	6.2	12.1
1979	18.2	6.0	12.6
1980	17.9	6.2	12.8
1981	18.3	6.9	13.6
1982	16.5	6.4	13.1
1983	16.3	5.2	11.8
1984	16.1	6.3	11.6
1985	15.7	5.2	11.4
AVERAGE	18.9	6.4	12.7

SOURCE: OECD, *Economic Surveys*, quoted in Jones 1987: 3.

industrial enterprise should not be a strictly "private" affair; they may well feel that they could not afford it! Yet as a nation deprived of natural resources, the people believed and apparently still believe that the survival of Japan, i.e., their own survival, will result essentially from their own efforts. The postwar high saving propensity bears testimony to this general conviction. Economic growth in the 1950s and 1960s and the affluence that ensued were due to the achievements of Japanese industry; such achievements in financial terms were themselves due, via loans, to the savings of the "man in the street." Although the saving rate has slowly declined over the 1975–1985 period, on average it has remained three times that in the United States and 50% higher than in West Germany (table 1).

Incorporation

Before the middle of the nineteenth century, Japan had known a most active commercial economy, which even today deeply influences corporate behavior. But industry and industrial enterprises had been almost completely ignored. These had to be started with the "Opening of Japan" in 1854. There was, however, a major hurdle to overcome internationally. The so-called unequal treaties had granted extraterritorial rights to foreigners residing in Japan and denied reciprocal treatment in trade and commerce. The reason given was that Japan did not have a modern (read

"Western") legal system. The treaties were not abrogated until 1899. By then, Japan had pieced together a "modern" legal system by importing what it found relevant in the systems of the Western powers (Henderson 1973: 166–172). Thus, a Western system was superimposed on native behavior.

Because much of the imported legal thought required introducing new and alien concepts, translation from English, French, or German into the Japanese language was a serious problem. For example, in Japanese tradition there was no term for "rights"; "reciprocal duties" had been at the source of social behavior. The current term for rights, *kenri*, is a translation of the French term *droits*, invented by a certain Rinsho Mitsukuri, whom the Meiji Government entrusted in 1869 with the translation of the Napoleonic Codes (Noda 1976: 44). It was only much later that clear statutory definitions were given (e.g., the concept of "merchant" in the Commercial Code was finally specified in 1938).

Book Two of the Commercial Code (1899), which is Japan's corporation law, was originally modeled after German corporation law, and subsequent amendments (1911, 1933, and 1938) continued to reflect German developments. After World War II under the U.S. occupation, this model was discarded, largely in favor of the corporation law of Illinois, when this part of the Commercial Code was thoroughly revised (Henderson 1973: 112).

Under this Code (Art. 53), three forms of private corporation are determined: *gōmei kaisha* (Arts. 62 to 145), *gōshi kaisha* (Arts. 146 to 164), and *kabushiki kaisha* (Arts. 165 to 456). In the Anglo-American system of law, the first would be a commercial partnership in which liability of the partners is unlimited; the second would be a limited partnership resembling commercial partnerships except that it has both general and limited partners. In Japan, however, because of the influence of German law, the idea of partnership is nonexistent. In prewar Japan, the *gōmei kaisha* was the popular form of the *zaibatsu*, the prewar form of industrial grouping under a holding company. Today it is fast disappearing, except as the form of incorporation of audit corporations (*kansa hōjin*), inaugurated in 1968 as Japan's equivalent of Western auditing firms. The *kabushishi kaisha* (joint stock company), the third form of incorporation, limits a participant's interest to his investment in capital stock certificates.

There is a fourth form, the *yūgen kaisha* (private corporation), an association formed under the Yūgen Kaisha Law (1938) modeled on the German GmbH Law (1892), itself modeled on the older Private Company Act of the United Kingdom. Certain articles of the Commercial Code apply to this law. The *yūgen kaisha* is a perfect form of incorpora-

TABLE 2.

Number of Companies by Legal Status and Capitalization (1975 and 1985)

	Capitalization (million yen)								Percentage
	Less than 5	5–10	5–50	50–1,000	10–100	100–1,000	More than 1,000	Total	
Kabushiki kaisha									
1975	397,179		255,342	20,972			1,890	675,383	55.8
1985	410,021	193,277			264,672	16,763	2,863	887,596	53.5
Yūgen kaisha									
1975	436,864		43,378	147			2	480,391	39.7
1985	572,287	112,989			38,106	136	5	723,523	43.6
Gōmei kaisha									
1975	6,283		1,206	23			0	7,512	0.6
1985	5,077	464			618	7	0	6,166	0.4
Gōshi kaisha									
1975	35,695		3,736	27			0	39,458	3.2
1985	27,965	3,008			2,270	23	0	33,266	2.0
Others									
1975	5,194		2,917	144			1	8,256	0.7
1985	4,362	1,654			3,283	158	2	9,459	0.6
TOTAL									
1975	881,215		306,579	21,313			1,893	1,211,000	100
1985	1,019,712	311,392			308,949	17,087	2,870	1,660,010	100

SOURCE: National Tax Administration 1977: 10, and 1987: 10.

tion for small/medium enterprises that require no public funding. As with the joint stock company, liability is limited to a member's capital contribution; the principal difference is that the ownership share may not be transferred to a nonmember without approval of the general shareholders' meeting. Although the Yūgen Kaisha Law was enacted to accommodate the needs of private companies, prestige-minded Japanese businessmen do not generally choose this vehicle for corporate formation but prefer to operate through the stock corporation, which seems to imply a larger size.

> [T]he primary reason why the *kabushiki kaisha* form is preferred to the *yūgen kaisha* form is that most of the difficulties and strict formal requirements designed for the protection of public shareholders are either circumvented in practice or have become almost moribund. . . . To quote an example: the public disclosure requirements in terms of corporate accounting and business records are now practically inoperative, partly due to the absence of any active interest in such information on the part of public shareholders. Shareholders' meetings in Japanese companies, which could technically have power to override management, are usually conducted almost as rituals. Shareholders' meetings of large corporations are more of a ceremony attended by a small number of hand clappers engineered by the management than an open forum for serious debate on corporate policy and management. On the other hand, in small companies with a small number of shareholders, shareholders' meetings are seldom held, nor corporate minutes prepared, and share certificates are very rarely issued to stockholders. It is clear, therefore, that the legislative intent to offer more convenient forms of limited liability company has been frustrated in the process of actual application within the particular environment that is Japan, where critical debate and group discussion are not commonplace attributes of society. (Takeuchi 1980: 157)

The joint stock company is thus the form of incorporation used by over 50% of all corporations. Their number increased from 675,000 in 1975 to 890,000 in 1985 (table 2). The legal requirements of the joint stock company were originally stipulated for major companies. Over the years, they were repeatedly revised to broaden relevance and protect shareholders and creditors. In 1963, for the first time since the Commercial Code was enacted in 1899, regulations concerning presentation of financial statements were strengthened to make them more meaningful.

Family Corporations

The family corporation *dōzoku kaisha* exists only in the eyes of tax legislation. According to the Corporation Tax Law (Art. 2.10), a family corporation is a company in which 50% or more of the capital is owned by no more than three independent shareholders (two or more shareholders belonging to the same family are deemed as one shareholder). Many small businesses (neighborhood grocery stores, drug stores, laundries) that are run by a family are in fact incorporated as *kabushiki kaisha* (rather than *yūgen kaisha*) and for tax purposes are treated as family corporations. Between 1975 and 1985, their number increased from 1.1 to 1.5 million, while the total number of corporations increased from 1.2 to 1.6 million. A number of successful, well-known large corporations with capitalization of over one billion yen also remain family owned: 749 out of 1,893 in 1975, and 185 out of 2,870 in 1985 (National Tax Administration 1977: 165, and 1987: 158).

Incorporation as a *kabushiki kaisha* allows small as well as large family corporations to take advantage of corporate income taxes, which are lower than individual income taxes, for two reasons. First, as of 1975 the effective corporate tax rate (including local taxes) is 38% for taxable income of ¥7 million or less for corporations with capital stock of ¥100 million or less, while the rate is 56% for all others. Individual income taxes range progressively from 15% (including inhabitants' tax), for an annual taxable income of ¥500,000 or less after various deductions (¥1.7 million for a married couple with two dependents), to 88% (Individual Tax Income Law, Art. 89). Second, if, in family corporations, corporate and private accounts are properly segregated, relations with tax authorities will be smoother and legitimate business expense deduction claims will be honored with fewer problems. Various tax provisions close loopholes in transactions between family corporations and their shareholders. The Corporation Tax Law (Art. 67) provides for additional income tax on retained (after-tax) income. This lessens the possibility of individual shareholders having lower income taxes if dividends are not distributed and remain as retained earnings in the corporation.

In 1987, the additional tax ranged from 10% to 20% of retained earnings, after deducting either ¥15 million, 35% of taxable income for the current year, or the amount of accumulated surplus lower than 25% of paid-in capital, whichever was larger.

A further tax provision (Art. 132) is the authority to recalculate the income of a family corporation if the corporate income tax has been unduly reduced. What is generally at stake is the sale of assets and services (including interest, rent, and so on) at an unduly low price and their purchase at an unduly high price. The balance between recalculated and reported income is usually deemed a gift expended or received and is taxable.

As a joint stock company, the family corporation must publicize its balance sheet. This is seldom done. If so stated in the articles of incorporation, share certificates are to be issued to shareholders; in reality, very few family-owned stock corporations do so. Needless to say, accounting and business practices in small corporations are usually below standard.

Commercial banks and loan associations usually prefer *kabushiki kaisha* to *yūgen kaisha* in granting loans, which may well exceed the amount of equity capital. However, the amount of loans will also depend upon the mortgage of land, collaterals (marketable securities), and the directors' personal property. Moreover, bankers do not like a situation in which loaned money is utilized for the personal use of the officers, something that frequently happens in a family business but is more readily suspected in a *yūgen kaisha*.

Large and Small Enterprises

So-called democratization of the Japanese industrial structure, heralded by the U.S. military occupation (1945–1952), was not directly concerned with the small-enterprise sector. Like the Meiji government, the Japanese government after World War II privileged those large firms involved in iron and steel, electric power, chemicals, shipbuilding, and other heavy industries that were profitable before the war and were important in the reconstruction of the Japanese economy. Further government directives in the 1950s and 1960s heightened favoritism toward larger corporations, while development of the postwar domestic market saw the appearance and rapid expansion of large-scale consumer goods companies. Small enterprises could hardly compete with modern capital-intensive companies. They did not have equal access to raw materials procured abroad, imported technology selectively controlled by the government, and financial sources no less selectively supplied by the banks. Many became subcontractors, subsidiaries, or affiliated firms of larger corporations. In the late 1960s, the situation looked as follows:

> In Japan, the technology gap took the form of a dualistic structure of industry and the labor market. There were marked differentials in productivity and wage rates. The productivity differentials reflected the scarcity of capital and the different capital intensities prevailing in modern and traditional sectors, and the wage differentials rested on the peculiar Japanese labor market institutions (permanent employment, seniority payments, etc.) that kept the modern sector wages high in the face of labor surplus. This combination of conditions produced a flexible labor supply response

to increases in demand for labor, and hence underlay a wage lag with respect to labor productivity that was itself the condition for high profits and
high investment and savings rate. (Ohkawa and Rosovsky 1973: 40)

It would thus not be appropriate to look at Japanese industry as irrevo-
cably split in two, large- and small-enterprise, sectors. Neither could have
survived without the other.

Quite naturally, Japanese industry is known abroad mainly through its
large corporations (*dai-kigyō*), be they manufacturers, financial institutions, or the unique general trading companies (*sōgō shōsha*). What is
striking about these companies is some uncanny capacity for quick adaptation to changing circumstances and their ability to make the most of
their being "latecomers" in technology, international marketing and
more recently foreign investment. Much of the available information is
about them and often presents them as the *Wunderkind* of global industrialization. This is not due, however, to some magic corporate management; what they are reflects conditions nurtured by Japan's society and
economy.

None of these large corporations stands alone. Each is the epicenter of
other enterprises, large and small, with which it has developed privileged
relationships more of a historical than a mere economic nature. At the
same time, each faces several equally large competitors in the domestic
market itself. The result is an unrelenting struggle for life of a peculiar
nature: the survival of the fittest does not necessarily spell the disappear-
ance of the rival, who reappears, equally challenging, in some other corner of the market. It is very much part of Japan's business culture to
formulate each industry in terms of the "Top Four" or "Top Five" and
rank them among themselves. This is a national game applied as well to
steel makers and department stores as to banks and breweries. Tally is
kept annually and widely reported in the media (exactly as for the national leagues in popular sports). This ranking is a rallying point for the
workforce, from top executives to clerks or mechanics, for suppliers and
distributors, for related companies no less than subcontractors. Hence,
there is an obsessive concern for corporate image.

At the same time, these national champions are also members of broad
industrial groupings that may include rivals. They share even broader
concerns of a national and international scope as members of the *Keidanren* (Japan Federation of Economic Organizations), often referred to as
Japan's second Diet. Hence, very few major corporate decisions are taken
without prior discussion with peers. It must also be noted that the bulk
of labor union membership (30% of the labor force is organized) is found
in these large corporations. To be a maverick in this context is sometimes
attempted, but it is indeed difficult to keep up.

Turning to the small enterprises, the first problem is one of definition. The official term is "small and medium enterprises" (*chūshō kigyō*), which was given a legal definition, although it is not used consistently by official instances themselves. As defined by the Basic Law of Small and Medium Enterprises (1963), Article 2, they are incorporated businesses capitalized at less than ¥100 million or with fewer than 300 (regular) employees, or unincorporated businesses with fewer than 300 employees. For wholesaling enterprises, the criteria are capitalization at less than ¥30 million or fewer than 100 employees, and for retail and other service enterprises, the criteria are capitalization at less than ¥10 million or fewer than 50 employees. Ministry of International Trade and Industry (MITI) statistics sometimes refer to "small enterprises," with the meaning of a business with fewer than 20 employees. For commercial and service businesses, this criterion is fewer than five employees.

Roughly half of the small/medium enterprises are in commerce, one out of five in services, and one out of six in manufacturing industries. They are much better known for their negative than for their positive aspects. However, they made a major contribution to the phenomenal growth of the Japanese economy after World War II, apparently larger than has been the case in other industrial countries (table 3). Reevaluating their role, the 1986 White Paper of the Small and Medium Enterprise Agency looked for the better sides.

First, the small and medium enterprises have, through their rapid opening, closing, and changes in scale, imparted a fluidity to Japanese industry, which contributed to the conversion of the industrial structure and injected new blood in industry. Further, [they] have, through their greater flexibility been able to cope with small changes in user needs which the large enterprises found difficult to handle.

Second, the small and medium enterprises have supported the basic foundation of Japanese industry through acting as subcontractors in an efficient production system wherein work is apportioned in an efficient manner, information costs are cut, and technology is smoothly propagated.

Third, the small and medium enterprises account for a large part in the nation's employment. Further, they play a great role in the creation of new employment, offering jobs for newly employed and others. They have therefore been contributing significantly to Japan's employment. Further, [they] are just as good as large enterprises in making use of the abilities and individual characteristics of their employees, being able to look through the entire organization when evaluating employees, and thus provide a worthwhile workplace. (MITI 1986a: 14)

These positive aspects notwithstanding, in the 1980s, when over 70% of the total private sector workforce is found in these enterprises, wages are only about 60% of those paid in large corporations (table 4). Wages

TABLE 3.

Small/Medium Enterprises in Manufacturing: International Comparison (1972–1982)

	1972			1977			1982		
	No. of Businesses	No. of Employees	Value-added Amount	No. of Businesses	No. of Employees	Value-added Amount	No. of Businesses	No. of Employees	Value-added Amount
Japan (A)	97.8	53.6	37.2	98.0	56.4	39.9	96.6	55.6	38.6
(B)	99.4	69.5	53.9	99.4	71.7	56.6	99.2	71.9	55.9
U.S. (C)	95.6	42.7	36.9	96.0	43.4	36.3	96.2	46.9	38.4
U.K. (D)	96.3	21.9	18.2	96.6	22.5	18.5	95.5	35.3	31.0
	(1975)		(1975)						

SOURCE: EPA (Economic Planning Agency) 1986: 175.

NOTES: (A) Ratio to the total manufacturing industries of businesses with fewer than 100 employees.
(B) Ratio to the total manufacturing industries of businesses with fewer than 300 employees.
(C) Ratio of businesses in manufacturing with fewer than 250 employees.
(D) Ratio of businesses in manufacturing with fewer than 200 employees.
In both Britain and the U.S., there is no legal definition of "small and medium-sized" enterprises as such. Generally speaking, for manufacturing industries, those with fewer than 200 employees (Britain) and fewer than 500 employees (U.S.) are considered to be small and medium-sized businesses, respectively. However, here we analyzed those businesses with fewer than 250 employees for the U.S. in order to facilitate making comparisons among the three countries.

TABLE 4.

Wage Differentials According to Size of Establishment (1965–1983)

(percentage)

Year	500 or More Employees	100–499 Employees	30–90 Employees	5–29 Employees
1965	100.0	80.9	71.0	63.2
1970	100.0	81.4	69.6	61.8
1975	100.0	82.9	68.7	60.2
1980	100.0	80.5	65.4	58.0
1981	100.0	80.0	65.3	57.0
1982	100.0	78.9	64.1	56.7
1983	100.0	79.0	64.0	56.6

SOURCE: Japan Productivity Center 1985: 37.

in small enterprises have increased, but compared to large corporations the gap remains wide enough to make it difficult to hire competent school graduates, especially college graduates. The productivity value per employee differs greatly between large and small enterprises and their working conditions no less. Lifetime employment (*shūshin koyō*) and a seniority wage system (*nenkō chingin seido*), entrenched practices in Japanese firms, are expected but not as often obtained in small enterprises. Allowances and fringe benefits are not as readily forthcoming. Labor unions are rarely found. Due to high job turnover and lack of continuity, it is difficult to organize a united front to increase wages, raise safety standards, reduce working time, and assure steady employment. Traditionally, the small enterprises have been ready victims (or beneficiaries) of the business cycle.

As reported in the 1987 White Paper of the Small and Medium Enterprise Agency, business conditions are currently worsening on three counts: (1) Appreciation of the yen has reduced considerably the export capacity of the small firms, in fact, much more than for the large enterprises. (2) Competition with the imports from the Asian Newly Industrializing Countries (NICs) keeps intensifying. Whereas in the recent past, competition was primarily about price, today it is also about quality and function, and on overseas markets as well. (3) Last but not least, parent companies are expanding their overseas investments and thus have reduced procurement from their domestic suppliers (*Focus Japan* 1987: 1–2).

Listed and Unlisted Corporations

Although stock exchanges were opened in 1878, listing was not regulated by law until 70 years later with the enactment of the Securities Exchange

Law in 1948. Of the more than one million joint stock corporations in Japan, fewer than two thousand are listed on the exchanges. The main reason for listing was greater ease in raising corporate funds, either as equity or, more important in postwar Japan, as bank loans. Listing also allowed shareholders to offer their shares as collateral for private loans (banks, as a rule, refuse to honor unlisted shares). The overwhelming motivation for not being listed was and is, of course, to maintain easier control and avoid financial disclosure. Listing requirements themselves exclude many corporations, according to amount of capital, minimum number of shareholders, and, most important, the requirement to have paid dividends continuously during the five years (recently reduced to at least one year) preceding application for listing and to expect to do so after listing.

Most unlisted stock corporations are, in essence, family-owned companies whose shares are held by one individual and his acquaintances who "lend" their names to the owner. In general, then, the owner does not call general meetings of shareholders. Required official reports are simply invented. The general meeting, however, becomes of real importance when potential successors to the founder fight for control.

A small number of unlisted companies are traded over the counter. Creation in 1961 of the Second Section (*Daini-bu Shijō*) on the Tokyo, Osaka, and Nagoya Stock Exchanges formalized the then over-the-counter (OTC) market. In February 1963, a system was established whereby the Japan Association of Securities Dealers publicly reported daily sales and price changes as well as corporate finance of some unlisted stocks. In 1976, the Japan OTC Securities Co. (Nihon Tentō Shōken K.K.) was inaugurated to facilitate trading and ensure fair prices. These unlisted stocks are either registered (for prominent companies not yet listed on the exchange) or delisted stocks. In November 1983, regulations for such registered stocks were changed so as to allow easier access by small/medium companies and thus promote venture capital.

Foreign Companies

There is no standard definition in Japan for a "foreign" company. Characteristic of the so-called foreign-capital affiliated companies (*gaishi-kei kigyō*) in Japan is their smaller share of output there compared with in other industrial economies (table 5). Statistics about foreign direct investment, on an approval and notification basis, are published annually by the Ministry of Finance: at the end of 1985, investment amounted to $6.6 billion, involving over 6,000 companies (Keizai Koho Center 1986:

TABLE 5.

Share of Output by Foreign-controlled
Companies: International Comparison
(1975–1980)

Canada	56%
Australia	36
France	20
United Kingdom	19
West Germany	18
United States	5
Japan	3
World	10–15%

SOURCES: French Government; MITI; OECD Estimates;
Bundesbank. Quoted in Abegglen 1984: 118.

58). The figure 6,000, however, does not indicate the number of companies active in Japan.

The Ministry of International Trade and Industry (MITI) conducts an annual survey of "foreign-capital affiliated companies," but their definition in terms of foreign capital ratio has varied over time: 15% in 1967, 20% from 1968 to 1974, 25% from 1975 to 1981, and 50% since 1982. In 1985, it sent questionnaires to 2,556 companies (in 1984, 2,268) of which 1,132 (48.5%) responded (1,127 or 49.7%, in 1984) (MITI 1986b: 26, and MITI 1987a: 7).

For its part, the Ministry of Labor has conducted, in 1983, its third survey of labor relations in foreign firms, by sending questionnaires to 2,355 companies of which 1,301 (55.2%) responded. It used the definition of more than 25% foreign capital ratio, but also included branches and offices of foreign corporations (MOL 1983: 4).

In fiscal 1979 based on *Fortune*'s annual lists, of the top 200 nonfinancial U.S. companies, 127 (63.5%) were present in Japan, each running an average of 3.9 subsidiaries and joint ventures. Of the top 100 non-American corporations, excluding 19 Japanese companies, 28 (34.6%) were active in Japan, with an average of 7.2 subsidiaries (JETRO 1984: 6). The 1980s witnessed a surge of direct investment in Japan: "In the late 70's annual direct foreign investment from all foreign countries averaged $269 million per year. Since 1980, the annual total has averaged $739 million per year. . . . Investments in Japan do not appear to provide exceptional profitability, nor do they generate dramatically lower profits. Overall, investing in Japan generates about the same level of profitability as investments anywhere else" (Booz, Allen & Hamilton, Inc. 1987: 7, 19). According to the MITI survey, although the percentage of all sales by "foreign" firms has been for many years a dismal 2%, their

TABLE 6.

"Foreign" Firms: Percentage of All Sales and Ratio of Current Profit to Sales (1975–1985)

Type of Firm	1975			1980			1983			1985		
	Foreign Firms: % of Sales	Ratio of Current Profit to Sales		Foreign Firms: % of Sales	Ratio of Current Profit to Sales		Foreign Firms: % of Sales	Ratio of Current Profit to Sales		Foreign Firms: % of Sales	Ratio of Current Profit to Sales	
		Domestic Firms	Foreign Firms		Domestic Firms	Foreign Firms		Domestic Firms	Foreign Firms		Domestic Firms	Foreign Firms
All industries	1.90	1.3	1.6	2.17	2.4	3.8	1.47	1.8	3.5	—	2.1	3.4
Manufacturing	3.85	1.2	1.7	4.66	3.6	4.3	2.91	2.9	4.3	3.2	3.6	3.7
Manufacturing, excluding petroleum products	2.11	1.4	3.7	2.26	3.7	6.2	1.36	3.0	6.8	1.5	2.1	6.3
Petroleum products manufacturing	29.36	(−)1.2	(−)0.3	38.07	1.7	2.8	29.42	0.9	2.4	35.6	0.6	1.7
Nonmanufacturing	0.97	1.3	1.3	1.00	1.8	2.7	0.78	1.3	2.2	—	—	—
Commerce	1.27	0.9	0.1	1.36	1.1	2.7	1.10	0.8	2.1	0.7	0.9	2.3
Services	0.84	2.0	4.7	0.52	3.3	3.9	0.22	2.9	4.4	—	—	—

SOURCES: 1975–1983, MITI 1986b: 34, 43; 1985, MITI 1987: 12.
NOTE: From 1982 on, the definition of foreign-capital affiliated companies changed from 25% to 50% foreign capital. For 1985, some figures are not given in the survey.

profits, of course depending on the industry, have averaged about twice those of domestic companies (table 6).

In 1985, for example, the ratio of current profit to sales in some industries was

	Domestic Firms	"Foreign" Firms
Chemical industry	5.2%	4.4%
Machinery industry	3.8%	3.4%
Electrical industry	6.0%	12.8%

(MITI 1987a: 12)

Few foreign corporations were listed on Japanese stock exchanges before recent changes in regulations. The number is now increasing very rapidly from 15 in 1981, 12 in 1982, 11 in 1983 and 1984, to 21 in 1985, and 52 in 1986 (Tokyo Stock Exchange 1986a: 14, and 1987b: 15). More than 60 are expected by the end of 1987. Corporations must satisfy the Securities Exchange Law, which engenders considerable discontent with the disclosure system and its costs: in particular, double auditing (abolished in January 1984, on the condition that CPAs and auditing standards in the home country be substantially equivalent to Japan's) and the format and content of notification statements and their filing periods (in July 1984, extended from within three months to within six months of the business year).

Business Environment

Today's Japanese enterprises are still expected to abide by the business philosophy of early industrialization: the creation of wealth for all and for each. Thus, value added (*fuka-kachi*) is of the essence. Stated simply, value added is the difference between sales revenue and cost of materials used; it is the most intimate linkage between market and production; and, last but not least, it is the overwhelming purpose of enterprise. It is perceived by the Japanese enterprise, its managers, workers, suppliers, distributors, and clients as the result of their collective effort, i.e., their interdependence.

A long-time Western observer of Japanese enterprises who has reflected on Western enterprises did not mince his words:

> In most Western countries, the enterprise belongs to the shareholders, while workers and managers alike are related to it only by contract for the performance of certain specified tasks. By no stretch of the imagination can either managers or workers be considered "members" of the enterprise, nor would they admit to "belonging" to it. They only "work for" the com-

pany. In principle at least, men at all levels of the enterprise work for the enrichment of the shareholders, who are themselves anonymous and transient. But the maximization of profits, a goal which some managers may willingly adopt, is not one with which the ordinary worker, nature being what it is, can easily identify himself. The short-term gains of stockholders are seemingly incongruous with his long-term vital interests in job security and pecuniary rewards in keeping with his increasing family obligations. Moreover, the perceived identification of management with pecuniary interests of the shareholders suggests to the wage-earner that the goals of the enterprise to maximize profits are pursued mainly at his expense. (Gregory 1982: 40)

The business environment is responsible for the Japanese style of management. A recent illustration is quality control (QC). Japanese industry learned it from the United States in the late 1940s but made it its own in a spectacular fashion, by looking at product quality as a corporate duty expressed through the interdependence of all actors in the enterprise as well as in the market. Quality is understood as *the* key product characteristic, simply because it encompasses the entire process from conception and design to commercialization and end-use. Quality control, then, affects product as well as job quality, requires constant upgrading of the human resource on the production floor no less than in the board room, and calls on corporate pride on the part of all participants. On the shop floor, operators are involved in the design of the equipment if not also in its construction and participate in production scheduling.

The standard method here is the QC circle, whose immediate purpose is participation in process improvement (Schonberger 1982) and whose suggestions are numerous and largely adopted (table 7). In regard to suppliers of parts and components, a long-standing relationship is sought, whereby mutual performance is enhanced and technical assistance is provided. "Just-in-time" (JIT) delivery is obtained in terms, again, of mutual assistance, and feedback is provided to suppliers on product performance. A similar network is attempted with distributors as well, providing them with financial assistance, bearing service costs, and promoting the general custom of generously accepting the return of unsold goods. Finally, a major effort is made at integrating the end-user, to whom product appeal is not so much stressed as corporate reliability. The outcome of all this is that the enterprise is not considered to be a mere economic entity for the benefit of shareholders but a social institution for the service of society at large.

In Japan, the business environment knows two poles, the enterprise and the market, linked by market share. The enterprise is an entity whose mission is economic as well as social, in regard to both its employees and

TABLE 7.

Suggestion System: International Comparison

	U.S. (1978)	Japan (1980)
Rate of worker participation	14%	54.2%
No. of suggestions/worker	0.15	12.82
Rate of suggestions adopted	24%	72%
Average reward/suggestion	¥30,530	¥466
Record reward for a suggestion	¥17,200,000	¥810,000

SOURCE: Japan Productivity Center 1982.

customers. It has been characterized as an "organic" organization in contrast with the "mechanistic" organization more common in Western economies. The organic organization thrives on group dynamics: it is the ideal and progressively practical embodiment of interdependence between man and machine, man and man, institution and institution. To a very meaningful extent, it stresses process over results, for instance, by giving greater weight to production strategy than to product strategy (Kagono, Nonaka, Sakakibara, and Okumura 1985: 34). Process stands for corporate survival, the dynamic survival resulting from growth, and growth comes from interaction with a fiercely competitive environment. Corporate objectives are, then, market share supported by new product ratio, rather than, as in the case of the United States, return on investment supported by share price (table 8). Share price is of very little importance to Japanese executives!

> Managements with a bias toward growth have distinctive mindsets which include the expectation of continued growth, decisions and plans formulated to produce growth, and the unfaltering pursuit of growth unless the very life of the organization is threatened. Companies with a bias toward growth add physical and human capacity ahead of demand. Prices are set not at the level that the market will bear, but as low as necessary to expand the market to fit the available capacity. Costs are programmed to come down to support the pricing policies and investments are made in anticipation of increased demand. (Abegglen and Stalk 1985: 6)

Such interaction between enterprise and market is, however, less the result of management decisions than of the vital necessity to respond to the expectations in the economy and society. What are elsewhere referred to as the social responsibilities of business, largely dependent on acceptance by management, in Japan are not open to debate in the boardroom (a most difficult aspect of doing business in Japan for "foreign" firms). For example, that a squeeze of the payroll starts with the company offi-

TABLE 8.

Importance of Selected Corporate Goals

Goal	U.S.	Japan
Return on investment	2.43	1.24***
Capital gain for shareholders	1.14	0.02***
Increase in market share	0.73	1.43***
Improvement of product portfolio	0.50	0.68
Efficiency of logistic activities	0.46	0.71**
Equity/debt ratio	0.38	0.59
New product ratio	0.21	1.06***
Public image of the company	0.05	0.20**
Quality of working conditions	0.04	0.09**

SOURCE: Kagono, Nonaka, Sakakibara, and Okumura 1985: 28.
NOTE: Mean scores of importance (3 points for the most important goal, 2 points for the second, 1 point for the third, and 0 points for others).
**Significant at .01 level of t-test of means.
***Significant at .001 level of t-test of means.

cers or that an unavoidable layoff places on managers the burden to find new employment for those dismissed is practice, not a lofty precept!

Corporate behavior is then directly influenced, if not determined, by the expectations outside as well as inside the corporation; financial behavior is cut of the same cloth. For example, the general practice for the company facing difficult times is to turn primarily to what is called its main bank and secondarily to other banks for financial and managerial assistance. It is then expected that, after successful rehabilitation, the company will attach great importance to its relationship with these banks out of a sense of moral obligation. There are, however, exceptions "that confirm the rule."

The following behavior was widely reported as most unusual: In the early 1980s, Daishowa Paper Manufacturing Co. (capital ¥10 billion) faced serious difficulties because of a slack in the paper product market. It turned to the Sumitomo Bank, its main bank and one of its major shareholders, for financial assistance and the seconding of directors. Some assistance was also provided by other financial institutions. By 1984, the problems had been surmounted, and the company started to refund its bank loans. The seconded directors returned to the Sumitomo Bank. In March 1986, the company had refunded the total of ¥28 billion to its main bank, implying that the relationship was severed.

Another example concerns the accountability of financial officers in one of the major city banks.

In mid-1984, the New York branch of a large Japanese bank incurred a loss in foreign exchange transactions of $40 million, roughly equivalent to the monthly profit of the bank. Responsibility was assumed as follows:

(1) profit-sharing for all 34 members of the board of directors in Tokyo including the chief executive officer was canceled, though most of them were not even involved in international business; (2) the senior managing director and managing director of the international office, who were based in Tokyo, were demoted to managing director and director respectively; (3) the general manager of the New York branch was fired because he had full responsibility for the branch; (4) the branch officer (manager) was transferred back to Tokyo; and (5) the assistant manager who handled the transactions directly was fired. Here we can see a typical pattern of responsibility-sharing in Japanese organizations. (Watanabe and Mochizuki 1986: 88)

It may well be misleading to look at a Japanese company without qualifying the Western experience of what a corporation is and is supposed to be. A Japanese company would not and could not survive if it were not also a reflection of Japan's business environment. Being legally incorporated, in terms familiar in Western economies, results in a different entity with different corporate behavior. Corporate behavior, financial and otherwise, reflects the dynamics of the industrial society itself.

2

INTERACTION WITH THE AUTHORITIES

COMPARED TO WESTERN COMPANIES, corporations in Japan display much less concern about their autonomy. Companies, no less than the individuals who work there, are embedded in a web of relationships in which the the bureaucracy is an active participant through regulations and administrative guidance. In regard to financial matters, the main actors on the government side are the Ministry of International Trade and Industry (MITI), the Fair Trade Commission (FTC), the Bank of Japan (BOJ), and, last but not least, the Ministry of Finance (MOF).

Administrative Guidance

Historically, Japanese society has not made a clear distinction between private and public. In Western experience, "private" evolved from individualism, spawned rights, and is appreciated in sharp contrast to "public." In Japan, even today the experience of "public" is appreciated in a collective context explicitly involving the individual, with the result that "private" tends to be equated with the negation of this interdependence (see Koschmann 1978: 1–30). The relationship between government and business is, then, like that of the two sides of a coin: each side is obviously different, but the reality is *one* coin. Japan does not have the Western tradition of *laissez faire* that supposes a gap between public sector and private sector.

It is a most remarkable exception in world history that Japan, notwithstanding its 2,000 or so years of continuous history, suffered its first successful invasion in 1945. As one consequence, in Japanese experience the authority of the "government" is not so much granted from the outside (by law and/or political process) as resulting from the inner needs of a homogeneous and highly integrated society. To use the apt contrast proposed by Koschmann, whereas in Western experience, power is based on "fear," in Japanese experience it is largely based on "faith" (Koschmann 1978: 13).

Another striking difference between the Japanese and the Western experience is that it was the "government," not private industrialists, that initiated Japan's industrialization in the second half of the last century. From the beginning and continuing today, the essential role of the government is not "regulatory" but "developmental" (Johnson 1982: 19–23). Admittedly, for many years after World War II, given the imperative needs of reconstruction of the economy, government authority was primarily expressed in "regulatory" terms. Today it has largely returned to its historical, "developmental," role, a most explicit manifestation of which is administrative guidance (*gyōsei shidō*).

In regard to the government-business relationship, the term "government" stands not so much for the political parties and the Cabinet, but for a comparatively small bureaucracy (table 9). Except for a few months in the late 1940s, the majority in the Japanese Diet has always been conservative. Continuity of basic policies was thus ensured. Careers in the bureaucracy are coveted, and thus the bureaucracy is staffed by the better talent available.

Administrative guidance might be understood along the lines of the pre-Meiji tradition in which the *samurai*, or warrior-bureaucrat, makes, interprets, and administers the "law" (as a rule of equity). It is not, but does not necessarily preclude, arbitrariness. The penalty for not accepting administrative guidance is not direct; it is indirect, on the basis of continuity of interaction. The aim of guidance is to help and encourage private initiative. At times this guidance may be ill advised but well intentioned. The fact that a number of higher officials, upon retirement, join private industry, mostly industries with which they were concerned (this movement into the private sector has been nicknamed *amakudari*, descent from heaven), helps the process substantially. Thus, former officials of the Ministry of Finance join financial institutions; officials of MITI join manufacturing companies; those of the Ministry of Health and Welfare join pharmaceutical companies, and so on.

> The relevant aspect is that the business community of Japan tends on the whole to see the bureaucracy of Japan as competent and well intentioned and as working toward the national interest. Equally important, the bureaucrats concerned with industry, trade, and finance are generally active in support of Japan's businesses as the necessary and appropriate instruments of economic growth and well-being. In Japan too businessmen

complain a good deal about unnecessary government regulations and inter-
vention. Bureaucrats complain about narrow and self-serving business behavior. But in comparison with other market economies, there is a basis of
cooperation arising out of history, out of a sense of shared purpose, and
out of a view that the roles of government and business can be mutually
supporting. (Abegglen 1984: 108)

The ultimate function of administrative guidance is consensus building. Consensus is a problem-solving technique. It does not mean an inherent unity of policy; it stands rather for a unique capability of resolving
conflict. Neither the various government agencies, nor the industries, nor
the members of a given industry, speak with one voice. A consensus,
however, is expressed in specific terms. It should not be construed as a
planning technique, except perhaps in the sense of an implicit agreement
at a given point in time on guidelines. On broad issues, interaction takes
place mostly between the Cabinet and/or ministries, and the Federation
of Economic Organizations (*Keidanren*). Particular issues are handled
between the specific industry and the specific bureau of the ministry
concerned.

Consensus requires flexibility upward. The bureaucracy drafts the
bills; the Diet legislates a broad charter law; the bureaucracy then interprets and administers the law. Thus, broad priorities are established
above the ministries, but expenditure and revenue allocation are dele-
gated to bureaucracy. Flexibility is also required downward. The respon-
siveness of the industry depends on its needs and the ministry's ability to
service these needs. To bring this flexibility to fruition, constant interaction takes place through joint deliberation boards or advisory commit-
tees (*shingikai*) (somewhat comparable to open public hearings in the
United States), trade associations, and the old-boys network (same school
or same year of entry into public service, or *amakudari*, whereby high

TABLE 9.

Public Employees per Thousand Population: International Comparison

	Japan (1980)	U.K. (1978)	F.R.G. (1979)	U.S. (1980)
National public employees	7.7	8.7	2.4	8.6
National defense	2.5	9.5	10.7	13.4
Government enterprises	8.1	37.4	14.1	—
SUB-TOTAL (A)	18.3	55.6	27.2	22.1
Local public employees (B)	26.6	53.7	48.5	60.4
TOTAL (A + B)	44.9	109.3	75.7	82.4
TOTAL (minus defense)	42.4	99.8	65.0	69.0

SOURCE: Adapted from Tsuji 1980: 73.

officials upon retirement join a large corporation in the industry with which they were familiar). In order to obtain consensus, the ministry bureau must often act as conciliator, if not also as arbitrator. This is where administrative guidance is brought to bear. In general terms, the Japanese bureaucracy considers that at the level of the individual firm, marketplace discipline is appropriate, but at the level of the industry, it has an important role to play in the redistribution of capital and labor and in technological development (Abegglen 1984: 101–114).

Much administrative guidance is credited to MITI. For example,

Yashica, a leading camera maker, ran into serious financial difficulties in 1974. On October 11, the president announced to the labor union that the company might close on October 31. He had been informed that the two largest stockholders and financial backers, Taiyo-Kobe Bank and Nissho-Iwai Co., intended to discontinue financial assistance. In recent years, Yashica's image had been damaged by public utterance of internal rivalry, a major embezzlement, and some window dressing. However, the Ministry of International Trade and Industry, apparently prompted by Yashica's recent business tie-up with Carl Zeiss of West Germany, requested further assistance and a reconstruction plan was finally agreed upon. A director of Nissho-Iwai was appointed president; the smaller of Yashica's two plants was to be sold to a computer maker, but the labor union objected. The plant was temporarily closed and the workforce reduced by 900, as employees resigned with extra retirement benefits (*Japan Economic Journal* 1975, February 25).

Administrative guidance often takes place in the context of tax incentives.

Every year, after extended negotiations, MOF and MITI agree on an aggregate ceiling for special tax measures. MITI is free to grant tax incentives in whatever amounts to industries of its choosing, so long as it stays within the limits of the aggregate ceiling. . . . In the complicated aggregation of interest within MITI, special tax provisions are considered one of the four interrelated policy measures designed for each industry; the others are subsidies, legislative measures, and administrative guidance. The General Coordinating Division (of MITI) tries to blend all four ingredients, each in appropriate measure, into an effective recipe that meets the needs and peculiar circumstances of each industry. Declining industries may get a stronger dose of administrative guidance and subsidies, while for the high tech industries, greater tax incentives and research support may be the most effective instruments of promotion.

The strength of Japan's system is that it (1) keeps a cap on the estimated losses due to special tax incentives, (2) forces all industries to compete with one another for special tax treatment on the basis of what lies in the best interests of the industrial economy as a whole, (3) gives MITI the leeway and authority to determine the optimal uses of special tax incentives, (4) holds parochial politicking in check, and (5) uses tax policies in relation to other tools of industrial policy. (Okimoto 1986: 72)

One current example of administrative guidance by MITI is related to its specific responsibility toward so-called depressed industries. Two temporary laws (1978–1983 and 1983–1988) permit MITI to identify such industries in addition to those legally designated if they satisfy specific criteria.

Once an industry has been identified, by statute or by MITI . . . consultation takes place between MITI officials and the firms in the industry to determine whether the firms favor designation. If two-thirds of the firms in the industry (measured both by number of firms and by the share of sales) agree, they apply formally for designation. MITI then makes a decision concerning designation.

After an industry is designated, the Ministry—in consultation with the industry's trade association, its individual firms, its major customers, and independent experts—develops an estimate of the amount of excess capacity to be scrapped. . . . In the course of its consultation, MITI attempts to forge an industry-wide consensus on a capacity reduction goal and a schedule for its attainment. Once consensus is reached, it is formulated as the industry's Basic Stabilization Plan and officially approved by the Ministry.

In practice, there is considerable overlap in the sequence of steps just outlined. Discussions with firms and trade associations usually begin before MITI identifies an industry as a candidate for designation. Indeed, MITI would be unlikely to initiate the process were it not more or less assured in advance that two-thirds of the firms favored designation. Similarly, formal designation of an industry does not strictly precede the development of a capacity reduction plan. Preliminary attempts to forge a consensus are made in the early rounds of negotiation concerning designation. (Peck, Levin, and Goto 1987: 84)

A most prevalent channel of administrative guidance is the trade association (*jigyōsha dantai*). Trade associations are found in all sectors of industry, nationwide, regional, industrywide, and product line. Their total number is over 23,000. Participation is high. They all come under the stringent Trade Association Law (1947), whose enforcing agency is the Fair Trade Commission.

[The collectivist proclivity of the Japanese people plays] an important role in the implementation of industrial policy, especially for administrative guidance. Government officials find it difficult to give guidance to individual firms. Trade associations, however, provide a useful conduit through which government policy can be relayed to member firms. These associ-

ations also provide a forum for negotiation and cooperation with government officials in formulating policy and the substance of the guidance to be
given. Like convoys providing protection for each member, these associations develop industry-wide cooperation but may at the same time be
criticized for protecting their members against the discipline of market
forces, for allowing them to stagnate and become inefficient. When carried
too far and resulting in cartels as defined by the Antimonopoly Law, collectivist behavior becomes an antitrust violation. (Iyori 1986: 61)

For its part, the Bank of Japan directs administrative guidance, called
"window guidance," at the city banks. In addition to the standard instruments of monetary policy, such as direct market operations in the call
and bill discount markets,

> the discount window is an extremely important avenue for supplying funds
> to banks. . . . The Bank of Japan decides on the level of bank borrowing up
> to a predetermined quarterly ceiling, the term of the borrowing, and there-
> fore the effective interest rate associated with the borrowing. Also, the in-
> teraction between city banks and the Bank of Japan through the discount
> window constitutes an important line of communication between banks
> and the monetary authority. . . . The large volume of discount window
> borrowings means that the Bank of Japan is able to confer substantial sub-
> sidies to individual banks. This practice may also give the Bank of Japan
> some leverage in influencing bank behavior, a process referred to as "win-
> dow guidance," although the extent and effectiveness of the activity is
> open to debate. (Dotsey 1986: 19–20)

Fair Trade Commission

The Law Relating to Prohibition of Private Monopoly and Maintenance
of Fair Trade, usually referred to as the Antimonopoly Law, was enacted
in 1947 during the U.S. military occupation. The original act was patterned after the American antitrust laws and included several new improvements that were deemed necessary for American purposes in Japan.

> Therefore, the Japanese Act was much more severe than . . . American
> antitrust laws. For the Japanese to whom the Act had no roots at all, the
> Antimonopoly Act was considered to be one of the irresistible results of
> defeat and measures forced on Japan. (Nakagawa 1984: 301)

The law was amended several times, usually to the effect of watering it
down, until finally the 1977 amendments reversed the trend. A major
objective of the law was to eliminate the possibility of a resurgence of
prewar *zaibatsu;* to that effect, holding companies were prohibited (Sec.

TABLE 10.

Maximum Shareholding by Financial Institutions (1977–1986)

Institution	Number of Companies in 1977 (A)	1980 Survey	1985 Survey	Dec. 1986 Survey (B)	Progress Rate (A − B)/A × 100
City banks	1,625	1,331	949	771	52.6
Long-term credit banks	269	236	150	127	52.8
Trust banks	205	159	121	96	53.2
SUBTOTAL	2,099	1,726	1,220	994	52.6
Local banks	521	419	290	245	53.0
Mutual banks	231	191	108	92	60.2
SUBTOTAL	752	610	398	337	55.2
TOTAL	2,851	2,336	1,618	1,331	53.3
Securities companies	286	—	124	106	62.9
of which top 12	268	229	114	100	62.7
TOTAL	3,137	—	1,742	1,437	54.2

SOURCE: FTC 1987.

9). Furthermore, financial institutions were allowed only limited share-holding in each of their clients. In its original version (1947), the law limited such shareholding to 5%; this was amended to 10% in 1952. The amendment of 1977 (Sec. 11) returned to 5% and gave the concerned institutions a grace period of ten years (which expired in December 1987) to divest themselves of the shares in excess. Progress has been slow (table 10). As of December 1986, 137 financial institutions still held shares in excess of 5% in close to 1,500 companies for a total amount of ¥56 billion (FTC 1987).

The enforcing agency of the Antimonopoly Law, the Fair Trade Commission (FTC), has always had as its head a former vice-minister of the Ministry of Finance. But despite the general interdependence so characteristic of Japanese corporations and the prevalence of administrative guidance, the Commission is often at odds with other government agencies, in particular MITI. In 1968, it succeeded in stopping the merger of the three major paper manufacturers, but failed in regard to the merger that resulted in the Nippon Steel Corporation (in both cases, the merging companies had been one company until the end of World War II).

The FTC has issued a number of "Guidelines" concerning specific business practices. In an effort to counteract the tendency of businessmen and officials as well to turn to trade associations for purposes that may run counter the Antimonopoly Law, the FTC issued guidelines addressing the activities of these associations (1979) and promulgated an "Interpretations Concerning the Relation between the Antimonopoly Act and Administrative Guidance" (1981).

> During 1953–1983, the FTC issued 621 decisions in connection with Antimonopoly Law violations, of which 357 (55%) involved trade associations violating Section 8-1 of the Law. Additionally, many of the 215 decisions about cartel activities of entrepreneurs in violation of Section 3 implicated trade associations. (FTC 1983: 236)

Stockholding by companies is checked under "Standards for Examination of Stockholding by Companies" (1981), and mergers and acquisitions are the object of FTC Guidelines titled "Administrative Procedures Standards for Examining Mergers, etc., by Companies" (1980) and "Approach to Examination of Mergers, etc., in the Retailing Sector" (1981) (Nakagawa 1984: 79–88).

As one would expect, the FTC is involved in the administration of measures whereby the government promotes contractual agreements among firms in the same industry, such as the Temporary Measures for the Structural Adjustment of Specific Industries Law of 1983. This law, among others, promotes business tie-ups that may cover production, transportation, and marketing agreements, if not also mergers. Thus the Commission will approve a common selling agent for several companies only if the participants have a combined market share of 25% or less (Peck, Levin, and Goto 1987: 121).

Ministry of Finance

But the most forceful guidance is, of course, provided by the Ministry of Finance (MOF) that "is by and large equivalent to the U.S. Treasury Department, the Office of Management and Budget (OMB), and the Securities and Exchange Commission combined, but because of its statutory and actual budgeting authority, it is probably even more powerful than such an aggregation would be in the United States" (Higashi 1983: 43). In terms of prestige, it enjoys the top position attracting every year the cream of the crop of college graduates entering the labor market. "The elite character of the MOF, rather like the British Treasury and the French Inspection des Finances, derive[s] in part from the selection of the intake [of career officers]" (Horne 1985: 194).

Besides its overall power in the Japanese economy resulting from its decisive role in the national budget and its process (Campbell 1977; Rukstad 1986), the MOF's impact on corporate finance is exercised in various ways: tax administration, intermediary financing, and regulation of the financial sector. More than administrative guidance may take place, as, for example, when the Ministry became an active participant in the operating results of city banks underwriting government bonds by sometimes forcing the bonds to be purchased below market price.

> Previously, the banks had been required to value their government bond holdings at either the market price or the purchase price, whichever was lower, a valuation method known to Japanese accountants as *teikahō*. From the six-month period ending March 31, 1980, the banks were allowed to value their government bonds at either the market value or the purchase price, a valuation method known to Japanese accountants as *genkahō*. The banks chose the accounting method that best suited their books at the time. . . . [Some banks] chose to list their bonds using the *genkahō* valuation method, to cover up paper losses on their government bond portfolios. . . . Only the Ministry of Finance knows for sure how much money Japanese banks are actually making. After each six-month period, the banks are required to report figures for net operating income that Japanese accountants refer to as *eigyō jun-eki*. This comprises net interest and dividend income plus fees received minus operating expenses. It does not include securities gains or losses, extraordinary gains or losses, or transfers to or from reserves. It also does not include local enterprise taxes that amount to 13.2% of net taxable income. Only by analyzing these figures can the Ministry determine the health of the country's banking industry. (Bronte 1982: 22, 23)

In the last ten years or so, several mutual banks have got into trouble because of poor management. How does MOF react to the problem?

> Instead of forcing the closure of the bank or arranging some form of takeover of assets, it organized a financial support plan from other large private financial institutions. The MOF stood by its policy of not allowing any financial institution to go into liquidation. It argued that the collapse of any financial institution would upset the confidence of the public and hence the financial order of the economic system. (Horne 1985: 209)

In such dire circumstances, but also as a matter of accepted custom, retiring career officials of the MOF are sent to sit on the board of financial institutions (table 11).

For almost three decades after World War II, until 1974, two different jurisdictions were involved in financial reporting. One was the Commercial Code, which gave general legally binding principles for recording and reporting corporate financial matters but did not require that this be done according to specific accounting principles. Its precepts are administered by the Ministry of Justice, usually with the help of the Legislation Deliberation Board (*Hōsei Shingikai*) and supported by a retinue of legal

TABLE II.

Former MOF Career Officers Holding Executive Positions in Financial Institutions
(May 1981)

Rank	Public Financial Institutions	City Banks, Long-term Credit Banks	Regional Banks	Mutual Banks, Credit Associations	Total
President, Deputy President	9	5	11	24	49
Executive Director (*Riji*)	13	—	—	—	13
Senior Managing Director (*Senmu*)	1	—	12	4	17
Managing Director (*Jomu*)	—	1	2	7	10
Advisor (*Komon*)	—	4	1	1	6
Other	—	4	2	11	17
TOTAL	23 (21%)	14 (12%)	28 (25%)	47 (42%)	112 (100%)

SOURCE: Adapted from Horne 1985: 207.

scholars and practitioners with little specific interest in accounting practices. The other jurisdiction was held by the Ministry of Finance in two areas. It is in charge of the Securities Exchange Law (regulating the listed companies) with the help of the Business Accounting Deliberation Board (*Kigyō Kaikei Shingikai*), itself supported by a retinue in which keen and professional interest is shown in corporate accounting and financial reporting. In addition, the MOF administers tax legislation that presents its own viewpoint on financial reporting, even though tax returns must be prepared based on financial statements as required by the Commercial Code. Caught in the middle and playing it safe, before 1974 corporations had largely opted for tax-oriented accounting and disclosure. Finally, in 1974 and thereafter, the Commercial Code was revised several times in order to bring financial reporting more in line with international practice.

It must be acknowledged that in this conflict between the Ministry of Justice and the MOF, as in other interministerial rivalries, protagonists on both sides often displayed exaggerated legalism. At stake was not just reconciliation of two different legal traditions and terminologies but traditional factionalism prevalent among government agencies and their supporters, in and outside business.

The participatory decision-making process, together with the paternalistic atmosphere of the "closed" organization, enable career officials at various levels in a given ministry to share information and ideas. Out of such knowledge come sectional interests, which play an important role in the interministerial conflicts over jurisdiction and responsibility. Consequently, the Japanese, who show remarkable skill in reaching a consensus within their own organization, often fail to cooperate in interorganizational situations. (Higashi 1983: 56)

The Ministry of Finance itself operates not so much as "one" ministry but as a not infrequently uneasy coalition of functional bureaus. At times, the Banking Bureau and the Securities Bureau are at odds, as are the Securities Bureau and the Tax Bureau. The Banking Bureau and the Securities Bureau are more directly responsible for developing and implementing domestic financial policy. The former, which regulates the banking industry, is basically in charge of the indirect financing of corporations by the use of its most powerful tool, control over interest rates (with the exception of the postal savings rate). The latter Bureau focuses concern on the development of the bonds and equities markets and thus supervises direct financing.

Each bureau, at the MOF as in other government agencies, sponsors various deliberation boards (*shingikai*). The Business Accounting Deliberation Board, referred to above, is an advisory body composed of government officials, leading businessmen, and experts. Its recommendations to the Ministry of Finance are held to be binding to the degree of a ministerial ordinance (*shōrei*), even though they are often presented as "opinion" or "principles."

Financial Intermediation

The role of the government as financial intermediary is played through post office funds and the Fiscal Investment and Loan Program (FILP). Postal deposits, insurance premiums, and pension payments together with funds from the national pension funds, from surplus funds of special accounts of the government, and from public corporations are entrusted to the Trust Fund Bureau (*Shikin Unyō-bu*) of the Ministry of Finance. The portion of these funds (over 80%) allocated to loans and investments is used as a source, among others, for the FILP, an official instrument for off-budget financing purposes. In recent years, the rough distribution of these funds has been 30% to public investment, 20% to local government, and 50% to policy implementation financing. The latter allocates in turn 70% to 80% of its funds to small business loans and housing loans. FILP is the main source of funds for the Japan Development Bank (JDB), whose basic lending policy is formulated yearly by the Cabinet. In the 1980s, about one-quarter of JDB funds went to the manufacturing sector: "Fiscal funds comprised a major proportion of new equipment funds throughout the (postwar) period, although their share has gradually declined. Their share was particularly large in the fifties, and especially for major strategic industries, electricity, shipping, coal, and steel" (Sakakibara, Feldman, and Harada 1982: 46). These funds were important not so much for their volume, but for the fact that they served as "pump priming" for private loans.

> If even 10 percent of new equipment funds come from public sector inter-
> mediaries, private intermediaries feel much more secure in extending large
> loans, since, in these cases, the government is assuming default risk. Thus,
> public financial intermediation acts as a catalyst to channel large amounts
> of funds to specific directions. This does not mean, however, that the Gov-
> ernment did as it pleased with industry. Funds could not be channeled to
> sectors where expected returns were low. Private financial institutions sim-
> ply would not lend to such sectors, even if the Government did assume a
> substantial portion of the default risk. However, in cases where both ex-
> pected returns and risk were high, the involvement of public entities could
> be quite significant. For gigantic projects, participation of a public financial
> intermediary as well as a long-term credit bank was often an integral part
> of the formation of loan consortia. Indeed, had it not been for public fi-
> nancial intermediation, basic industries such as energy, steel, shipping and
> petrochemicals would not have developed so smoothly. (ibid.)

Financial pump priming is but another facet of the developmental role of the Japanese government. It combines neatly with other official efforts in the promotion of private initiative, in particular the "national projects" (in technological development) sponsored by MITI and other agencies. One illustration of its effectiveness is the fact that although Japan's total trade in technology licenses is still in deficit, the balance of trade in new technologies, in value terms, shifted to Japan's favor as early as in 1972 (Wheeler, Janow, and Pepper 1982: 126).

In conclusion, there is on the part of Japanese officialdom, at most times and in most respects, a predominant concern for contributing to the momentum of the economy. Constant interaction between industry and bureaucracy is thus required. The process need not be fastidious. If, as is felt, the survival of Japan depends on, say, technological innovation, "dangers of overall systems inefficiency are largely obviated by leaving decisions as to appropriateness of technology to the entrepreneur and the market place, keeping government agencies free to make and coordinate general policies. In this process, the distinctive competencies of both government and business enterprise are strengthened. Since both government and business have as their goal pushing forward the frontiers of technology to maximize wealth creation, there tends to be an identity of basic purposes which serves as a sound footing for cooperation and mutual support rather than conflict and adversarial postures" (Gregory 1985: 62).

3

INTERACTION AMONG COMPANIES

INTERACTION AMONG COMPANIES takes various forms at different levels. Long-ingrained social behavior commonly observed among Japanese themselves is reflected in business transactions among the commercial and industrial organizations they staff. The vertical relationship between a company and its subsidiaries and that between contractor and subcontractors are common expressions of such corporate behavior. But Japanese social behavior also determines the Japanese outlook on mergers, acquisitions, and business relations in general.

Related Companies

"Related companies" (*kankei-gaisha*) are a deeply rooted aspect of Japanese business with far-reaching consequences in determining corporate financial behavior. In Japanese usage, the term applies to a vertical relationship among firms, to be distinguished from the more horizontal relationship among the members of an industrial grouping (described in detail in chapter 4). The major members of such industrial groups, e.g., the trading company, have themselves numerous related firms. Both horizontal and vertical relationships are facets of concentration resulting from a general predisposition to corporate interdependence.

The relationship among so-called related companies is, first of all, culturally determined by the age-old *oyabun-kobun* relationship:

> The functioning of the Japanese social system is based on interpersonal relationships, maintained through a variety of groupings, both vertical and horizontal. The former are exemplified primarily, though not exclusively, by the *oyabun-kobun* relationship . . . (a simulation of father-son or

parent-child relationship). . . . There is no more basic interpersonal relationship in Japanese society than *oyabun-kobun*, a legacy of feudalism
based on a Confucian concept. In its many forms it constitutes the main-
spring of Japanese behavior and provides a sense of loyalty and obligation
outside the familial framework. Mentor-protégé, senior-junior, superior-
subordinate, master-apprentice, teacher-student, and many other relationships all come under this rubric. (Yanaga 1968: 12–13)

One often hears the expression *oya-ko-gaisha* (*oya* = parent; *ko* =
child; *gaisha* = company). Such a parent company exercises de facto
control over its child company by offering it business, financing it when
required, sending a director to represent the parent's interest, and giving
a general feeling of security to the child's employees. The authority of the
parent is not formulated in writing, and, in some sense, independent operations by the child are expected. Yet one should not mistake this for
freedom in which there is no commitment to the parent. The relationship
is intended as an exclusive parent-child relationship between the related
companies.

In Western industrial nations, consolidated financial statements usually
include fair presentation of the financial condition and operating results
of parent and subsidiary companies as a group. Generally, if a company
owns a controlling interest in another company, this is a sufficient criterion for inclusion in the consolidated statement. Yet such a criterion
would not be sufficient for Japanese related companies. What may be
quite specific in sociological terms is not so clear in economic terms.
"Related companies" is a popular expression, rarely defined and most
loosely used. For companies having to file financial statements with the
Ministry of Finance, two categories are defined: "*One*, if more than 50%
of issued shares is owned by the registrant (parent), or *two*, if 20% or
more of issued shares is owned by the registrant and thereby a major part
of the business activities is under his control by uninterrupted and close
relationship" (MOF 1962).

Under this definition, related companies can thus be distinguished as
follows: the subsidiary company (*ko-gaisha*) belongs in category one; the
affiliated company (*kanren-gaisha*) belongs in category two; and the subcontracting company (*shita-uke-gaisha*) may be in category two, if the
parent contractor owns 20% or more of the shares. Since 1977 the Ministry of Finance has required all listed companies to submit audited
consolidated financial statements as attached supplementary financial
statements in addition to the parent-only statements at the time of application for listing.

The Japanese entrepreneur, for his part, reviews with glee the many
reasons he has for establishing subsidiaries:

From the management viewpoint: Because management techniques should be adjusted according to the type of business, a separate entity with separate management is sometimes preferable to a different type of business within the same company. Thus, it is common to find a wholly owned trading subsidiary handling all sales of the parent manufacturer.

When foreign technology and know-how cannot be obtained on a straight license basis, the joint venture subsidiary is a convenient second choice.

It is also generally felt that overseas business is best handled by a subsidiary, even wholly owned, rather than by a branch office.

From the personnel viewpoint: Given the prevalence of lifetime employment and promotion by seniority, it is common practice to transfer redundant management personnel to subsidiaries. Subsidiaries can also provide excellent training for promising executives (see Inohara 1972).

Also, given the prevalence in postwar Japan of enterprise unionism (one union for the entire company), the same employment conditions apply to all union members in the same company in spite of quite different work circumstances. It is reasonable, then, to establish a different corporate entity in order to enforce different employment regulations, for example, in the Tokyo-based and the locally based businesses, for production and marketing or servicing, or for assembly and component parts businesses.

From the financial viewpoint: The subsidiary may be a minority shareholder of the parent, thus broadening capital contribution to the latter and providing a stable shareholder.

In some cases, loans and trade credit from financial institutions are larger when granted to plural entities than to a single entity and intercompany guarantees on loans (often not reported in financial statements) can be obtained.

Subsidiaries can be beneficial for tax purposes. For example, the limitation on allowable entertainment expense can be repeated among several entities, or the subsidiary can simply be used as a loss company enjoying the five-year tax loss carry-forward.

The subsidiary can also be used to smooth profits of the parent by adjusting prices of intercompany dealings, even by reporting unrealized sales, and by the use of differing financial period endings.

Intercompany sales and purchases are the most attractive benefit of parent-child companies. Notes to the financial statements of the parent company (according to the Commercial Code) should disclose sales to and purchases from its subsidiaries, and the balance of account due from and to its subsidiaries. However, the terms "sales" and "purchases" are interpreted in the sense of products or services transacted in the ordinary course of business, *not* transactions regarding land or buildings. Furthermore, these terms are *not* restricted to legitimate transactions. In many cases, including cases of unaffiliated subcontractors, the parent supplies materials for processing largely at cost and buys back the processed products or parts at the original cost (to itself) plus the cost of labor for processing. Although not permissible under sound accounting principles, it sometimes happens that the transaction is recorded in the parent's sales and cost of sales, with the result that both the value of the sales and the cost of sales are inflated by the cost of materials supplied to the subsidiary. This practice goes back to the prevailing custom in Japan of ranking companies by reported sales.

Admittedly, a delicate balance between the parent's interests and the need to respect those of the child company must be maintained in order not to damage the morale of the latter's management and workforce. For example, intercompany pricing (often a fixed price) must be such that loss to the subsidiary (as well as to the subcontractor, but to a lesser degree) is not enough to drive it out of business and profit is not enough to allow it to become financially independent and escape the parent's control.

Since the fist oil shock, the top six general trading companies have substantially increased their shareholding in related companies.

The total amount in billion yen was 210 in 1970, 734 in 1975, 851 in 1980, and 966 as of March 1982. This last amount concerned 5,804 domestic related companies; in 67.2% of these companies, the stocks held by the trading company amounted to less than 10%, in 14.9% between 10% and 25%, in 9.6% between 25% and 50%, in 4.0% between 50% and 100%, and in 4.3% the trading company held 100% of the shares (FTC 1983/4: 26–29).

Particularly in the 1980s, subsidiaries are more and more perceived as instruments for diversification, often essential for corporate survival. On the basis of its 1987 databank of Japanese listed companies, *Tōkei Geppō* reported a total of over 16,000 subsidiaries and affiliates, one-third in manufacturing and two-thirds in nonmanufacturing. In recent years, the total has increased yearly by about 400, whereas before 1973–1974, it had been by about 300. The purpose is twofold: (1) to promote an entirely new business by a subsidiary of the group, and (2) to make the parent company "slim." For example,

The Nippon Steel group entered the fields of electronics and ceramics through newly established subsidiaries.

Daicel Chemical launched Daicel Finance to earn profit on financial investment.

Ohbayashi Gumi, one of the top construction companies, started Ohku Systems to develop and sell construction software.

Misawa Homes together with Hazama Gumi started Hazama-Misawa Urban Development to capitalize on their real estate information networks.

TABLE 12.

Six Major Industrial Groups and Their Related Companies: Number of Companies and Percentage of Assets, Capital, and Sales (FY 1981)

	Number of Companies	Assets (%)	Capital (%)	Sales (%)
Six groups	182 (0.011%)	25.94	16.46	15.78
Subsidiaries: 50% and more	4,271 (0.249)	2.05	3.48	3.55
Affiliates More than 25% and less than 50%	4,251 (0.248)	2.65	5.75	4.01
More than 10% up to 25%	3,278 (0.191)	3.36	6.95	4.29
TOTAL	11,982 (0.699)	34.00	32.64	27.63

SOURCE: FTC 1983/6: 23.
NOTE: Percentages are of all 1,710,000 companies in Japan.

Takara Shuzo, a manufacturer of *sake* (rice wine) entered bio-tech and medical services by the establishment of subsidiaries.

Toray (textiles) launched Toray System Center to sell on-line systems and production systems. It established its apparel division as a separate company.

Sansui Electric separated its distribution center from the factory. Etc., etc. (*Tōkei Geppō* 1987, May)

Financial institutions are no less active in diversification through the establishment of new affiliates, for example, in management consultation, software, venture capital, office management, investment advice, and real estate.

The Employment Promotion Agency reported that, as of July 1986, 73.6% of the companies surveyed had increased the number of their subsidiaries in the last five years; the number had not changed in 20.3%; and it had decreased in 6.1% of the companies. One-third of the companies intended to increase the number in the near future. Presently, subsidiaries and affiliates have a workforce that usually does not exceed 100 in number but whose average age is substantially higher than that at the parent company (ibid.).

The importance of related companies has been detailed in regard to the six major industrial groups (*keiretsu*). The member companies themselves account for 25% of all corporate assets, but this percentage is raised to 34% when their related companies are added (table 12).

Subcontracting

The dismal position of subcontractors in the interwar years has improved considerably since World War II by dint of protective legislation and official financial help. In essence, their role has changed from one of subordinate to one of equal.

Especially in manufacturing, the system of subcontracting (*shita-uke*) in Japan divides the production process into numerous stages.

> A comparison of the rate of intermediate input by enterprise size in Japan and the U.S. for the industries in which the subcontracting system is widespread in Japan shows that, in Japan, the larger the enterprise size, the higher the intermediate input rate, while, in the U.S., no such trend is apparent. In the Japanese subcontracting system, parts of the production process are commissioned to smaller sized enterprises to create a chain of labor linking up the large enterprises to medium enterprises, and the medium enterprises to small enterprises and to thus form a single overall production system. All processes are thus subdivided into numerous stages. As opposed to this, in the U.S., enterprises of all sizes feature high in-house production rates. (Small and Medium Enterprise Agency 1986b: 23–24)

The system calls for regional concentration around one plant of the manufacturer who produces in-house only 20% to 30% of the components required. It consists of various tiers, only two of which handle business relations. The local factory deals only with the first tier of subcontractors, who in turn deal only with the second tier, down to a third and fourth tier, if not further (the bad reputation of the system often originates at these lower levels). In recent years, a common feature has been the existence of study groups involving contractor and subcontractors, especially between manufacturer and first tier, and between first and second tier. The flow of information from the manufacturer, ranging from machine layout and quality control to accounting and market feedback has been of decisive importance. Quality is then built in rather than tagged on.

The context of slow economic growth combined with the impetus of product quality as competitive edge helped subcontractors to a significant extent (table 13). The well known *kanban*, or "just-in-time," system requires from the parent companies' greater responsibility toward their subcontractors. Parents are now often encouraging their subcontractors to procure some of their raw materials and semifinished components on their own, thus making them less dependent. The entire system operates not as a chain of contracts (through open bidding and set periods) but as a chain of relationships where each link is nurtured over time.

When the manufacturer and his first-tier subcontractors or first- and

TABLE 13.

Main Reasons for Subcontracting (1986)

Subcontractor		Parent Company	
Reasons	Percentage	Reasons	Percentage
Steady amount of orders	50.1	Know-how of subcontractor not held by oneself	57.6
Product design and development difficult by oneself	45.8	Efforts concentrated into best suited work	48.2
Difficult to obtain orders by oneself	42.4	Past business relations with and reliability of subcontractor	46.5
Efforts concentrated on production activities	38.7	Increased flexibility through size of orders	37.1
No worries about default or debts	27.7	Lower personnel costs and lower unit cost of products	36.5
Improved reputation	26.2	Small lot sizes and thus greater efficiency through production by small enterprises	30.6
Supply of raw materials, etc.	21.7	Overly large size of own company would reduce operating rate	9.4
Technical assistance provided	14.7	Competition among subcontractors ensures high quality and lower unit price	8.8

SOURCE: Small and Medium Enterprise Agency 1986b: 24–25.

second-tier contractors work closely together over a period of time, the contractor is often requested to participate in the ownership of his more important subcontractors; eventually the smaller company asks the larger one to buy its shares. Therefore, rather than the larger company simply buying out the smaller ones, acquisition is by mutual agreement.

Thus many related companies are, in fact, subcontractors. They are often used as buffers to equalize or stabilize the periodic profit of their parent company. Financial statements, under such circumstances, include to a significant extent non-arm's-length deals that are equivalent to parent-subsidiary transactions.

Subcontracting of services to so-called manpower supply companies (similar to temporary help companies in the United States) has been growing steadily since the late 1960s in such areas as catering, security, building and equipment maintenance, and technical services such as computer programming, translation, and interpreting. The main reason is a saving on labor costs. Such service companies are often started by transferring surplus personnel to a new enterprise, which is at first totally dependent but is soon fending for itself. As of January 1987, 26% of the listed companies had established indirect work divisions as separate companies, and many more planned to do so. Already 25% of such separate supply companies had 100 or more employees (MITI 1987b: 61). General trading companies, banks, and others sometimes use these companies to keep former female employees on tap. It is reported that 80% of these manpower companies' staff consists of women employed part-time.

Legal protection of subcontractors has improved steadily. A strengthened Fair Trade Commission is able to improve its role as watchdog: it administers the Law Against Delay in Payment of Subcontract Proceeds, etc., to Subcontractors (1956), and the Law Against Unjustifiable Premiums and Misleading Representations (1962). Inquiries about the application of these laws are entertained by the Commission. Between 1979 and 1985, the number of such inquiries by parent companies has increased by 50%, but those by subcontractors themselves have more than quadrupled. The prosecution of violations has increased by 180%; about half of such violations have to do with contract deficiencies. Upward adjustment of payment under FTC guidance appears to be progressing: from 5 cases affecting 52 subcontractors and a total amount of ¥80 million in 1979, to 111 cases affecting 1,791 subcontractors and a total amount of ¥585 million in 1985 (FTC 1986: 147–150).

It is inappropriate to regard Japanese subcontracting as a drag on the economy. The lower wages paid by subcontractors do not result from subcontracting as such but from lower capital investment plus lower productivity per worker, in a word, from their smaller size. The subcontracting system must be appreciated for its contribution to the resilience of the economy. It is generally recognized that much of the success of the large manufacturing corporations is due to small/medium subcontractors consistently providing parts of reliable quality. From 1976 to 1981, the percentage of manufacturing companies using subcontracting increased from 32.5% to 37.0%; in the electric machinery industry in particular, it increased from 55.1% to 57.9% (MITI 1987b: 113).

Mergers

According to the Fair Trade Commission, between 1951 and 1970, there were about 8,100 mergers, 500 or so yearly; during the 1970s, the number was over 10,000, or more than 1,000 per year (table 14). Mergers occur mostly in the wholesale and retail sectors (over 35%) where small enterprises predominate. One may well wonder whether the Japanese term *gappei*, translated as merger, corresponds fully to the Western notion. Both refer to a "marriage," yet marriage is approached differently. Whereas marriage in the West is basically a relationship decided upon by two parties for their own sake, in Japan many marriages are still arranged through a third party, at least in form. Similarly, Japanese business "marriages" are effected mostly through the advice of third parties— government, banks, business leaders. Despite the various types of mer-

TABLE 14.

Number of Mergers by Type (1970–1985)

Type of Merger	1970	1975	1980	1985
Horizontal	472	261	204	360
	(36.1%)	(23.4%)	(16.7%)	(28.2%)
Vertical	107	159	119	204
	(8.2)	(14.2)	(9.7)	(15.9)
Forward	46	88	49	66
	(3.5)	(7.9)	(4.0)	(5.1)
Backward	61	71	70	138
	(4.7)	(6.3)	(5.7)	(10.8)
Diversified	574	614	833	669
	(44.1)	(54.9)	(67.9)	(52.5)
Geographic market	205	129	372	221
Extension	(15.7)	(11.5)	(30.3)	(17.3)
Product extension	109	128	119	99
	(8.4)	(11.5)	(9.7)	(7.8)
Conglomerate	260	357	342	349
	(20.0)	(31.9)	(27.9)	(27.4)
Other	150	84	70	43
	(11.5)	(7.5)	(5.7)	(3.4)
TOTAL	1,303	1,118	1,226	1,276
	(100)	(100)	(100)	(100.0)
Number of mergers[1]	1,147	957	961	1,113

SOURCES: 1970–1980 from Iyori and Uesugi 1983: 200; 1985 from FTC 1986a: 225.
[1]The actual number of mergers is lower than the total computed because some mergers were of more than one type.

gers distinguished by the Fair Trade Commission, whose approval must be obtained, *gappei* is usually arranged either by the government as part of some overall policy, and/or by the banks for more immediate reasons, and/or by influential business leaders concerned about the objectives of the government, the policies of the banks, and the strengthening of the industrial grouping. In the early postwar years, mergers of trading companies, chemical companies, and textile companies were successfully "arranged" by their main banks. This was to eliminate duplicate investment, realize the merits of large-scale operation, reduce so-called excessive competition, and amortize past losses by future earnings from expanded operations.

The reorganization movement in the automobile industry in the 1960s, enthusiastically supported by MITI, is a good case in point. In at least two major episodes, the Industrial Bank of Japan played a key role, by successfully participating in the Nissan-Prince merger and by stopping three smaller makers, Mitsubishi, Isuzu and Fuji (BCG 1972a: 125). The 1969 merger of the two steelmakers, Yawata and Fuji, offered a similar instance of interaction of protagonists, bureaucracy, and banks, the initial rejection by the Fair Trade Commission notwithstanding (BCG 1972b: 150–151).

In most cases, the best protection of an enterprise's autonomy comes from permanent employment with its double effect of loyalty to the enterprise and restriction of labor mobility. In well-established companies, employees are promoted by seniority; some of them have waited 20 or 30 years to be promoted to department head or director. If a change in corporate structure were to ignore such seniority, employee morale would soon collapse or, at least, internal dissension would greatly damage the chances of the new set-up. Furthermore, as labor unions generally restrict membership to the permanent employees of the company, a merger implies necessarily the merger of two enterprisewide labor unions as well. These considerations may destroy a merger's economic rationale and make it even more difficult in Japan than in other industrial countries to merge two different groups of people into one group or to subordinate one to the other.

A merger thus becomes a major organizational headache for management (assuming that the two enterprisewide labor unions have agreed to cooperate). To give equality to both groups, directors from each company will retain their positions until, over a period of time, older executives retire and a new leadership of the united company emerges. The older of the two former presidents will be made chairman of the board (*kaichō*), the younger one president (*shachō*). Sometimes the same dual pattern of positional allocation is kept for many years throughout the management hierarchy.

Some mergers are referred to as *taitō gappei*, merger on equal footing, where shares of the old companies are exchanged for those of the new company on a one-to-one basis, but other considerations are at work as well.

In April 1986, at the instigation of MITI's wanting to strengthen the competitive position of the domestic oil companies, Cosmo Oil (capital ¥27 billion) resulted from the merger on equal footing of Daikyo Oil (capital ¥6.7 billion) that provided the new chairman, and Maruzen Oil (capital ¥20.4 billion) that provided the new president (in Japan, the Chief Executive Officer is generally the president).

Another well-known merger on equal footing was, in 1975, that of the Daiichi Bank and Nippon Kangyo Bank resulting in the present Daiichi Kangyo Bank. Both sides contributed a comparable amount of capital stock, comparable amounts of deposits, and a comparable number of directors.

Merger in Japan is thus similar to a pooling of interests aimed at unifying two companies in terms of management and personnel. Both managements remain in the surviving company, but shares in the surviving company are exchanged for outstanding shares of the liquidating companies.

Toward the end of the 1970s, a new trend started to surface. Whereas most earlier mergers were of the "arranged-marriage" type, now they result more from discussion among the companies directly involved: 52% of the mergers in 1985 versus 10% in 1975 resulted from direct negotiations (FTC 1986b: 237).

Often, where in the West one would expect a merger, in Japan, affiliation is preferred. In some cases, the affiliate company is a candidate for merger in due course. But quite often Japanese-style affiliation is, in human terms, more acceptable than a merger. The employees of many affiliates feel happier working with the employees of the parent company; they maintain their independence from the parent company, yet at the same time freely utilize the services and benefits of the parent.

In the case of merger (or acquisition), tax regulations do not permit the surviving company to utilize the tax losses of a dissolved company to offset taxable income of the surviving company in a future profitable period. Therefore, a merger (or acquisition) sometimes takes the form of a loss company absorbing a profitable company.

Acquisitions

Among Japanese companies, acquisition is no less delicate to handle than merger. Most takeovers are achieved quietly and peacefully. As opposed to a Western-style takeover, in Japan the acquiring company rarely takes the initiative; rather, the acquired company takes the first steps, usually indirectly through a director of its main bank or perhaps through an influential business leader. The company to be acquired seeks business or financial assistance from the acquiring company.

The fate of an acquired company will largely depend on its profitability at the time of acquisition. Within a profitable company, except for share ownership, heavy borrowing, and a substantial amount of business from the new partner, interference by the new owner is avoided as much as possible. Specifically, the acquired company will not be treated as would be a subsidiary of the parent created on its own initiative. If, however, the acquired company is weak, unconditional surrender is expected, expressed by the acquisition of the majority of shares. There is always the fear that the weak company will impair profits of the acquiring company; thus, the process of combining accounts is done over time in order to progressively strengthen the acquired company.

Takeover by acquisition of shares without the consent of the acquired company is by far the less popular form of takeover. In this form shares are collected confidentially, both through negotiations with large shareholders and through market purchases, without registering the name of the true shareholder. The transaction takes place in two phases: *kaishime* (collecting shares) and *nottori* (management takeover). Often, the first phase ends with the resale of shares to the existing management at a substantial premium, and therefore the second phase does not material- ize. There is in Japan strong dislike, if not public opprobrium, for this type of takeover.

But the environment is changing. Japanese business circles now look at acquisitions in a different light.

In September 1985, a survey of the top 100 companies listed on the First Section of the Stock Exchange was reported. Of these companies 48% acknowledged that acquisitions would become an important corporate strategy for two major rea- sons: (1) to obtain technology not presently possessed, and (2) to enter into new product areas. Nonetheless, 40% expressed a persistent negative attitude to- ward divestment, and 33% stated that unfriendly acquisition would provoke strong opposition in the business community (*Nihon Keizai Shinbun* 1985, Sep- tember 2).

Minebea, a manufacturer of miniature ball bearings that diversified into electronic devices and machinery components, is a perfect example of changing attitudes toward takeovers.

Established in 1951 with a capital of ¥3 million, Minebea was listed on the Second Section of the Tokyo Stock Exchange in 1961 and moved up to the First Section in 1970. The company is popularly described as the maverick par excel- lence. It has no main bank and is not a member of an industrial group. But, most of all, it is recognized as the only company in Japan that achieved its success through mergers and acquisitions, domestically and abroad. And it did it by rais- ing funds in the capital markets—as of the mid-1980s to the tune of almost ¥200 billion. In the late 1960s and early 1970s, three attempts at takeover, considered as unfriendly, ran into strong opposition and failed. The company, encouraged by a successful takeover in the United States (1971), started a string of acquisi- tions of domestic companies that were performing poorly but provided diversifi- cation. It rehabilitated them. In 1979, it started diversification into textiles and household goods. In the 1980s, the strategy is continued, this time in regard to ongoing companies, several listed as well, and consolidation took place. Minebea maintains that all these activities evolved without personnel lay-off (Doi [Ma- sako] 1986: 51–78).

Many company executives are interested in acquiring other companies for inclusion in their own industrial grouping.

The president of Misawa Homes, Chiyoji Misawa, aged 49, declared that by the age of 55 he will have ten listed companies in his group. So far, he has six: three were acquired during the three years from 1983 to 1985, and three more between January and March 1987 (*Nikkei Business* 1987: 40–42).

Mergers and acquisitions appear most feasible among new and growth corporations, which are more liberal in their methods of achieving growth and success. The process always remains delicate. One thing is sure: economic rationale for an acquisition is not sufficient; human and subjective considerations must be taken into account.

Hamamatsu Photonics is a fast growing R&D venture. It came in need of fresh capital. In March 1987, by the purchase of two million new shares for ¥3.8 billion, Toyota Motor became the number two shareholder (8.1%), after the Association of Employee Shareholders (17.1%). For these employees, the infusion of new capital was the much needed recognition of their research potential; for Toyota, it meant some diversification in its high-tech development effort. Toyota also sent two part-time directors (*Nikkei Business* 1987: 34–35).

The Foreign Takeover Bid and Stable Shareholders

In Japan, acquisition invariably evokes a specter of takeover by non-Japanese interests. The expression "TOB" (takeover bid) is used almost exclusively to describe major foreign threats to Japanese companies, usually to grossly undercapitalized firms. The old Foreign Exchange and Foreign Trade Control Law (Art. 26) and its relevant regulations restricted control of a Japanese company to the effect that when a nonresident intended to acquire more than 10% of a listed company's stock, he first had to notify the Ministry of Finance. Within this limitation and as part of the capital liberalization program started in the latter half of the 1960s, takeover bids by foreign interests have been made possible through the 1971 revision of the Securities Exchange Law (Arts. 27.2 and 27.8), which permits public purchasing of corporate shares (in contrast to "public offering").

When the Japanese government began to liberalize foreign capital entry into Japan, management became increasingly concerned about the thin capitalization of Japanese companies in general, which seemed to offer too ready a temptation for takeover by foreign capital. It was a challenge altogether different from the technological lag faced by industry in the earlier postwar period. In order to acquire foreign technology, licensing had been practiced on a grand scale. When foreign interests demanded management participation as a condition for the transfer of technology, the result was an increased number of international joint ventures. Government authorities repeatedly expressed interest in promoting this form of business cooperation, and industry relied on the resilience of industrial grouping to assimilate a system of equity cum management participation. But the vulnerability resulting from heavy dependence on borrowed technology was only compounded by the new threat—takeover—now possible because of the "free" entry of foreign capital. The solution to this problem was "stable shareholders," who would not allow shares to be acquired by foreign interests planning a takeover.

Stable shareholding is a further development of the long-standing mutual shareholding (*mochi-ai*), which evolved from the prevalence of "related" companies. The dynamics of industrial groupings, with the ever-present concern about strengthening business relations, made mutual shareholding insufficient. The problem came to a head in 1969, when General Motors and Isuzu made public the intention that the former would buy shares of the latter. MITI finally announced that it would accept up to 35% foreign capital participation, on the condition that a substantial portion of the shares be held by stable shareholders. The term was used to indicate shareholders of Japanese nationality who could be counted on to retain their shares, even if the stock declined in market value and favorable prices were offered by foreign interests. (The creation of a holding company could serve this purpose, but it would run counter to the Antimonopoly Law.) A feasible means of finding stable shareholders would be for companies in a group or in the same industry to hold each other's shares. An executive of Fuji Motors clearly expressed this sentiment at the time of the break between his company and Isuzu in 1968 (although later Fuji Motors gave up this shareholding):

> I think it is advisable for our company (Fuji Motors) and Isuzu Motors to continue holding each other's shares in spite of their liquidation of ties, so that we can remain each other's stabilized shareholders. Also it is desirable that the automobile firms as a whole hold one another's shares regardless of group affiliations, in order to defend native capital. (*Nikkan Kōgyō* 1968)

It became, then, a major duty of financial executives to find stable shareholders (banks, life insurance companies, suppliers) able to subscribe to frequent new-share offerings and retain their shares even when the market value is high enough to induce shareholders to sell. They are required to obtain approval of the issuing company if they wish to transfer or sell rights. It is, however, understood that they are not interested in management participation. (Obviously, the practice is not without danger, especially on the part of aggressive trading companies. It is recognized that it does not take long before their "stable" shareholding in smaller companies turns out to be the first step toward participation in management.)

Personal contact is the most efficient way to find stable shareholders. When a capital increase is planned, financial executives usually visit the major shareholders who might be willing to subscribe to new shares and request their cooperation in purchasing the new shares at par while retaining both old and new shares. However, a request for further subscription of shares frequently implies a favor in return. Thus, the firm planning a capital increase may be required, in the case of an insurance company, to invest in a new life insurance contract for its officers and employees; an unwritten commitment may be made to a supplier, offering a favorable purchase of its goods; the company raising capital may promise in turn to buy outstanding shares of related companies, thereby expanding mutual shareholding. Or the firm may at this time confirm its friendly relationship with the bank by promising (albeit unwillingly) to buy more bank shares.

Promotion of stable shareholding got underway in the early 1970s. It was fully endorsed by the securities companies in 1974, when brokers were faced with a drastic downturn in the securities market and were frantically searching for additional business. For them, this was but new vigor in the older practice of *oyabike*, whereby new shares were allocated selectively. One may well wonder where a company finds the needed shares, since stabilization of shareholding is not legally approved for holding treasury stock (Commercial Code Art. 210 specifies the approved reasons for holding treasury stock). Apparently, this is not a deterrent; listed companies, with the cooperation of their securities brokers, have methods for producing whatever shares are required to increase stable shareholding. However, this enthusiasm for stable shareholding was strongly criticized by government authorities as unduly reducing the percentage of readily marketable shares (*fudō kabu*) in the total shareholding of Japanese corporations.

Here too, the environment is changing as many large companies are reducing their shareholdings in "related" companies. Financial institutions themselves faced a December 1987 deadline for reducing their shareholdings in any given company to a maximum of 5%.

> Cross-holdings would not come onto the market unless companies needed cash instantly. . . . But the Tokyo market is changing in this regard, as several large manufacturing companies, among them Nippon Steel, recently have been unloading shares of group companies onto the market in order to raise cash. A worsening of the manufacturing recession could only accelerate this trend. (Roscoe 1986: 112)

Ironically, most of these transactions have been prearranged with buyers agreed upon beforehand. Not surprisingly, the majority of buyers

, a large European chemical company faced the dire prospect of not
g able to abide by a delivery contract with a major Japanese client.
l counsel at the home office advised cancellation of the contract and
payment of appropriate damages so that the long-term business rela-
ship would be maintained. Instructions to that effect were sent to the
idiary in Japan, where the expatriate executive who had worked in
n for many years recalled some instances when Japanese clients had
ght up "changed circumstances" and proposed a new course of ac-
without the slightest reference to the contract in force. Would it
k the other way around? Because the lowest estimate for damages
a six-digit dollar figure, it was worth trying—and it worked. The
rminant consideration was the existing relationship; in fact, adversity
reinforced it.

appears futile to the Japanese to expect full control of performance
legal provisions. Reality, at least as the Japanese see it, is always more
n what is spelled out in writing. This reasoning, however, does not
ly directly to foreign firms. It is not their view of the contract, and
s the Japanese have learned the techniques of what they call "inter-
ional" contracts. Trade associations and the like continue to hold
ining sessions about the negotiation and formulation of an "interna-
nal" contract. Carefully crafted contracts are more than ever indispen-
le for the foreign party, but it should not ignore or deny the Japanese
int of view.

turns out to be fellow stable shareholders, in particular life insurance
companies.

Little can be said yet about the decline of stable shareholding. It would
have profound repercussions on the stock market and the Japanese
economy as a whole. At the very least, an increased supply of actively
traded shares would serve to reduce share prices in the short run. Given
the pervading impact of administrative guidance, the chances for takeover bids, junk bonds, insider trading, and the like on a substantial scale
appear remote indeed.

Contractual Relations

In the Western legal tradition, the business contract is a relationship that
respects the autonomy of each party, qualified only by the conditions of
the contract. Documentation is key: the written word prevails, and external forces such as courts and arbitrators are part of the process. Western
law, however, was introduced into Japan only about one century ago.
Traditionally, dealings in Japan were (and largely remain) based on a social, rather than legal, basis. Personalities are key: consultation among
parties and recourse to third parties for conciliation are common techniques for resolving conflict.

> A few years ago, a well-known Japanese professor of law was asked by one
> of the TV channels to chair a round-table discussion on international con-
> tracts. He was considered as a foremost expert in the matter, having stud-
> ied it in Germany and in the United States. Concerned about refreshing his
> memory, he called up an American acquaintance who had studied law in a
> Japanese university and was involved in business in Japan for many years.
> Their encounter started by a rather forceful statement on the part of the
> Japanese that, stripped of Japanese-language circumlocutions, was as fol-
> lows: "You know what is the matter with you foreigners? When a deal is
> negotiated, you foreigners negotiate a contract, we Japanese negotiate a
> relationship." The essence of the difference had been clearly stated. Of
> course, any contract is a relationship, but not every relationship is a mere
> contract! (Ballon 1985b: 3)

East and West equally appreciate that successful business is not the
result of a contract but of a relationship. However, in Japan, emphasis is
taken away from the legal aspects of performance and shifted to more
subjective aspects, in fact, to the performers. Consider these instances:

Foreign companies expect open bidding to be the rule, in particular for building
projects, if not also for any local procurement. However, among their local com-

petitors, there is the general conviction that greater benefit can be expected from an ongoing relationship than from a temporary contract (see Kobayashi 1987).

Land is purchased by contract. But the contract has established a relationship between the buyer and seller that all too often requires outlays well beyond the contract and well after the contract has been consummated.

Regular employment, as opposed to part-time, is not on the basis of an individual labor contract. Secure employment results from a relationship governed by a sense of obligation between company and employee, extending on both sides deeper and wider than any contract.

The customary tone of written contracts among Japanese companies contrasts sharply with the legal, professional tone common in the West. Companies have little, if any, recourse to legal professionals, be they attorneys-at-law or judges. It has often been pointed out that Japan counts only 12,000 lawyers, and the problem of law consciousness of the Japanese has been addressed with much controversy (see Haley 1978: 359–390; Brown 1983). Although some major cases of pollution and product liability have demonstrated that collectivities have active recourse to litigation against corporations (Upham 1987), it remains true that the role of judges is perceived differently.

> Japanese not only hesitate to resort to a lawsuit but are also quite ready to settle an action already instituted through conciliatory processes during the course of litigation. With this inclination in the background, judges are likely to hesitate, or at least not to seek, to expedite judicial decisions, preferring instead to reconcile the litigant parties. . . . Complaint about delay in reaching judicial decisions is almost universal, particularly in recent years, and the reasons for the delay are diverse. But one reason may be this judicial hesitancy to attribute clear-cut victory and defeat to the respective parties. . . . Furthermore, it seems that judges are rather commonly inclined to attach importance to the status quo or to a fait accompli. . . . Considering these facts, parties in a dispute usually find that resort to a lawsuit is less profitable than resort to other means of settlement. (Tanaka 1976: 265)

A standard contract between two Japanese companies encompasses two to three pages and contains a dozen articles. It does not state definitely the matter at stake, in order not to restrict the flexibility judged indispensable for satisfactory performance. The final clause apparently throws the contract to the winds: "Concerning matters not stipulated herein or any doubt about the stipulation, both parties shall settle them upon deliberation." This flexibility is echoed throughout the contract by the frequent use of expressions such as "mutually acceptable," "as soon as practical," or a statement such as "Should a disagreement arise, the

parties will settle it amicably by consultation." resort to judicial proceedings. The need for obligations is recognized, but means for adjust to consultation!

In the Japanese corporate structure, legal m handled in a unit so labeled; it would make the tic! The preferred label is *bunsho-ka* (archive se a section, even in the largest companies, is comp ees who have learned corporate legal practice th company. These male employees are provided wit employees. The total staff of "legal" sections in tions tends to be below ten (Commercial Law Ce Kenkyūkai 1982). If a case has to be litigated, t practicing attorneys or law teachers (law faculty cludes lawyers admitted to the bar). The main jo ever, is to prevent litigation.

> In the words of the head of the Legal Department of th tion, "For a private firm, once a dispute occurs, dam company eventually wins the suit, in the process it will urable and very often irreparable harm, economically more important for our Legal Department than preventi (Commercial Law Center 1979: 8).

In practice, therefore, the legal aspects of busine various departments, if not neglected altogether. Fo

> Sales sections have wide discretion to adjust contractua generally avoid informing other sections [including the their difficulties. They feel that disagreements with thei from their failure in choosing business partners or from starting deals without reaching sufficiently specific unde the details of the performance. Thus they hate to publici they consider reflect their mistakes, and the facts of the known only to the members of a particular section or de 1968: 167)

The contract determines a time frame, and changing they occur, are supposedly controlled by legal theory the Japanese businessman remains intimately convince unpredictable and that, therefore, the circumstances t tractual performance are unforeseeable. Flexibility i taken for granted. The age-old legal principle of sup interpreted in the broader context of the relationship ra row context of the contract. Because of the sudden ju

4

THE INDUSTRIAL
GROUPING

O N OCTOBER 31, 1945, fifteen Japanese firms (*zaibatsu*) and their subsidiaries and affiliates were, by a directive of the military occupation, restricted from the sale, trade, transfer or adjustment of their capital stocks, bonds, debentures, voting trust, or other forms of capital securities. One week later, the four major holding companies (*honsha*), Mitsubishi, Mitsui, Yasuda, and Sumitomo, were directed to transfer all securities and ownership of other firms to the Holding Company Liquidation Commission for the purpose of public distribution of these securities. Soon, more *zaibatsu* shared the same fate. Securities were not to be sold back to the original holders, but were to be issued first to employees of the respective firms, then to the inhabitants of the areas in which the firms were located, and finally to the public at large when the stock exchanges were reopened in May 1949. Although the sale of stocks was not officially permitted, they were in fact traded in over-the-counter transactions, and group trading was prominent. "The Occupation did not eliminate groupings, only the family role in them and their top holding companies" (Hadley 1984: 320).

The Antimonopoly Law (1947), enacted to prevent the reappearance of monopolistic domination of the economy, explicitly prohibited holding companies. Numerous smaller companies emerged immediately after the war, but economic reconstruction requiring huge amounts of capital soon put banks in the limelight. Major commercial banks, also called city banks (*toshi ginkō*), replaced the *zaibatsu* and were increasingly relied upon as the primary source of corporate funds.

Commercial banks became key to financing because a) Japanese citizens overwhelmingly put their savings in bank deposits, b) by relying on commercial banks for external capital savings could be enhanced through credit creation and c) it gave the government a handle for steering investments which it would not have had financing been done through the capital market. (Hadley 1984: 320)

Compared to the prewar holding companies, whose domination took a well-defined form, postwar concentration is a dynamic force, never fully crystallizing into an institutionalized shape but always in the making through mutual shareholding, bank and intercompany loans, business transactions, and multiple human ties. Although former *zaibatsu* names and trademarks initially discontinued were in most cases revived after 1952 and the term *zaibatsu* is still used by the mass media, the economic phenomenon referred to is basically different from the prewar one. The standard Japanese term for the postwar form is *keiretsu* (literally, alignment; commonly translated as "grouping"). Because stockholding control is formally lacking, it cannot be called a conglomerate. It has the following characteristics:

1. The members are all "independent" major firms in their own oligopolistic industries.

2. The *keiretsu* is a confederation pursuing the "one-set" formula (i.e. excluding competitors but aiming at representing all lines within the confederation).

3. Service firms (for example: banking, trading, insurance, and shipping companies) from within the *keiretsu* perform special functions for industrial member firms in varying degrees (not usually to the complete exclusion of outsiders).

4. Between the firms there are several cross-ties: e.g. borrowing from the same banks, mutual shareholding, interlocking directors, using the same trademark, the same trading company, and liaison planning by presidents' clubs.

5. Much interfirm business, horizontal and vertical, is done within the group of firms.

6. Holding companies at the top (as in the prewar *zaibatsu*) have been eliminated so that the relationship between these groupings is now more cooperative than controlled. (Henderson 1973: 131–132)

A helpful distinction is usually made between *kin-yū* (financial) *keiretsu*, such as those around city banks or the Industrial Bank of Japan (IBJ), and *kigyō* (enterprise) *keiretsu*, such as those around Hitachi or Matsushita. Most typical are the groupings around the six major city banks that are periodically investigated by the Fair Trade Commission. The FTC distinguishes two classes: the three former *zaibatsu* groups, Mitsubishi, Mitsui, and Sumitomo, and the other three groups, Fuyō

TABLE 15.
Six Major Industrial Groups: Shares of the National Economy
(FY 1977 and 1981)
(percentage)

	Total Assets	Net Assets	Paid-up Capital[1]	Amount of Sales[2]	Current Profit[3]	Total Profit	No. of Workers[4]
Total of six groups							
1977	24.99	19.39	19.13	15.66	18.51	26.66	6.05
1981	25.94	18.08	16.46	15.78	19.23	25.31	5.11
Former *zaibatsu* three groups							
1977	11.72	9.13	8.44	7.49	8.36	11.68	2.39
1981	12.42	8.23	7.53	7.38	8.49	11.71	2.03
Other three groups							
1977	13.26	10.26	10.68	8.17	10.15	14.97	3.66
1981	13.53	9.85	8.93	8.40	10.74	13.61	3.08
All companies	100.00	100.00	100.00	100.00	100.00	100.00	100.00

SOURCE: FTC 1983/6: 22.
[1]Excluding life insurance companies.
[2]Excluding financial companies.
[3]Excluding non-life insurance companies.
[4]Excluding insurance companies.

(Fuji Bank), Daiichi-Kangyo, and Sanwa. These six groups, comprising fewer than 200 companies (members of the group's presidents' meeting) and each including a major trading firm, represent a substantial portion of the Japanese economy (table 15). The privileged role of the bank is essentially the result of the early postwar circumstances that placed them at the heart of the reconstruction of industry and the subsequent high rate of economic growth.

> Group financing needs can be to a considerable extent complementary, seasonal fluctuations in demand for funds can be smoothed, and cyclical variations in the strength of economic demand can be more easily financed. In addition, the existence of different types of financial institutions within the group—typically a commercial bank, a trust bank and an insurance company—enables the differing financial needs of the group to be met. Finally, a group trading company, itself financed to a significant extent by the group bank, provides trade finance to smaller companies in the group with which it is in more knowledgeable contact and thus provides a buffer to the bank against the riskier end of the lending spectrum. A final advantage for the bank comes from the availability of a large number of group employees who are encouraged to put their savings with the group bank and thus provide a source of stable deposits. (Elston 1981: 513)

A recent study attempts to explain the phenomenon of Japanese industrial groupings in terms of basic economic analysis, stressing that they are not an unmitigated blessing. The study concludes that

> (1) the level of profits and growth rates of the G (group) firm are generally lower, (2) distribution of output within the firm is biased in the G firm in favor of the employee, (3) the fluctuation of profit as well as growth rates is relatively smaller for the G firm, and (4) financial policy of the G firm differs significantly from that of the I (independent) firm. That is, the debt-equity ratio is much higher, and the ratio of dividend over paid-in capital much lower for the G firm. It is of interest to ask why group-affiliated firms show a tendency towards lower profits or growth rates and have smaller variations in these measures. The tendency may be attributed to the risk attitude of management which seeks to stabilize corporate performance at the cost of lowering the *level* of performance itself. Indeed, stability of performance is likely to guarantee the *status quo* of the managers, unless they perform too poorly when compared with the average firm. It may also improve the welfare of other corporate constituents, particularly workers, if they are sufficiently risk-averse. (Nakatani 1984: 230, 228)

Close interaction between banks and enterprises is not limited to the large industrial groups. It is most common throughout Japanese industry. As a practical consequence, the first piece of information the Japanese businessman inquires about when encountering a lesser-known company is about its "main bank" (*shuryoku ginkō*).

The Main Bank

Contrary to general expectations in other industrial countries, Japanese banks are not "outsiders" in the eyes of their clients, small and large. It is vital for any enterprise to cultivate a close relationship with its main bank. More often than not, this bank at some point in time has had to stage a rescue operation for its major clients with the cooperation of other parties concerned. Especially in the 1950s, many companies found themselves in dire straits and turned to their main banks.

For example, Marubeni, a major trading company, had the Sumitomo Bank as main bank. In 1955, it absorbed Takashimaya-Iida, a smaller trading company of the Fuyō (Fuji's) *keiretsu*, at the request of the Fuji Bank, which was rescuing Takashimaya-Iida. Marubeni suffered a large loss that year as it took over Takashimaya-Iida liabilities. But the understanding was that progressively the loss would be more than made up by future business introduced by the Fuji Bank and its *keiretsu*. The Fuji Bank became its main bank. Today, Marubeni is the leading trading company of the Fuyō group.

Most growth companies initially borrow from as many banks as make themselves available, because the banks try to finance a large number of borrowers with a limited amount of lendable cash in order to share the risk of loans to a particular company. At a certain stage in the lender-borrower relationship, a specific bank becomes the main bank. However, even when a bank has become the main one, loans continue to be taken in large amounts from other banks. A rather exceptional case would be the switch from one main bank to another. It may happen, however, that the client's needs are larger than the main bank can provide. Thus Mitsui & Co., the general trading company at the core of the Mitsui Group, has far outgrown the capacity of the Mitsui Bank; it has now three main banks: Mitsui Bank, Fuji Bank, and the Industrial Bank of Japan. The process by which a company is integrated into the group could be sketched as follows:

1. The company develops substantial business with a given group; naturally, it involves the core bank of the group.

2. This bank promotes business volume by obvious readiness to favor new loans related to business with the group; it also increases its shareholding in the company.

3. The bank proposes that it be given preference in loans and shareholding (over a second bank).

4. The second bank reacts by requesting that loan amount and shareholding percentage be kept at least equal. The company must now decide whether or not to join the group of the first bank.

A standard variation of step 3, immediately eliminating step 4, would be for the bank to be instrumental in a merger with some other company under its wing, or, if the company is weak or not yet well established, to make further support conditional on some tie-up (shareholding or dispatch of a director) with a member company of the group.

The complex interaction of banks and clients is well illustrated by the case of a major trading company, C. Itoh.

C. Itoh started in Osaka. After World War II, when it launched its development as a diversified trading company, naturally enough it used the Osaka-based Sumitomo Bank as its main bank. However, in the process of building up the Sumitomo *keiretsu*, the bank strongly promoted Sumitomo Trading, smaller than C. Itoh. Meanwhile, C. Itoh reinforced its ties with the Daiichi and Nippon Kangyo banks. When these two banks merged in the early 1970s, Daiichi Kangyo Bank became the first main bank and Sumitomo Bank the second main bank of C. Itoh.

Sumitomo Bank had been the main bank of Ataka & Co. (the last on the then standard list of the top ten general trading companies). When this company was in dire straits in 1977, the bank after lengthy negotiations succeeded in convinc-

TABLE 16.

Equity and Debt Capital Extended by the Top Nine Trading Companies (1978)

(million yen)

Company	Equity Investment at Home and Abroad (A)		Loans at Home and Abroad (B)		A + B		Rate of Return on Equity Investment (percentage)	Overseas Financing (equity and loans as percentage of A + B)	
Mitsubishi Corp.	177,955	(38.6%)	283,361	(61.4%)	461,316	(100.0%)	9.4	140,200	(30.4%)
Mitsui & Co.	283,536	(39.0)	443,056	(61.0)	726,582	(100.0)	3.1	248,700	(34.2)
C. Itoh & Co.	239,958	(42.1)	329,625	(57.9)	569,583	(100.0)	2.2	115,300	(20.2)
Marubeni Corp.	159,727	(53.5)	138,695	(46.5)	298,422	(100.0)	2.2	126,100	(42.3)
Sumitomo Corp.	109,554	(63.8)	62,053	(36.2)	171,607	(100.0)	2.0	59,300	(34.6)
Nissho Iwai	65,217	(40.9)	94,325	(59.1)	159,542	(100.0)	2.0	61,000	(38.2)
Tomen	42,376	(43.3)	55,457	(56.7)	97,833	(100.0)	2.0	41,700	(42.6)
Kanematsu-Gosho	34,461	(31.8)	74,021	(68.2)	108,482	(100.0)	1.3	25,200	(23.2)
Nichimen Jitsugyo	24,538	(33.2)	49,319	(66.8)	73,857	(100.0)	1.2	29,600	(40.1)

SOURCE: Kojima and Ozawa 1984: 89.

NOTE: The trading companies do not make public the breakdown between overseas equity investments and loans. One estimate made from their financial statements for fiscal 1980 (April 1, 1980–March 30, 1981) puts the equity-debt ratio of overseas investment for Mitsubishi at 80 to 20, for Mitsui 65 to 35, for C. Itoh 82 to 18, for Marubeni 87 to 13, for Sumitomo 87 to 13, for Nissho Iwai 64 to 36, for Tomen 89 to 11, for Kanematsu Gosho 86 to 14, and for Nichimen Jitsugyo 91 to 9. These figures, however, do not include offshore-arranged loans, which are known to be quite substantial in amount but for which no statistics are available. Hence the equity-debt ratios shown here are concerned only with financial flows made directly from Japan.

ing C. Itoh to absorb a substantial portion (the steel division) of Ataka, which subsequently dissolved. For its part, Sumitomo wrote off over a three-year period ¥106 billion that it had loaned to Ataka.

Group cohesion must be nurtured with care and over time, and is determined as much by intangible as by tangible factors. The main bank greatly influences group transactions, which are on a semi-arm's-length basis. Member companies are often persuaded to buy products and services from within the group. The bank may even elicit deposits to build up its deposit record (the major criterion for size among Japanese banks); it can also persuade companies to borrow when money is abundant. However, the bank must respect the autonomy of member firms; normally, it neither contributes positive advice nor takes action unless so requested. Otherwise, a company can turn to another bank with which it already has substantial loans.

Kubota, a successful company listed on foreign stock exchanges, has had for several years as board members the presidents of both Sumitomo Bank and Fuji Bank from which it borrows heavily. Consequently, the company has two main banks. The business rationale is that Kubota, an Osaka-based company, is related to the Sumitomo Bank but considers it essential to have also a Tokyo-based bank, the Fuji Bank, as main bank. The president of Kubota thus participates in the regular meetings of company presidents of the Sumitomo as well as the Fuyō *keiretsu*.

General Trading Companies

In Japan, industrial producers have long been involved solely in manufacturing; in principle, purchase of raw materials, sales and distribution of the finished product, as well as all ancillary services were activities largely undertaken by the general trading company (GTC) (*sōgō shōsha*) attached to the industrial group. The term "general trading company" is restricted to the top nine trading companies (they were ten until the failure of Ataka & Co. in 1977.) Periodically the Fair Trade Commission surveys the top six trading companies, in line with its surveys of the six major *keiretsu*. Undoubtedly, GTCs are the most powerful single concentrated force in Japanese business (table 16).

These firms, as their name implies, are involved in all types of trading, nothing excluded. Because their primary interest is in import and export for Japan, they are able to bring in a large supply of exchange and to contribute in no small way to Japan's favorable balance of payments. They have also established themselves in third-country trade, performing substantial off-shore business, an activity from which they make large profits. They raise funds through financial institutions, Japanese as well as foreign, to finance development of overseas natural resources for export to Japan with payment on a deferred basis. They serve as information centers, not only for their own trade but also for other companies, or liaison between foreign governments and corporations. Finally, GTCs have invested heavily in such large-scale projects as petroleum exploration, ocean development, raw material resource development in iron ore and timber, and in the so-called information industry, all areas of major concern for future development of the Japanese economy. Quite naturally, executives of the *sōgō shōsha* refer to their companies as "world enterprises" (*sekai kigyō*) and often suggest with legitimate pride that they should more properly be called "general development corporations." "Without the trading companies many small Japanese firms could not hope to exploit foreign markets. The trading companies have effectively become the overseas procurement, sales, and financing departments for thousands of Japanese companies" (Bronte 1982: 113).

Domestically, GTCs are assured a leading role because they participate heavily in the steady development of the domestic market and are by nature involved in physical distribution and its financing. They serve an inventory function, acting as reservoir to adjust supply and demand. Particularly in textiles and foodstuffs, they play a vital role for many subsectors of the economy by providing raw materials and credit to producing and processing firms. Leasing is also one of their major lines. The ease with which *sōgō shōsha* combine domestic and international operations by being able to readily transfer personnel where needed is one of their most striking features.

Though the GTCs indeed boast of their hefty volume of transactions, their merit is not so much in the benefits they themselves derive from these transactions as in the intermediation itself, in particular financial intermediation. The overall business talent of the general trading companies is backed up by substantial financial means, both received and provided. Obviously, the huge borrowings by the six major trading companies mainly from the city banks cannot be generated from within their own industrial group; all other groups cooperate (table 17). The main purpose of these borrowings is to cover financial arrangements with suppliers and customers, large and small. Credit in the Japanese economy is thus expanded in successive waves. Enterprises can simultaneously borrow from the trading companies to purchase raw materials and sell finished products while to a certain extent financing themselves, their subsidiaries, and their subcontractors. For many reasons, this interme-

TABLE 17.

Top Six Trading Companies: Borrowings from Major City Banks (End FY 1981)

(million yen)

Bank	Mitsubishi Corp.	Mitsui & Co.	C. Itoh & Co.	Marubeni	Sumitomo Trading	Nissho-Iwai
Daiichi-Kangyo Bank	52,418	49,405	82,597	26,630	—	67,835
Fuji Bank	46,203	62,465	37,756	85,505	—	11,385
Sumitomo Bank	40,187	57,108	66,551	23,085	72,573	2,685
Mitsubishi Bank	70,154	51,752	5,443	52,763	23,709	12,178
Sanwa Bank	58,542	55,220	7,010	44,872	—	78,020
Mitsui Bank	13,857	69,793	36,175	32,711	—	14,222
(for comparison)						
Bank of Tokyo	64,979	64,381	68,801	90,850	59,074	56,643

SOURCE: FTC 1983/4: 9.
NOTE: Figures are taken from the securities reports of the respective companies. Bold figures are not mentioned in these reports.

diary financing function of the trading companies has the support of the banks, which originate it, and that of the enterprises, which benefit.

For banks, the assumption is that the trading company is more knowledgeable and involved in marginal loans.

> The trading companies were able to expand their lending facilities because they were willing to assume risks which the large banks would not touch. In this respect, they evolved into what were essentially venture banks. They provide the missing services that the city banks would not, or could not offer. Because they often knew better than their clients the markets for raw materials and end products, they could afford to take risks. And, while banks would accept only relatively liquid assets as loan collateral, such as cash, securities, time deposits, and sometimes land, the trading companies would accept any marketable product. . . . The trading companies can secure their loans in a number of ways. Although the banks receive priority in the event of a bankruptcy, the trading companies will accept mortgages on fixed assets, including even the personal property of the client's corporate officers. They can accept promissory notes issued by healthier companies and endorsed by the client, and may request extra guarantors for loans. Since trading companies often store commodities for clients after delivery, because of the shortage of warehouse space in Japan, they also have property which can be seized. Perhaps the most important protection against losses on loans is the knowledge which the trading companies possess about their clients' markets. (Bronte 1982: 114–115)

Furthermore, the trading company is better able to sustain a loss in one area and make up for it in another because of the types and quantity of goods it handles, one item being usually a very small percentage of total turnover in the wide portfolio of products. For a bank to lend to a trading company that is financing an enterprise is much less a default risk than a direct loan to the enterprise, because the trading company can, if necessary, absorb the loss. Banks usually ask their smaller customers to consolidate small notes receivable into one note of a trading company. The note from a major trader is readily rediscounted by the Bank of Japan. A meaningful advantage is that smaller firms can borrow from trading companies at more favorable interest rates than at the banks and without compensating balance. If receivables are in jeopardy, the trading company can come to the rescue with much less adverse publicity than if banks are involved. For the trading company itself, because its popular image and ranking in the industry is determined by sales volume and because the trading company is not subject to the governmental checks and controls on financing that restrict the banks, its financial operations are a direct contribution to sales. As a result, GTCs are able to contribute substantial integrative power to the *keiretsu*, both vertically and horizontally.

> In short, as financial institutions, Japan's general trading companies are unique. They combine the roles of the British merchant bank, which was founded to provide medium-term loans for foreign trade, and the German universal bank, which is heavily committed to financing its affiliated industrial group. But the important difference is that Japan's trading companies are quite willing to accept an extremely low rate of return on financial investment in exchange for other business transactions that enable them to earn commissions. The financing services of a trading company may perhaps be likened to what in marketing jargon is called a "loss leader," which is used to attract customers to other items the store sells. (Kojima and Ozawa 1984: 25)

It is no surprise then that the two main financial features of *sōgō shōsha* are thin margins and high leverage: (1) Low gross trading profit margins are caused by the nature of their business—the pursuit of economies of scale to reduce business risks and bulk transactions—as well as their accounting practices—reporting gross amount of transactions as gross trading volume when in fact only the services of a broker are provided or when the revenues from a transaction are in reality only a commission. For the fiscal year that ended March 31, 1986, the nine GTCs reported an average gross trading volume exceeding ¥10 trillion and an average trading profit margin of less than 2%. (2) Leverage is by far the highest among Japanese companies. This is because the GTCs, as trade creditors or organizers of large projects, are frequently in a position to provide large amounts of financing in various forms for their customers and suppliers and for companies that participate in the projects. To finance their operations, the *sōgō shōsha* rely primarily on the banks, for they are perceived as excellent credit risks by the Japanese banking community. As of March 31, 1986, the average ratio of debt to equity of the nine GTCs was 18:1 (Touche Ross 1986: 8—14).

Since the mid-1970s, for reasons beyond their control, the ability of trading companies to finance clients' transactions has been seriously eroded. Japan's international trade has changed substantially as it has worked its way into higher levels of technology and more and more Japanese corporations have entered trade on their own account. Also, city banks themselves have had to revise their own credit policies and are competing directly with the financing provided by trading companies. This is reflected in the top six GTCs' increased shareholding in related companies and their attempts at playing a role in world markets more similar to that of merchant banks.

The Mechanics of Grouping

Basically, the *keiretsu* is a loosely knit organization of independent companies with a balanced combination of growth industries. At the same time, it is well organized in the sense of its competitive position vis-à-vis other groups. Interdependence within the group, with the main bank at its center, is cultivated by business and human ties.

In the early postwar years, mutual shareholding was a powerful instrument in the formation of the major *keiretsu* attempting to reestablish their prewar importance. Later, much mutual shareholding took place under the label of stable shareholding. City banks, within the constraints of the Antimonopoly Law, are among the largest shareholders of their major corporate clients, followed closely by the other financial institutions in the group (trust banks and insurance companies).

According to an FTC survey (1981), the average percentage of stock in each member company by another member company was 2.0% for Mitsubishi, Mitsui, and Sumitomo groups (former *zaibatsu* groups) and 1.5% for Fuyō, Daiichi-Kangyo, and Sanwa. For cross shareholding ratios (the average proportion of each *keiretsu* member firm's outstanding shares held by all other member firms in the *keiretsu*), the former *zaibatsu* groups averaged 32%, and the other three averaged 19% (FTC 1983: 5—8).

Business transactions within the group manifest a similar trend; currently they average about 10% among nonfinancial members (table 18). On the basis of the FTC's internal documents for the year 1984, intragroup transactions in major product categories were reported as follows:

	Purchases	Sales
Textiles and apparel	3.1%	1.2
Food and agricultural products	0.5	0.6
Mining, metal materials, and chemicals	9.9	6.7
Machines and equipment	1.1	.8

(Higashi and Lauter 1987: 41)

Human ties play an important role in group cohesiveness as well. They take the form of presidents' meetings, interlocking directorates, and transfer of personnel. Meetings of presidents of the *keiretsu*'s major member companies are held regularly, often backed up by meetings of directors and of upper-level managers. These meetings are not organs of decision making in the sense that a majority vote would carry the day, but they are manifestations of the very dynamic process of consensus. Views are exchanged, opinions heard, and actions reciprocally adjusted, more on an ad hoc basis than in terms of binding policy, a process that characterizes Japanese management.

The dispatch, permanent or temporary, of executives among group members is standard practice in ordinary times. In troubled periods a former bank official may be installed as president or board member of the company concerned. It is also fairly common that when the president or a director of a bank retires he becomes president or director of a related company (although the reverse is never seen!). For example, at one time or another, presidents of Yamaichi Securities, New Japan Securities, Wako Securities, Nissan Motors, Cosmo Oil, and Nissan Chemical were all former executives of the Industrial Bank of Japan.

The top six trading companies, as of March 1982, had dispatched executives to 57.5% of the companies in which they held 10% or more of the shares (an average of 1.4 directors per company or 14.2% of the Board), to 89.6% of their affiliates (2.7 directors per company or 30.1% of the board), and to 97.6% of their subsidiaries (5.0 directors per company or 66.2% of the board) (FTC 1983/4: 32).

Interlocking directorates are a feature of the *keiretsu* found in 70% of the member companies, and in about half of the member companies at least the main bank (or the trading company) has dispatched one executive to them. But no less effective than interlocking directorates are the close personal relations among alumni of the same university, pupils of the same teacher, intermarriage with or without adoption by the other family, previous service in the same military organization, or the

TABLE 18.

Six Major Industrial Groups: Intragroup Transactions (1981)

(percentage)

	Nonfinancial Members		Member-Manufacturers	
	Purchases	Sales	Purchases	Sales
Total of six groups	11.7	10.8	12.4	20.4
Former *zaibatsu* groups	14.8	13.4	18.6	29.0
Other three groups	9.1	8.6	8.2	14.9

SOURCE: FTC 1983/6: 19, 20.

comradeship that resulted from working together in the same prewar *zaibatsu*.

In addition, human ties within the group are accumulated by transfers of personnel (*shukkō*). This practice is identical to the one found among related companies. It takes one of the following two forms: either the transferee, initially sent on a temporary basis, later becomes a permanent member of the company, or the transfer is only temporary, usually for a term of two or three years. The transfer may supply the following benefits to the two corporations: manpower supply and technical assistance; training (the parent's) personnel, especially young promising managers, through broader experience and business contacts; strengthening the subsidiary's managerial and financial operations, if not also directly controlling it; promoting (the parent's) managerial staff by transferring them to the subsidiary after the mandatory age limit. When reduction of personnel must take place, it is a major responsibility of management to first seek the transfer of surplus personnel to other companies. This practice has been nicknamed the "Japaneselike lay-off," as when the shipbuilding industry, hit by the oil shock, transferred some of its workforce to the automobile industry.

Interdependence is thus the key to a thriving group life: "it stabilizes corporate performance substantially" (Nakatani 1987: 188). It flourishes in times of prosperity but works best in times of need. During tight-money periods (a recurring phenomenon in postwar Japan) as well as in the face of oil shocks or yen appreciation, cooperation among member companies remains the first privileged recourse.

5

BUSINESS
FAILURE

THE JAPANESE TERM *tōsan*, translated in Japanese statistical reports and in mass media as "bankruptcy," is generally used in reference to business failure with liabilities of ¥10 million or more where default, excessive debts, or difficulties in business operations come to light owing to the following:

1. Suspension of bank transactions
2. Public announcement of voluntary dissolution
3. Filing under the Corporate Reorganization Law
4. Filing for commencement of composition
5. Filing for commencement of liquidation (Commercial Code, Art. 381)
6. Filing for special liquidation (Commercial Code, Art. 431)
7. Filing for voluntary petition of bankruptcy

For many years, between 15,000 and 20,000 enterprises failed annually. Although corporate insolvency as a statistical category is defined differently in different countries, an international comparison appears to reveal a Japanese peculiarity. The constancy over the years of the number of insolvencies indicates that the phenomenon is less of a cyclical than of a structural nature (table 19). Remarkably, in postwar Japan there has not been a single case of bank failure. In 1986, the number of business failures was 17,476 (18,812 in the previous year), including 4,611 unincorporated enterprises, with total liabilities of ¥3,752 billion (¥4,186 billion in 1985) (table 20). The vast majority of these failures (13,332 cases in 1985) are the fate of small companies capitalized at less than ¥10 million; they display certain characteristics by industry.

Firstly, by industry the non-manufacturing industry accounted for a large portion of the total. This reflects the fact that the business conditions of

construction and commerce . . . became stagnant as a result of the slow
growth in personal consumption and private housing investments against
the steady increase in exports. Secondly, as a whole, the ratio of small-scale
bankruptcies increased with the amount of debt per case being small. This
trend toward small-scale bankruptcies is particularly notable in the manufacturing industry, which indicates an increase of bankruptcies centering
on small-scale enterprises highly dependent on domestic demand. (MITI
1984/10: 7–8)

Among the older (more than 20 years of operations) small enterprises,
bankruptcies reflected companies' delay in responding to structural
changes in demand and supply environments (MITI 1985a: 8).

In general terms, failure is the result of a set of causes:

   Remote causes: business downturn in the industry; decrease of
sales turnover; severe competition
   Immediate causes: accepting orders at a loss; entry into a new area
or new product line; overinvestment in facilities; bad debts
   Trigger causes: problem with the circulation of bills; chain reaction
of bankruptcies; shortage of funds (Teikoku Data Bank 1985: 21)

By far, the largest business failure in postwar Japan has been that of
the Sanko Steamship Co. with liabilities of ¥520 billion, in 1985 (Stewart 1986). Other failures with liabilities of over ¥100 billion were Kojin
(1975), Eidai Sangyo (1978), Osawa Shokai (1984), and Riccar (1985).

When a Japanese company faces severe financial difficulty and reaches
the point of seeking protection from or settlement with its creditors, it
has two legal options: to apply for bankruptcy or composition under the
Bankruptcy Law, or to file for reorganization under the Corporate Reorganization Law. (To try to reach a settlement with creditors under the
Composition Law [1922] would generally be more appropriate for small

TABLE 19.

Insolvency Cases: International Comparison (1978–1986)

Year	Japan	United States	United Kingdom	F.R. Germany	France
1978	15,875	6,619	8,988	5,952	—
1979	16,030	7,564	8,037	5,484	15,863
1980	17,884	11,742	10,928	6,312	17,375
1981	17,610	16,794	13,747	8,496	20,895
1982	17,122	24,908	17,767	11,915	20,462
1983	19,155	31,334	20,438	11,845	22,708
1984	20,841	52,078	21,950	12,018	25,018
1985	18,812	57,067	21,674	13,625	26,425
1986	17,476	—	21,557	13,500	27,802

SOURCE: Bank of Japan 1987: 170.

TABLE 20.

Cases of Business Failure by Size of Capital, Size of Liabilities, and Cause
(1975–1986)

	1975	1980	1984	1985	1986
Total number of failures	12,605	17,884	20,841	18,812	17,476
Unincorporated enterprises	2,505	3,838	5,937	5,280	4,611
(Amount of their liabilities in billion yen)	(1,913)	(2,707)	(3,626)	(4,186)	(3,752)
Incorporated enterprises, by capital size (million yen)					
Less than 1	870	803	678	577	521
1–less than 10	7,754	10,760	11,300	10,091	9,416
10–less than 50	1,326	2,306	2,697	2,664	2,687
50–less than 100	83	130	165	161	174
100 and over	67	47	64	39	67
Incorporated enterprises, by liabilities size (million yen)					
10–less than 50	7,331	8,563	9,805	8,394	7,614
50–less than 100	2,240	3,949	4,504	4,106	3,794
100–less than 500	2,437	4,361	5,362	5,085	4,735
500–less than 1,000	312	567	666	700	759
1,000 and over	285	444	504	527	574
Incorporated enterprises, by cause					
Stagnation of sales	2,959	5,230	7,805	6,519	6,219
Deterioration of sales bills collection	1,063	2,528	1,938	1,761	1,902
Reckless management	5,025	5,778	5,868	5,245	4,348
Failure of business planning	1,707	2,110	1,944	1,868	1,581
Other	1,851	2,238	3,286	3,419	3,426

SOURCE: Statistics Bureau 1987: 384.
NOTE: The source translates *tōsan* as "bankruptcy."

estates.) But in Japan business failure is popularly equated with suspension of bank transactions.

Suspension of Bank Transactions

Banks suspend transactions after two dishonored notes within six months are reported by the clearinghouse. The experience may, of course, befall an individual (25,000 cases in 1975 declining to 7,000 in 1986) as well as unincorporated (21,000 to 10,000 cases) and incorporated enterprises (16,000 to 13,000 cases) (table 21). It means that the issuer cannot open a current account or receive loans for a period of two years. Therefore, the issuer's home bank is to cancel his current and loan accounts, while collecting unused note forms and loans (Namiki 1984: 27). Moreover, if the suspended party establishes a new corporation or becomes the representative of an established corporation, and that corporation is seen as the same reality as the suspended (having the same president, same business content, and no change in capital), the same sanctions are to be taken in regard to that corporation. An exception to the rule of suspension is possible for so-called loans for preservation of credit (*saiken hozen*): loans already made to the debtor could be renewed, for example, for two to five years, until the debtor is able to pay them back. Most suspensions of business transactions with banks are triggered by notes being dishonored, for whatever economic "causes," and the large majority of cases affect companies capitalized at less than ¥10 million. Most reports mention only the number of enterprises whose liabilities amount to ¥10 million or more (the number of suspensions of enterprises whose liabilities are less than ¥10 million would be about one-third of the former) (table 22).

When business failure is imminent and corporate management is faced with unconditional surrender to the banks, it will often try as a last desperate move to turn to a *kōri-gashi* (loan shark). A note sold at usury rates is not recorded; only a cash transaction is recorded as receipt for cash sales. Expert opinion has it that most dishonored notes have been notes issued to loan sharks. Many small companies have failed in such a way. The usual practice is to obtain the necessary cash by depositing a ten-day maturity note to be settled at the issuer's bank and bearing an interest rate of 3% to 10% for the period. The receiver is requested not to turn in the note at the bank on the promise that it will be refunded in cash. The management hopes that during the ten days the banks will agree to further financing. If there is a delay, however, new short-maturity notes are issued or the loan shark uses strong-arm tactics. If he simply cashes the note, pandemonium occurs: the short maturity is a clear sign to the banks. They may back out, or at least will not take long to decide on a course of action.

Business failure is the standard hard luck of small companies that do not have the necessary leverage on banks or others to bail them out. It is often caused by a chain reaction: when a parent company fails, some of its subsidiaries and subcontractors share its fate. Unlike the small firms left to fend on their own, most large companies are tightly involved with an industrial grouping. They may find themselves in a shaky financial position, but it is expected that well before anything as dangerous as

TABLE 21.

Cases of Suspension of Bank Transactions by Size of Capital and Cause
(1975–1986)

	1975	1980	1984	1985	1986
Total number of cases	64,307	62,766	48,283	39,949	32,451
Persons (nonenterprise)	25,651	25,472	13,343	10,057	7,115
Unincorporated enterprises	21,730	18,777	16,300	13,252	10,746
Incorporated enterprises capitalized at less than one million yen	2,320	1,606	1,429	1,153	872
Incorporated enterprises capitalized at one million yen and over, by capital size (million yen) (Amount of liabilities in billion yen)	(1,056)	(1,446)	(2,028)	(1,861)	(2,041)
1 and over	14,477	16,635	16,976	15,337	13,578
1–less than 3	8,271	7,860	7,397	6,400	5,407
3–less than 10	4,624	6,459	7,029	6,405	5,730
10–less than 50	1,421	2,025	2,190	2,171	2,125
50–less than 100	57	75	76	82	68
100 and over	104	216	284	279	248
Incorporated enterprises capitalized at one million yen and over, by cause					
Overinvestment in inventories and plant equipment	1,345	1,274	1,045	1,069	942
Stagnant sales	5,883	5,865	7,236	6,530	5,818
High cost of production, shortage of labor, and deterioration of profits	1,992	2,608	2,223	1,971	1,823
Deterioration of proceeds collection	1,496	1,646	1,495	1,333	1,240
Allied enterprises failures	1,322	1,878	1,661	1,631	1,458
Financing by accommodation bills	2,040	2,517	2,598	2,205	1,943
Other	2,887	5,078	5,874	5,246	4,834

SOURCE: Statistics Bureau 1987: 384.

dishonoring a bill could happen, the main bank, if not also the entire group, will move to the rescue.

It is unlikely that the investing public, particularly the foreign investor, would be involved in the business failure of a small firm. But between the small firms and the large corporations that enjoy group support, there remains an intermediate level at which the investing public may well get caught. This would be the listed medium-size company, not affiliated with one of the large groupings and having no main bank. In the ten years from January 1965 to May 1974, 26 companies in a similar position were

TABLE 22.

*Cases of Suspension of Bank Transactions with Liabilities of Less Than
10 Million Yen (1979–1985)*

(number and percentage)

Year	Business Failures		Of Which Liabilities Are Less Than ¥10 Million	
	Total	Cause: Suspension	Total	Cause: Suspension
1979	25,909	24,998	9,470	9,461
	(100.0)	(96.5)	(100.0)	(99.9)
1980	27,326	26,322	9,197	9,185
	(100.0)	(96.3)	(100.0)	(99.9)
1981	28,004	27,152	10,703	10,642
	(100.0)	(97.0)	(100.0)	(99.4)
1982	26,921	25,677	9,581	9,336
	(100.0)	(95.4)	(100.0)	(97.4)
1983	19,958	18,742	9,703	9,685
	(100.0)	(93.9)	(100.0)	(99.8)
1984	28,959	27,419	8,603	8,535
	(100.0)	(94.8)	(100.0)	(99.2)
1985	25,945	24,273	7,627	7,611
	(100.0)	(93.5)	(100.0)	(99.7)

SOURCE: Small and Medium Enterprise Agency 1986a: 50–51.

bankrupted or reorganized. All were listed on the Tokyo Stock Exchange, nine of them on the First Section. Two on the First and nine on the Second Section were bankrupted; all others reorganized (Bonds 1974: 23).

Bankruptcy

Medium and large corporations, if other means fail, have access to legal recourse: adjudicated bankruptcy (*hasan*) or reorganization (*kōsei*). As is true generally in Japanese civil courts, however, judges are less concerned about passing judgment than about helping parties settle a matter between themselves. In a business failure, there is the further imperative of seeking to prevent the dissolution of a company, which would deprive employees of the security they expected from lifetime employment. Adjudication of bankruptcy is, then, not a practical solution; it is preferable to rule on corporate reorganization.

The Bankruptcy Law (1922) was substantially amended in 1952; it recognizes three causes of bankruptcy: insolvency, suspension of payment, and, in the case of joint stock companies, total liabilities exceeding total assets (Arts. 126–127). A debtor may file a petition for voluntary bankruptcy. The majority of bankruptcies, however, are involuntary and

TABLE 23.

Corporate Bankruptcy Cases by Industry (1985)

Size of Capital (million yen)	Total	Construction	Manufacturing	Retail and Wholesale Restaurants	Real Estate	Transportation and Communication	Services	Miscellaneous
					Industry			
Total	1,243	288	372	376	29	35	59	84
Less than 5	613	146	164	206	13	10	32	42
5 and over	245	68	67	65	9	11	13	12
10 and over	323	64	118	89	4	13	9	26
50 and over	42	7	16	12	1	1	4	1
100 and over	18	3	5	4	2	—	1	3
500 and over	1	—	1	—	—	—	—	—
1,000 and over	1	—	1	—	—	—	—	—

SOURCE: Supreme Court Secretariate 1985: 299.

involve corporations or persons doing business. A petition of bankruptcy can be filed on behalf of joint stock companies by the company directors (Art. 133). After filing, the court, typically, appoints a receiver (*kanzainin*) (Art. 157). A judgment of bankruptcy is rendered if the obligor is found to be insolvent.

In 1985, close to 40,000 bankruptcy cases went in front of the courts, of which 17,000 were new cases brought during the year, and 17,000 cases were settled. Of these, corporate bankruptcies accounted for 1,243 cases. A total of 962 cases were settled, 20 by adjudication and 666 by liquidation, of which 20 involved money lenders. The remaining cases were settled by the creditors themselves (Supreme Court Secretariate 1985: 12, 299–300) (table 23).

Generally, in bankruptcy cases Japanese creditors are only interested in obtaining their share of liquidation; they rarely spend time and money on investigating criminal conduct, although they may make threats based on the right to do so.

Corporate Reorganization

The Corporate Reorganization Law (1952) was part of the legal reform initiated by the American Occupation. It applies only to joint stock companies. Its purpose is to regenerate a business on the basis of its prospects for rehabilitation through adjustment of the interests of creditors and shareholders, even at the cost of complete alteration of the corporate shell. The first problem is to determine who is to come to the rescue, a search that involves primarily the main bank if not also the court itself. If such a prospect is found, the court approves the start of reorganization. Often, major secured creditors become shareholders; capitalization is reduced, and a new top management takes over. The brunt of the reorganization falls on the unsecured creditors.

Reorganization under the original law required consent of all interested parties. It resulted in questionable deals being made in order to obtain unanimity. A 1967 amendment required an 80% favorable vote (Art. 205). The court considers the information obtained from the hearings and investigations, and decides whether to proceed with or dismiss the application. If a company's main customer applies for reorganization or if his livelihood depends upon payment of the debt, the court may allow the trustee to pay the claim prior to reorganization approval; it may also permit prior payment of small claims. Normally, an order of suspension is issued, suspending any procedure such as bankruptcy and ordering preservative measures, such as prohibition of payments except

TABLE 24.

Approved Reorganization Cases (1985)

Size of Capital (million yen)	Total	Number of Creditors					Credit Extended (million yen)						
		Fewer Than 100	100 and More	200 and More	300 and More	500 and More	Less Than 100	100 and More	500 and More	1,000 and More	3,000 and More	5,000 and More	10,000 and More
Total	19	11	4	3	1	—	—	5	—	7	3	3	1
Less than 5	1	1	—	—	—	—	—	1	—	—	—	—	—
5 and more	2	2	—	—	—	—	—	1	—	—	—	—	—
10 and more	3	3	—	2	—	—	—	3	—	3	—	—	—
30 and more	3	1	—	1	—	—	—	—	—	2	1	—	—
50 and more	4	3	3	—	—	—	—	—	—	1	2	1	—
100 and more	4	1	—	—	1	—	—	—	—	1	—	1	—
200 and more	2	1	1	—	1	—	—	—	—	—	—	1	1
500 and more	1	—	1	—	—	—	—	—	—	—	—	—	1
1,000 and more	—	—	—	—	—	—	—	—	—	—	—	—	—

SOURCE: Supreme Court Secretariate 1985: 307.

employee wages, prohibition of borrowing, and prohibition of assets disposal. If the court reaches the decision to commence reorganization, it issues an order to that effect, appoints one or more trustees, specifies a transfer of corporate authority, and orders restriction of payments, suspension of and restriction on the levy of taxes, and the creation of a new accounting period.

In 1985, 409 reorganizations were pending in the courts, 72 cases for ten years or more. Forty-one new cases were initiated, 18 in manufacturing and 17 in transportation and communications. Of these new cases, 18 pertained to companies with up to 50 employees, and 11 to cases of 50 to 100 employees. During the year, reorganization was approved in 19 cases (Supreme Court Secretariate 1985: 306) (table 24).

Many companies, listed and unlisted, have gone through legal reorganization and are now normally operating companies. Window dressing itself does not affect the court's approval of reorganization procedures.

Window Dressing

The Japanese term *funshoku kessan* is usually translated as "window dressing." It denotes an effort to present the financial condition of a company as better than it actually is. *Gyaku funshoku kessan*, window dressing in reverse, presents the financial position as worse than it actually is. "Fair presentation" is thus a problem that must be considered in both directions.

The penalty for window dressing may, of course, be business failure, or it may be prosecution for fraud and embezzlement. Public disapproval must also be considered. Japanese mass media follow the worldwide fashion of complaints and accusations against business—big business that is—through press campaigns against specific instances of industrial pollution or, more recently, profiteering. Publicity about embezzlement or other obvious malpractices is feared because it may embarrass financial backers, especially banks, which are highly sensitive about the public image on which their main source of income, deposits, depends. The Ministry of Justice itself gives adverse publicity to audit reports that were "qualified" by independent auditors.

Under the Securities Exchange Law, the Ministry of Finance has the authority to order a stock exchange to delist a company "when an issuer violates this law or its enforcing regulations, and delisting is necessary to protect the public interest and investors" (Art. 119). Stock exchanges, on their part, enforce delisting, admittedly not only for reason of malpractice. When the independent auditor has expressed an adverse opinion or a disclaimer, the stock may be delisted; hence the decrease in the number of delisting cases for reason of false presentation. The recent failure of Riccar Co., Ltd., Japan's third largest manufacturer of home sewing machines, is enlightening.

Riccar Co., Ltd., a listed company, was capitalized at ¥8,020 million and a workforce of 2,302 employees. On July 23, 1984, it applied for a court-mediated compromise with its creditors. The court issued an order for preserving Riccar's assets; apparently company executives would remain in their positions and work out a reconstruction plan. It was estimated that there were about 300 large creditors and some 600,000 small creditors, consumers who contracted with Riccar to make prepaid installments every month for two to three years and receive products in the future. At the time, the company had around 50 institutions lending to it, including foreign banks, domestic regional banks, and life insurance companies; foreign bank loans amounted to 10% of the declared debts. In its compromise proposal, Riccar asked the court to write off 40% of its debts totaling ¥82.6 billion and suggested negotiating the remaining 60% over a six-year period commencing three years after a settlement was reached.

One month later, August 1984, having failed to obtain agreement of the majority of its creditors, Riccar was forced to apply for reorganization. This allowed outsiders to examine the company's financial records. In February 1985, window dressing with respect to sales and inventories was officially disclosed, revealing that major losses had been suffered since 1979. In October 1985, five former executives were arrested on suspicion of falsifying company accounts and paying directors' bonuses, dividends and corporate taxes, in violation of the Commercial Code (breach of trust) and the Securities Exchange Law.

Riccar did not belong to a *keiretsu* (industrial group), but one of the major city banks was its main bank, providing over 10% of the loans, seconding executives, and being the major creditor. Foreign banking circles in Tokyo bitterly criticized the bank for having upheld Riccar until the last moment (Petach 1986).

In September 1987, Daiei, the largest supermarket chain, announced that its chairman/president would become the receiver (*kanzai-nin*) of Riccar to develop its nonstore sales. According to the reorganization plan, 60.3% of total liabilities of ¥93.4 billion will be repaid to creditors between 1988 and 1993 (*Nihon Keizai Shinbun*, 1987, September 14).

TWO

CORPORATE FINANCING

6

DEBT
FINANCING

INTERDEPENDENCE in Japanese business occurs along vertical as well as horizontal lines: companies are related through affiliation with their parent company, parent companies are related among themselves in the industrial group, and stable shareholders are found throughout the system. For the foreign observer, this phenomenon is readily understood and perhaps accepted in sociological terms, but it is less easily understood in economic terms, for such extensive interdependence is little consonant with Western business practices. It remains, however, at the root of Japanese corporate behavior, where it is eloquently manifested in its debt financing.

Even in the mid-1980s, the typical capital structure of a Japanese corporation appeared as follows:

Liabilities (77%)
Current liabilities
    Accounts payable   18
    Short-term borrowing   17
    Others   14
Fixed liabilities
    Long-term borrowing   14
    Bonds   9
    Others   5
Net worth (23%)
Paid-in capital   6
Capital surplus   4
Earned surplus   12

Abegglen describes the contrast between Japanese and Western companies in economic terms:

There are real differences in financial policies and strategies between Western and Japanese firms, but the extent of these differences is often overstated. Moreover, it is within the capacity of Western firms to reduce these
differences, and concomitantly reduce the advantage of the kaisha [Japa-
nese corporation]. The critical issue is the value placed on growth of the
company, and the drive of management to achieve growth targets that will
ensure long-term competitive success. The competitive advantages of the
kaisha derive as much from the selection of aggressive financial policies as
from any special characteristics of the Japanese situation. Their policies are
driven by their experience with and focus on growth. . . . The controversy
over Japanese financial practices is made more complex by the fact that
profitability has no single, definitive measure. Western executives tend to
focus on return on sales as the measure of profitability. By this measure,
Japanese companies are less profitable than U.S. companies. . . . But when
profitability is measured by after-tax return on shareholders' investment,
the position is reversed. (Abegglen 1985: 148–149)

In the prewar years, one-third of the supply of funds to industry came
from internal sources and two-thirds from external sources, with stocks
representing one-third of the total; however, in the postwar years, shares
soon fell well below one-tenth of the total (table 25). When the exchanges
were reopened in 1949 and until the 1980s, when slower economic
growth and the development of capital markets drastically changed Japanese top executives' outlook on sources of funds, stocks were not to be a
favored method for raising corporate capital.

The ranking of the main capital sources by Japanese executives has
been contrasted for the 1970s and the 1980s as follows:

	1970s	1980s
Bank loans	1	7
Depreciation allowance	2	2
Retained earnings	3	1
Issue of stocks	4	3
Issue of bonds	5	6
Issue of convertible bonds	6	4
Use of foreign capital	7	5

(Adapted from Shibakawa 1985: 196)

In the listed manufacturing companies surveyed by MITI in 1984, reliance on internal reserves, after increasing in the 1970s, has stabilized in
the 1980s. Long-term borrowings are half of what they were ten years
ago. Stocks and bonds, however, are increasing steadily (table 26). In
1984, the sources of fixed funds for the companies in the survey were as
follows:

	First Section	Second Section
Listed on		
Internal reserves	65.6%	63.0%
New stock issue	4.2	8.5
Corporate bonds (domestic)	4.5	1.2
Bonds (overseas)	8.2	3.6
Long-term borrowings	17.5	23.6

(MITI 1985a: 275)

TABLE 25.

Supply of Funds to Industry (1931–1980)

(percentage)

	1931–1940	1941–1950	1951–1960	1961–1970	1971–1980
Internally generated	36.8	28.6	42.7	48.6	48.8
Retained earnings	9.6	10.0	15.6	18.7	7.0
Depreciation	27.2	18.6	27.1	29.9	41.8
Externally raised	63.2	71.4	57.3	51.4	51.2
Stocks and shares	31.1	9.8	8.1	4.8	3.2
Industrial bonds	4.3	2.7	2.5	1.8	2.1
Borrowings	27.8	58.9	46.7	44.8	45.9
Private	27.3	53.4	41.5	40.5	40.3
Government	0.5	5.5	5.2	4.3	5.6
TOTAL	100.0	100.0	100.0	100.0	100.0

SOURCE: Bank of Japan, *Economic Statistics Annual*, various years.

TABLE 26.

Listed Manufacturing Companies: Sources of Funds
(1976–1984)

(percentage)

Year	Internal Reserves	Long-term Borrowings	Stocks and Bonds
1976	48.6	40.2	10.7
1977	55.1	32.0	11.4
1978	61.5	26.3	11.4
1979	70.1	17.8	10.7
1981	69.4	18.3	11.0
1982	67.6	18.6	13.7
1983	66.4	20.0	13.6
1984	64.7	19.6	15.7

SOURCE: MITI 1985a: 149.

TABLE 27.

Trends of Capital and Liabilities: International Comparison (1979–1985)

(percentage)

	Japan		United States		United Kingdom		F.R. Germany	
	Equity Capital	Liabilities	Equity Capital	Liabilities	Equity Capital	Liabilities	Equity Capital	Liabilities
1979	15.4	84.6	64.8	35.2	46.5	53.5	34.7	65.3
1980	16.2	83.8	65.4	34.6	46.6	53.4	34.3	65.7
1981	16.6	83.4	65.4	34.6	45.6	54.5	33.8	66.2
1982	16.6	83.4	65.0	35.0	45.0	55.0	34.6	65.4
1983	17.1	82.9	64.5	35.5	46.0	54.0	35.3	64.7
1984	17.3	82.7	61.8	38.2	46.3	53.7	36.2	63.8
1985	18.5	81.5	59.5	40.5	—	—	36.9	63.1

SOURCE: Bank of Japan 1987: 150.

Borrowing from the Banks

How was it that Japanese companies dared assume the level of risk associated with an 80% or more debt ratio (table 27)? In short, Japan (the total system of social as well as economic dynamics) stood behind the debt position of the companies. The network of financing had three important characteristics.

(1) Long-term credit involved various institutions.

> Private financial institutions, particularly long-term credit banks established to facilitate long-term finance, play a dominant role in this field. Recently, however, trust banks, mutual loans and savings banks and credit associations have increased in importance as suppliers of long-term funds. The rise in the relative weight of life insurance companies also commands attention. As for financial institutions outside the private sector, long-term finance by Treasury funds contributed substantially to the reconstruction of the Japanese economy, but . . . its relative importance has gradually declined with the completion of reconstruction. (Bank of Japan 1973: 201)

Furthermore, "commercial banks hold about one-quarter of outstanding bank debentures, the issues of which is the chief source of funds for long-term credit banks, while commercial banks' portfolios include about 50% of outstanding industrial debentures" (Bank of Japan 1973: 165).

(2) Personal savings were deposited largely with commercial banks, which have traditionally been engaged in long-term finance as well as commercial banking. Short-term lending was repeatedly renewed and used for long-term purposes. More than 70% of the loans, advances, and discounts of the city banks went to large companies, and more than half of the loans of regional banks went to small companies. "Commercial banks also lend money for subscription to newly issued shares of corporate business, while they themselves take up about 10% of such shares" (Bank of Japan 1973: 165).

(3) City banks were, however, in a perennial state of "overloan," and large continuous borrowing from the Bank of Japan compensated for the shortage of their cash reserves. "Therefore, in effect, the Bank of Japan stands as guarantor to the commercial banks" (Abegglen 1971: 5). The shortage of funds was also alleviated by borrowing from the call loan market, mainly the provincial banks. City banks "have had to ensure their liquidity by holding bonds and debentures which may be bought or sold by the Bank of Japan, and they also hold bills and debentures eligible for rediscount or as collateral security for borrowing from the Bank. Regional banks, however, are differently situated. Although they are

commercial banks, they have more liquidity, borrow little from the Bank and are substantial lenders in the call loan market" (Bank of Japan 1973: 166).

Most Japanese companies, including many major ones and major banks as well, are, in terms of capital, "thin" corporations. Due to high debt and consequent high interest expense, companies have been able to reduce income tax. Neither the Corporation Tax Law nor any other tax law prohibits thin capital. Starting soon after the war, all balance sheets looked similar—large debt and little equity—and most income statements looked similar—high sales and low net income. This was not the case in the prewar years, but after the war as companies frantically tried to keep up with economic growth, the debt portion ate progressively into the equity portion (table 28). In 1966, the Ministry of Finance amended the Special Taxation Measures Law (effective 1966–1968) to encourage improvement of the debt/equity ratio by permitting a credit against tax. Because the result was far below the expected target, the amendment was terminated in 1970 after a two-year extension. However, a turning point had been reached. During the period from 1969–1970 to 1973–1974, the situation appeared thus:

> The conventional view that Japanese companies have very high levels of bank borrowings, while generally true, is by no means universal. There are large systematic differences within the economy as a whole that can make generalizations regarding debt levels misleading. For the industrial and commercial sector as a whole, leverage is high and increasing. At the same time a large and prosperous sector of the economy is, if not debt free, at least no more in debt than Western companies. Light industry as a whole has significantly less debt than heavy industry. Leading companies within the light industry sector have been reducing their debt dependence steadily over several years. This suggests significant variations of [debt to equity] ratios within given industries. It should also be noted that these measures of debt levels take no account of sharp increases in the value of such assets as land and securities, which, if reflected in equity positions, might well cause the financial position of many Japanese companies to appear far more secure than is now the case. (Habgood 1975: 17–18)

Whereas in other industrial countries financial statements may often be rearranged according to liquidation value in case of heavy loss or heavy debt, in Japan they remain arranged on a historical cost (going concern) basis. The need for rearranging according to liquidation value is practically never mentioned, except in the following cases:

    1. Liquidation due to bankruptcy or termination of business (the latter happens rarely).

TABLE 28.

Financial Structure of Major Industrial Organizations (1960–1985)

(percentage)

	1960	1970	1980	1985
ASSETS				
Current assets	47.7	56.7	58.0	54.8
Quick assets	26.2	39.0	36.4	32.3
of which: (cash and deposits)	(8.9)	(9.7)	(9.0)	(9.4)
(trade receivables)	(17.3)	(28.1)	(23.4)	(22.9)
Inventories	15.0	13.2	16.6	14.0
of which: (finished goods)	(5.2)	(6.4)	(7.5)	(6.5)
(raw materials)	(3.3)	(2.0)	(3.0)	(1.5)
Fixed assets	51.9	43.0	42.0	45.2
Tangible fixed assets	43.6	32.4	29.8	31.5
Investments	7.8	10.1		13.2
Deferred Account	0.5	0.3	0.0	0.0
TOTAL ASSETS	100.0	100.0	100.0	100.0
LIABILITIES, NET WORTH				
Current liabilities	45.2	51.6	53.2	49.5
of which: (trade payable)	(15.5)	(23.7)	(21.4)	(18.3)
(short-term borrowing)	(16.5)	(15.9)	(16.6)	(17.3)
Fixed liabilities	25.8	29.4	29.9	27.8
of which: (long-term borrowing)	(16.4)	(19.4)	(17.6)	(14.4)
(debentures)	(6.9)	(5.2)	(7.0)	(8.5)
Net worth	28.9	19.0	16.9	22.8
of which: (capital)	(14.1)	(9.8)	(5.8)	(6.0)
NUMBER OF COMPANIES	512	475	518	620

SOURCE: Bank of Japan, *Shuyō Kigyō Keiei Bunseki* [Management Analysis of Major Enterprises], Tokyo, respective years.
NOTE: These percentages are based on the balance sheets of companies in all industries at the end of the second half of the fiscal year (April–March).

2. Assessment as required by the Inheritance Tax Law, when a company is transferred to an heir and its stock has no quoted market value.

3. Sale of the business. Whereas the future earning power should be the major criterion for its evaluation, liquidation value (mainly land value) is persistently used. However, when agreement is difficult, a compromise between future earning power and liquidation value is often reached without valid theoretical grounds.

The preference for debt over equity can be attributed essentially to three closely interrelated reasons: (1) The operation of the stock market, as it developed after World War II, considerably reduced the attractiveness of equity financing. Namely, a relatively fixed cash dividend yield of 10% to 20% of par value coupled with rights offerings at par value, was generally expected by Japanese investors. (2) It was more convenient to obtain loans for project financing than to obtain such financing from stocks or debentures. It was also cheaper in the sense that, in terms of expenditures, interest is considered before tax and dividends after tax. Because the overall corporate tax rate was roughly 50% to 60%, the dividend costs the company twice as much as the interest. (3) Banks were most anxious to finance the rapid expansion of the industrial sector. They were the link between savers and investors.

> About 53 percent of gross domestic investment (average 1960–69) have been formed in the personal sector. Of net savings—that is, after deduction of provisions for capital consumption—51 percent (average of 1960–69) is represented by personal net savings. Thus the corporate business sector and the personal sector have played important parts in economic development, the former as the principal investor and the latter as the principal saver. (Bank of Japan 1973: 59)

The Western observer may wonder whether it makes sense to expect independence from a company whose net worth is, say, less than 30%. Does such high debt make for control by the banks? The query is indeed Western. In Japan, the independence of company operations in such cases has rarely been questioned. In Japanese cultural as well as economic terms, more value is attached to interdependence than to a go-it-alone independence. Security through mutual assistance, readiness of emergency resource, mutual business referrals, and constant business advice are only a few of the advantages. From the viewpoint of international competitiveness, corporate financial policy may be crucial: other things being equal, "a firm with higher debt can price lower and earn a comparable return on equity. Or if it chooses to divide its financial advantage between a lower price and a higher return on equity, it can sell more competitively and perform better for its shareholders" (Hout 1974: 12).

The point of debt leverage in the eyes of both lender and borrower has been cogently argued as follows:

> A Japanese business must earn enough money to pay the interest on what is legally a bank loan but economically is equity investment in business and industry. The profit in the Japanese economy—the return on venture capital—is essentially the difference between what it costs a Japanese bank to attract and hold deposits, and the interest it charges for the loans to industry. . . . Business earnings over and above what is needed to cover the interest charge with a fair safety margin are of no benefit to the bank. . . . From the point of view of the Japanese business executive, however, faced as he is by the high cost of the capital on which he depends, minimizing the cost of capital is the most rational business objective. Maximizing profit makes no sense to him: there is no benefit to his company and incidentally, with

stock options being practically unknown in Japanese management, no benefit to him personally. But minimizing the cost of capital—that is, trying to operate the business with the very minimum of borrowed money—is indeed a major rational business objective. His business strategy, therefore, focuses on profit only to the extent to which it represents a minimum requirement. That minimum is quite high by Western standards. It is nonsense to say that the Japanese executive is not profit conscious. But he is not "profit-minded" in the sense that profit is an objective. It is a necessity; "minimizing the cost of capital" is the objective. (Drucker 1975: 233–234)

But the environment changed in the 1970s with slower economic growth, and the problems of the 1980s—trade frictions and rapid appreciation of the yen—created a new climate for corporate financing. Although borrowing as a means of procuring corporate funds appears to have remained quite constant, in actuality, a profound change has occurred: large firms borrow less; small firms borrow more. The overall percentage of borrowing has not changed much, with present-day domestic borrowing still accounting for 73.3% of all corporate funds and overseas bank borrowing for approximately 9.0% (Bank of Japan 1986/11). However, a sharp deviation became apparent by the mid-1980s, when borrowers were split into large and small corporate borrowers.

Large corporations that historically have dominated private borrowing no longer find it necessary to finance their operations through heavy debt, mainly because reduced investment requirements and substantial retained earnings have resulted in nonoperating profits. Many Japanese manufacturers built up their capacity during the 1960s and 1970s in order to cope with a rising demand for their products. Recently, however, demand in some sectors has decreased, causing a reduction in the demand for new capital investments, while depreciation and profits (retained earnings) have accumulated without much subsequent need for such funds (Cottrell 1985: 49). The result is that large corporations have been experiencing an unprecedented accumulation of surplus funds. One additional factor facilitating the decrease in bank borrowing by large corporations is the proliferation of alternate fund procurement methods, primarily direct financing. "Bank lending that accounted for over 80 per cent of total funds procured in the early 1970s has dropped to 59.4 per cent in 1984" (*Japan Economic Journal* 1985/12).

In view of this development, banks have had actively to seek new borrowers. Many small/medium corporations whose needs had been neglected while the banks channeled funds to large corporate borrowers have been finding borrowing restrictions easing. In fact, banks have steadily increased their lending to smaller companies.

The targeting of small- and medium-sized enterprises constituted part of the banks' strategy to cope with financial liberalization. Behind these moves were the shrinking of loan-deposit interest rate margins, on which the banks' profits mainly depend, and the sluggishness of loans to large enterprises. In the case of 12 city banks (excluding Bank of Tokyo), the ratio of loans to small- and medium-sized enterprises exceeded the 50 per cent line for the first time as such loans accounted for an average of 53.5 per cent of their total loans as of the end of September 1985. (Sakurai 1986: 24)

Loans

When a company wants to open an account or start transactions with a bank, it is required to sign a general-purpose agreement, the form for which is fairly standard. The agreement usually contains a clause to the effect that, for all present and future loans from the bank, the company shall provide collateral or guarantors immediately upon the bank's request. Further, any collateral furnished pursuant to such agreement will be applicable to all indebtedness present or future to such bank. Usually the guarantor is the company president and one or more of the directors. The guarantor, as an individual, is held liable jointly and severally with the principal for all obligations. There have been a few cases in which a guarantor's personal properties were seized by the bank upon a company's bankruptcy or refinancing. Although a company is required to sign such a general-purpose agreement providing favorable clauses for the bank, no bank, for fear of losing an important client, would charge penalty interest on delayed repayment, although such penalty is provided in the agreement. The agreement also stipulates (and this is the universal practice) that the interest rate fluctuates.

Long-term loans (by Japanese standards; until recently five to seven years, now ten years) have been supplied jointly by both long-term credit banks and commercial banks. Banks encouraged corporations to borrow in order to advance into new and diversified fields in which competition is still relatively weak. Cooperative expansion among the bank's clients into undeveloped areas has been essential for group growth. But banks were especially anxious to lend in order to concentrate on new, growth fields. On their advice, companies have borrowed to buy heavy equipment for plant expansion in electric power generation, heavy machinery, automobiles, synthetic fibers, petroleum, and so forth (for growth industries, shareholders' equity capital amounted to no more than 20%). Loans for expansion in areas as these cannot be amortized for five to seven years, and bankers have been well aware of the need to refinance within three to five years after the loan was granted, extending the term of repayment for another five years for a total repayment period of ten to twelve years. Such an extension allows enough time to take full depreciation of the purchased equipment. A long-term debt such as this has generally been secured by a mortgage on property.

The major enterprises, in 1985, had 17.3% of their financial structure in the form of short-term borrowing and 14.4% in long-term borrowing (see table 28). In Japan, however, short-term loans can be long-term. Because of strict supervision over bank lending by the Bank of Japan and the convenience of adjusting the interest rate to the current market situation, loans are often made for a three- to six-month period, with the implicit understanding that they will be renewed. Although these loans are officially labeled as given for "working capital" (*unten shikin*), it is understood that they can also be used for capital equipment. Thus, considerable current liabilities are created and current ratio is low, although these short-term loans are constantly renewed. A large portion of such loans is unsecured; the remaining portion is secured by promissory notes and securities. Mortgage is not common.

The consolidated financial statements of Mitsubishi Heavy Industries show that out of total bank loans of ¥733.58 billion, ¥2.29 billion was secured by a pledge of time deposits, notes receivable and securities, the balance being unsecured (March 31, 1985).

Heavy bank involvement in corporate financial structure has had the expected result that "at-arm's-length" relations are rarely found. Many widespread practices have evolved, not all of them open, that are extremely difficult to track down in financial reporting. Two major ones are collaterals and compensating balances.

Banks will take mortgages (fixed assets) or collaterals (receivables and securities) as a basis for a loan, rather than only short-term liquidity or long-term earning power. However, the mortgage value is limited to 60% to 80% of the current appraised value of fixed assets. (It is common practice for Japanese companies to place more emphasis on mortgage and asset value than on future earnings.) Often, in order to secure the long-term loan, the bank will take as mortgage the plant to be built through the loan.

It is also customary for banks to demand compensating balances (*kōsoku yokin-gaku*) whenever loans or discounts are granted. Strongly discouraged by the Ministry of Finance, the practice was general and supported by the postwar lenders' market. The borrower was to "understand" that 20% to 30% of his borrowing should be kept with the bank in the form of time or other deposits. The smaller the financial institution, the smaller the deposits were compared to the loans and the

TABLE 29.

Percentage of Compensating Balances and Loans over Deposits: Small/Medium Enterprises in Five Sectors (May 1986)

	"Explicit" Compensating Balances (A)	"Implicit" Compensating Balances (B)	A + B	Loans over Deposits
City banks	1.2	7.5	8.7	45.8
Local banks	0.6	5.7	6.3	38.9
Mutual banks	1.1	8.9	10.0	36.0
Credit associations	3.0	8.1	11.1	38.0
Credit unions	8.5	7.9	16.4	38.9
Other	0.2	6.1	6.3	19.3
AVERAGE	1.2	7.1	8.3	39.3

SOURCE: FTC 1986a: 1, 12.
NOTE: In May 1986, this survey was conducted for the 38th time. The questionnaire was sent to 7,445 small/medium enterprises selected at random in five sectors (manufacturing, construction, wholesale, retail, and services); 2,546 answers were usable.

larger the compensating balances. Notwithstanding the current borrowers' market, the practice persists and is implemented in various elusive ways, as one manifestation of the continued interdependence among business institutions. The Fair Trade Commission is concerned about the practice, and periodically since 1964 it has conducted surveys of several thousands of small/medium enterprises, and reported what percentage of such compensating balances are "explicit" (loan/discount is backed up by collateral and some agreement stipulates compensating balance) and "implicit" (when it is understood that the debtor cannot withdraw the compensating balance because of some loan/discount) (table 29).

Trade Note Discount

Trade note discount is the other form of indebtedness to the banks. For the major corporations surveyed annually by the Bank of Japan, trade payables amounted in 1985 to 18.3% of their financial structure (see table 28).

Promissory notes (*yakusoku tegata*) are an age-old and ubiquitous method of payment in particular among small/medium enterprises. The two centuries of Japan's seclusion (1632–1854) witnessed an extraordinary expansion of domestic commercial activities and the development of an elaborate system of payment based on trust, fostered by the inward-looking nature of a society untrammeled by alien inputs and creating interdependence among all its members. This tradition has been at the core of Japan's modernization and industrialization, with a bank as a first joint stock company. One contemporary manifestation of this heritage is the promissory note. This credit instrument, vital to business more often than not, may also be fatal.

On April 11, 1986, Dainichi Sangyo K.K., a company that had been backed by Japan's largest venture-capital raiser, filed for bankruptcy in the Tokyo district court. At the time, the press laid much of the blame on large dealings with a known speculator, Sanyo Kosan. The dealings were described as follows:

> The transactions apparently involve the sale of goods down a chain of companies, with each member in the chain issuing an IOU for the same merchandise. The IOUs are then presented to an outsider—usually a cash-rich concern such as Dainichi—for an advance. Once a profit has been made, the IOUs are redeemed, giving the outsider a windfall. The practice, called *korogashi*, or "rolling-over," began in postwar Japan as a genuine credit arrangement between cash-strapped businesses and their suppliers. But as commonly applied nowadays by speculators such as Sanyo Kosan, which used the cash primarily for stock-market speculation, *korogashi* entails significant financial risk for lender and borrower. Even so, the practice is condoned because it is regarded as a legitimate transaction between parties that understand the risks involved, Japanese businessmen and government officials say. (Wong 1986: 5)

Promissory notes are welcomed by the banks for two good reasons: (1) They are self-liquidating, namely, on the due date they are settled and the loaned money is automatically paid; and (2) they are a "two-or-more-names" credit in the sense that if the issuer is unable to meet the note, the bank customer and endorsers are liable for returning the borrowed amount. The practice of payment by promissory note shows many variations. Because clerical costs of handling these notes are high, as in the case of a consumer-credit company delivering innumerable small notes issued by individuals, the bank practice is changing toward not discounting them but granting a straight loan amounting to nearly 100% of total notes as collateral. Or, in a recent variation, the large manufacturer groups many payments due to parts suppliers in one promissory note issued to his bank; in turn, the bank, if so requested by the supplier (as is often the case), pays in cash with discount before the due date. Still another common variation, especially in smaller companies handling large numbers of promissory notes of small amounts, is for the bank to advise the company to turn first to a trading firm. The firm acts as a financial agent and dealer; it consolidates the notes into one. The trading firm thereby increases its trade volume (which determines its ranking among trading firms), and the bank covers its risk better, while reducing its work load.

Overdraft agreements are exceptional; they are granted only to the customer from whom other benefits are expected. They are, however, commonly negotiated with foreign companies. Overdrafts, after all, contradict the prevailing practice of compensating balances. Instead, a general practice is to negotiate what is called a "line of credit" (the English wording is always used).

Debt Security Financing

Currently, government bonds are by far the single largest type of bond issue, comprising two-thirds of total bond volume on the Tokyo Stock Exchange. Government bonds were first issued in postwar Japan in 1966, at which time the Tokyo Securities Dealers Association began to publish bond prices. Following the first oil shock, even larger issues of government bonds appeared, creating a rapidly growing bond market (table 30). The bond issue market is not a free market. Issues are controlled: coupon rates on corporate bonds are fixed and linked to those on long-term government bonds. In addition, straight bond issues are regulated by the *Kisai-kai* (Bond Flotation Committee), a committee primarily composed of city banks.

> In the system as devised by the Kisaikai, the wishes of the issuing bodies are totally ignored and issuing conditions are determined mechanically (based on industry grouping, size of company, etc.). As a result, the system succeeded in directing funds to priority sectors and achieved the reconstruction of Japan's industry. However, the problem is that times have changed and even though this type of priority financing is no longer needed the Kisaikai continues to exist and its policies have changed hardly at all. (Arai 1986: 28)

Recently, however, corporate bond issuance as a means of fund procurement has been gaining popularity. According to the Commercial Code (Art. 297), corporations cannot issue bonds exceeding the total amount of capital stock, capital surplus, and legal reserve or total shareholders' equity, whichever is lower. At present, however, the limit is twice that stipulated by the Commercial Code (Tentative Measures on Limit of Bond Issue Law, 1977). Long-term credit banks can issue financial bonds up to 20 times their capital and legal reserve (Long-term Credit Bank Law, Art. 20). Other developments that will help to increase the popularity of corporate bonds in the future are deregulation and liberalization.

> Japanese securities companies will revise their methods of underwriting domestically-issued straight corporate bonds for the first time in 39 years. At present, there exists no competition between underwriting securities

TABLE 30.

Volume of Bond Transactions on OTC and Exchange Markets (1974–1984)

(100 million yen)

Year	OTC Market	Exchange Market	Total
1974	323,459 (97.0%)	9,983 (3.0%)	333,442 (100%)
1975	509,036 (97.0)	15,889 (3.0)	524,925 (100)
1976	648,970 (96.6)	22,908 (3.4)	671,878 (100)
1977	1,131,643 (96.8)	37,887 (3.2)	1,169,530 (100)
1978	1,931,988 (94.9)	102,776 (5.1)	2,034,764 (100)
1979	2,042,351 (97.4)	54,188 (2.6)	2,096,539 (100)
1980	2,725,029 (96.9)	88,131 (3.1)	2,813,160 (100)
1981	2,884,292 (95.7)	130,002 (4.3)	3,014,294 (100)
1982	3,271,080 (95.4)	157,243 (4.6)	3,428,323 (100)
1983	3,850,972 (91.7)	348,796 (8.3)	4,199,768 (100)
1984	6,924,697 (90.3)	746,905 (9.7)	7,671,602 (100)

SOURCE: Japan Securities Research Institute 1986: 84.

houses because bond-issuing conditions are decided almost mechanically on the basis of the issuing firm's financial indicators. This method will be revised, however, so that an issuing firm will let the underwriting securities houses offer their own floating conditions and then choose the lead manager which has the best offer. Thus, issuing conditions will be made more flexible. (*Japan Economic Journal* 1987/3)

Along similar lines, bond rating organizations have been emerging in Japan. As long as corporate bond issues were restricted and heavily regulated, Western-style rating organizations were not required. With the recent trend toward deregulation and a freer market, a need for rating services of this kind became more apparent.

Despite the fact that even the concept of bond rating was hardly even known until a few years ago in Japan, today a number of domestic bond rating institutions are vying with each other. . . . At present there are five bond rating institutions in Japan. These are Mikuni & Co., the Japan Bond Research Institute (JBRI), Nippon Investors Service Inc. (NIS), Japan Credit Rating Agency (JCR) and the Japanese subsidiary of Moody's Investors Service, Moody's Japan K.K. In addition, Standard & Poor's Corp. of the U.S. has a representative office in Japan. (Arai 1986: 28)

Secured versus Unsecured Bonds

One unique characteristic of the issuance of Japanese corporate bonds was the Ministry of Finance's requirement of collateral. In contrast to many Western countries, Japanese corporations issuing debt certificates have long been required to secure their debt with collateral. Prior to the

TABLE 31.

Secured and Unsecured Domestic Bond Issues (1980–1985)

	Straight Bonds		Of Which Unsecured		Convertible Bonds		Of Which Unsecured	
Year	Cases	Amount Raised (million yen)	Cases	Amount Raised (million yen and %)	Cases	Amount Raised (million yen)	Cases	Amount Raised (million yen and %)
1980	101	993,500			12	96,500		
1981	127	1,269,000			52	526,000	1	60,000 (11.4%)
1982	91	1,047,500			46	417,500	1	45,000 (10.8%)
1983	62	683,000			67	861,000	9	257,000 (29.8%)
1984	55	720,000	1	10,000 (1.4%)	125	1,611,500	36	921,000 (57.2%)
1985	63	943,500			142	1,585,500	32	725,000 (45.7%)

SOURCE: Ministry of Finance, Securities Bureau.

First World War, only straight (unsecured) bonds existed, but major defaults in the 1920s led to financial reforms and by the 1930s secured bonds had become the norm.

In the postwar economy, collateral requirements were not a substantial burden on most manufacturing corporations, for most of them were able to provide assets such as land and factories. Japan's economic structure has changed, however, with service and other nonmanufacturing corporations accounting for a growing portion of the economy. For companies with few large assets, collateral requirements began to represent prohibitive barriers. Thus, as many corporations improved their financial position, uniform requirements were no longer acceptable.

In March 1979, Sears Roebuck offered through its subsidiary the first unsecured yen-denominated bond issue. This was followed by an unsecured convertible bond issue by Matsushita Electric Industrial Co., Ltd., the following month and by Nissan Motor Co. in February 1982 (Japan Securities Research Institute 1986: 71).

When the Ministry of Finance further relaxed issuing conditions of unsecured bonds in January 1983, within the same year the number of corporations eligible to issue unsecured straight bonds grew to about 20, and those eligible to issue unsecured convertible bonds increased to about 100 (ibid.). In 1985, over 45% of all convertible bonds in Japan were unsecured. This is even more remarkable when the sharp increase in their total issuance during the last five years is taken into consideration (table 31).

Domestic Issuance of Bonds

In contrast to the steady expansion in overseas issuance of corporate bonds, domestic issues of straight bonds have decreased markedly despite various measures to improve market functioning. Requirement of collateral has been mainly responsible for the decrease. After peaking at ¥1.4 trillion in 1975, domestic issuance of straight bonds had fallen off to ¥589.5 billion in 1985 (table 32). This corresponds to the increasing availability of alternate fund-raising avenues, namely overseas issuance.

Previously, industries not earmarked by the government were rarely able to issue corporate bonds and therefore issued convertible bonds as an alternative. The 1966 amendment of the Commercial Code (Art. 341.7) made it possible for the holder of convertible debentures to convert them into stock shares even during the period when the shareholder register is closed. The first issue of convertible bonds under the new law was by Nippon Express Co. in 1966. (It met with strong opposition,

TABLE 3.2.

Issuance of Straight and Convertible Bonds and of Warrants, Domestic and Overseas (1974–1985)

| | Straight Bonds | | | | Convertible Bonds | | | | Warrants | | | |
| | Domestic | | Overseas | | Domestic | | Overseas | | Domestic | | Overseas | |
Year	No. of Issues	Amount Issued (million yen)	No. of Issues	Amount Issued (million yen)	No. of Issues	Amount Issued (million yen)	No. of Issues	Amount Issued (million yen)	No. of Issues	Amount Issued (million yen)	No. of Issues	Amount Issued (million yen)
1974	159	889,870	8	43,039	58	248,750	4	15,730				
1975	306	1,405,900	42	267,850	57	408,000	10	104,595				
1976	179	1,137,200	36	208,156	15	59,000	24	208,923				
1977	131	1,131,100	27	176,822	17	115,000	30	192,717				
1978	152	1,295,500	25	148,455	31	292,500	62	339,162				
1979	116	1,182,200	25	186,640	33	371,000	104	604,749				
1980	101	1,032,500	35	184,060	14	104,000	72	510,648				
1981	123	1,219,000	15	767,138	39	363,500	105	803,977	3	20,000		
1982	94	1,113,500	50	375,482	51	447,500	94	656,679	8	44,000	12	98,006
1983	58	595,000	86	637,617	60	827,000	137	1,082,008	3	10,000	16	128,578
1984	51	765,000	55	617,708	108	1,208,500	167	1,310,942	2	13,000	53	451,126
1985	49	589,500	131	1,491,099	150	1,918,800	121	1,301,793	2	10,000	89	692,904

SOURCE: Tokyo Stock Exchange 1986b: 111.

because it was considered a modification of public offering of shares at market value, something to which the Japanese investor was not yet conditioned.) Almost all convertible bonds, unlike regular corporate bonds, are now listed on the Tokyo Stock Exchange.

Domestic issuance of convertible bonds has increased by 771% since 1974 and in 1985 stood at more than ¥1.9 trillion, with a record 150 issues being made. Furthermore, 1985 was also the first time in ten years that domestic issuance of convertible bonds surpassed that of overseas issuance in both amount issued and number of issues. The increase can be attributed to the relative easing of standards for the issuance of unsecured convertible bonds in 1983: in that year alone, the amount of convertible bonds issued nearly doubled. Other reasons were lower coupon rates and rising stock prices.

Another factor that favors domestic issuance of convertible bonds is that foreign investors usually convert their bonds into equity at a rapid pace, whereas Japanese investors have tended to hold them longer, many holding them until maturity. This factor is also undergoing change, as both individual and institutional investors increasingly seek to maximize returns.

Amendment to the Commercial Code in 1981 (Art. 341.8) made it possible for corporations to issue bonds with preemptive right of new shares (commonly called warrants in Western countries). Daiei, Inc., was the first to issue bonds with warrants, in December 1981, although Daiei's bonds with warrants were basically the equivalent of convertible bonds (i.e., the warrants are not detachable and the bonds must be used for payment on exercise). Daiei apparently chose warrants of this form because the market acceptance of the "new" style of debt was not entirely predictable. Currently, although they are gaining in popularity abroad, warrant bonds have remained quite negligible in the domestic market, because of the different regulations imposed on them. Whereas in most overseas markets warrants are separable from their underlying bonds, under self-imposed restrictions of the securities industry, warrant bonds issuable on the domestic market were initially restricted to those of the nonseparable type. In December 1985, detachable warrant bonds were issued by the Tokyu Department Store Co., Ltd.; by the end of July 1987, 14 issues of detachable warrant certificates were listed on the Tokyo Stock Exchange (Tokyo Stock Exchange, Monthly Statistics Report, July 1987).

In the 1970s, financial institutions and business corporations held bonds until maturity, a practice considered adequately profitable. More recently, given structural excess liquidity and low interest rates, bonds have become profitable only with the addition of the capital gain from their sale before maturity. In the ten years between 1975 and 1984, the volume of bond trading more than decupled. Except for government bonds amounting to approximately 82% of the total, financial debentures were the most actively traded, for approximately 4.2% of the total. Banks (city, local, long-term credit, and trust) were major participants, for about 20%, city and local banks as net sellers and trust banks as net purchasers. Business corporations investing their funds on a relatively short-term basis accounted for 7.2%.

More than 90% of the trading takes place on the OTC (over-the-counter) market, where the leading participants are securities companies acting as dealers. Since 1984, a number of banking institutions have been licensed to deal in public bonds. The Securities Dealers Association selects a certain number of issues and publicizes daily their selling and buying prices. On the Exchange markets (Tokyo, Osaka, and Nagoya), close to 500 issues of yen-denominated foreign bonds, over 400 issues of convertible bonds, and only a dozen issues of corporate bonds are listed (Japan Securities Research Institute 1986: 81–86).

In summary, a trend toward increased issuance of corporate bonds in Japan is in motion. This relative shift toward domestic issuance is linked to efforts to deregulate financial markets. As collateral requirements are relaxed, issuance procedures simplified, and terms of issuance improved, corporate fund procurement through domestic issuance of bonds is becoming more favorable.

7

EQUITY FINANCING

THE JAPANESE STOCK EXCHANGES are one century old. The first was opened in Tokyo in June 1878 and the second in Osaka the following August.

> The exchanges developed in a sense outside of the rest of the financial world, having little connection at that time with banking institutions or the general capital and loan markets. . . . Public savings were deposited almost exclusively in banks, as long-term postal savings, and in trust companies. Thus trust companies, banks and the government Deposit Bureau, which handles the postal savings, were the only truly large sources of investment capital. (Adams 1953: 32)

From about the turn of the century, corporations alternately relied more on stocks or more on debentures for their financing, depending upon the business situation. Not until the 1920s were any stocks of the *zaibatsu* open to public purchase.

> Illustrative of the public's desire to share in the ownership of the zaibatsu subsidiaries is the report . . . that at the time 400,000 shares of Mitsubishi Heavy Industries were offered for sale in 1935, 250,000 were made available to the "public." 45,580 people applied to buy 6,777,170 shares, roughly 27 times the number offered. (Hadley 1970: 25)

It became customary for private investors to pay for shares in installments, if not to hold a fraction of a share. "Payments made on stocks are only part of the capital values in most cases as it is common practice in Japan to issue stock partially paid up. Thus, on a share of ¥50, one quarter, i.e. ¥12.50, is generally the accepted first installment" (Japan Economic Federation 1940: 45). The practice of payment in installments was

TABLE 33.

Key Statistics of Listed Stocks (1949–1986)

	1949	1960	1970	1980	1986
No. of listed companies	681	785	1,580	1,729	1,866
No. of listed issues	819	843	1,698	1,737	1,873
Capital stock of listed companies (billion yen)	83	1,888	6,755	12,875	18,974
No. of shares listed (million)	1,680	33,485	118,988	216,023	277,570
Total market value (billion yen)	128	5,643	16,824	79,952	293,027
Trading volume (million shares)	425	43,331	57,099	118,931	238,354
Trading value (billion yen)	61	9,334	12,030	42,161	193,058
Average value (yen)	143.88	215.42	210.69	354.50	809.97

SOURCE: Tokyo Stock Exchange 1986b: 8, 9.

prohibited in 1951 and replaced by the U.S.-inspired concept of authorized capital.

After the reopening of the stock exchanges in 1949, the evolution of the stock market (table 33) was largely determined by the policies of the Ministry of Finance. The Japanese view of equity financing is a reflection of the nature of this market, but it is also the result of prewar experience.

> In point of fact, the Japanese mistrust of equity financing . . . is rooted in the experience of many Japanese business leaders with equity financing during the pre-Pacific War period. . . . In prewar Japan, new investment was commonly equity financed. Equities in major industries, such as textiles, were characteristically pledged by owners as collateral for the bank loans that permitted their purchase. The interests of equity holders that dominated the prewar boards of directors of Japanese enterprises often demanded that unrealistically high dividends be paid out so that equity holders' bank loans might be serviced. (Saxonhouse 1986: 124)

A current manifestation of this "mistrust" of equity financing is the often-heard criticism Japanese businessmen level at their American counterparts, accusing them of shortsightedness. "Decisions are allegedly made with undue concern regarding how any given action will affect the next quarterly earnings statement. Reliance on equity financing has led to compensation packages for top-level American managers that tie bonus payments to the market performance of company equities" (ibid.). Whatever the validity of these Japanese views, present-day Japanese practices must be understood in the light of past practices, many of a routine nature and rarely questioned. For example, when a company is established, authorized capital (*juken shihon*) and issued capital (*shihon-kin*) are usually in a maximum ratio of four-to-one (Commercial Code, Art. 166.2). Since treasury stock is not allowed, issued stock in Japanese balance sheets is equal to what in Western accounting is called "outstanding stock" (after deducting treasury stock from issued stock). Future capital increases can then be made more easily without the cumbersome procedure of shareholders' approval. Given the predominance of interdependence among corporations, Japanese executives, if not also society at large, do not perceive equity financing as a purely financial transaction. It is also the manifestation of some long-standing relationship, where strong social undertones are at work and much subjectivity, often of a personal nature, is at play.

Equity Issuing at Market Price

The Commercial Code (Arts. 199 and 222) provides for various kinds of stock: common, preferred, and no-par-value stock. In practice, almost all Japanese stock is common stock. Shortly after World War II, the traditional par value of ¥50 was increased to 500, and since October 1982, the minimum par value share has been ¥50,000 (Commercial Code, Art. 165). (Corporations established prior to October 1982 are allowed to retain their previous par value. Most listed corporations have thus a par value of ¥50 for their outstanding shares but adopt 1,000 shares as one unit to meet the ¥50,000 minimum requirement.)

New stock issues take three forms: offering to shareholders, public offering, and private placement. Over the years there has been a steady increase in "public offerings" (*kōbo*). In the 1960s, new stock issues were almost entirely in the form of offering to shareholders; a mere 0.1% was offered to the general public. Between 1965 and 1974, the percentage of public offerings fluctuated sharply with a high of 66.3% recorded in 1972; more recently, it represents approximately 71.3% with a peak of 87.2% in 1984 (table 34). However, the term "public offering" as used in Japan may be somewhat misleading. A large portion of new capital issues turned out to be subscribed to by a limited number of investors. In this practice, called *oyabike* (literally, "withheld by parent"), the underwriter, with the cooperation of the issuing company, allocated subscription rights to specified investors. These were mostly stable shareholders, but they also included individuals who sold shares immediately after purchase at a significant profit (because the market price in a thin market was higher than the predetermined subscription price). To curtail such blatant violations, in early 1975, the Ministry of Finance decided to progressively reduce the ratio of new shares coming under *oyabike*.

Public offering is generally followed by a free share distribution with prior consent of the stock exchange concerned.

TABLE 34.
New Stock Issues (1955–1986)
(million yen)

Year	Offering to Shareholders			Public Offering			Private Placement			Total of Stocks[1]		
	No. of Cases	Amount Raised	Excess over Par	No. of Cases	Amount Raised	Excess over Par	No. of Cases	Amount Raised	Excess over Par	No. of Cases	Amount Raised	Excess over Par
1955	126	64,145	—	4	454	70	11	175	—	141	64,774	70
1960	275	331,371	—	100	34,672	245,241	4	695	160	379	366,738	24,401
1965	95	114,537	—	19	159	103	8	2,666	189	122	117,362	292
1970	316	538,049	—	203	138,025	115,868	18	5,148	1,535	537	681,222	117,403
1975	166	771,374	3,945	103	221,502	194,764	16	8,228	5,180	285	1,101,105	203,890
1980	34	90,329	—	218	880,849	799,261	28	80,898	65,330	280	1,052,077	864,592
1985	40	182,607	121,188	103	505,738	463,405	18	33,488	27,838	231	859,114	726,829
1986	27	69,442	50,605	76	399,950	378,456	16	30,427	26,512	235	872,515	784,574

SOURCE: Tokyo Stock Exchange 1986b: 118–119.
[1] Since 1982, also including "Exercise of Warrant."

Under "Shareholders' Equity," a note to the financial statements of Sumitomo Corporation (1987) reads as follows:

> The Company may issue without consideration and upon approval of the Board of Directors new shares of its common stock to existing share-holders. The Code permits the Board of Directors to distribute (1) an amount of additional paid-in capital or legal reserve, transferred to stated capital and (2) the portion of the issue price of new shares in excess of the par value accounted for as stated capital in the form of free or partially free shares to shareholders.

In September 1987, the Industrial Bank of Japan issued new stock to shareholders at a distribution ratio of 0.05 for each share at the price of ¥2,100 per share. This price had been determined at approximately half the market price when, three months earlier, the new issue was approved by the directors.

In postwar Japan, capital increases were made at par value and issued as a rights offering to existing shareholders. Two separate objectives were thus combined in one: stock was sold both to raise capital and to please shareholders by giving them more shares (in foreign eyes, a partial stock split) with prospects for enhanced dividends. In the mid-1960s, however, with reorganization of the stock market and support of the underwriters, increases at par value were, to a great extent, replaced by offerings at a price close to the market price. Such offerings were initially heralded as the proper means for improving corporate debt/equity ratios.

Market-price offering has enabled issuing companies to decrease the number of new shares issued: issuers are now able to raise the same amount of funds by issuing only a fraction of the (par-value) shares formerly required. Consequently, the present ratio of market-price to par-value issues is approximately three-to-one. Market-price offering also promotes the valuation of shares on the basis of price/earnings multiples, and growth of earnings per share is now carefully watched. One piece of evidence illustrating the increased preference for market-price offering is that since July 1984, most capital increases by the major banks have been entirely public offerings at market price.

New share offering at market price is undoubtedly the most effective way to substantially enlarge equity capital. But several conditions remain desirable before such offering is planned. First, the company should be advised to engage a reputable audit corporation to certify its financial statements rather than an individual certified public accountant who might be easily influenced; underwriters should not accept underwriting engagements without such assurance. Second, underwriting firms should consider manipulation of market price or price-supporting operations as criminal acts rather than merely as undesirable, except where such an operation is officially approved (Securities Exchange Law, Art. 125.3,

TABLE 35.

Proportion of Holdings by Type of Shareholder (FY 1950–1985)

(percentage)

	1950	1955	1960	1965	1970	1975	1980	1985
Government and local government	3.1	0.4	0.2	0.2	0.2	0.2	0.2	0.2
Financial institutions	12.6	23.6	30.6	29.0	32.3	36.0	38.8	40.7
Investment trusts	—	4.1	7.5	5.6	1.4	1.6	1.5	1.4
Securities companies	11.9	7.9	3.7	5.8	1.2	1.4	1.7	2.1
Other business corporations	11.0	13.2	17.8	18.4	23.1	26.3	26.0	25.6
Foreign corporations	—	1.5	1.1	1.4	3.0	2.5	4.0	6.0[1]
Individuals and others	61.3	53.2	46.3	44.8	39.9	33.5	29.2	25.4
Foreigners	—	0.3	0.3	0.4	0.2	0.1	0.1	—
TOTAL	100.0	100.0	100.0	100.0	100.0	100.0	100.0	100.0

SOURCE: Tokyo Stock Exchange 1986b: 288–289.

[1]In 1985, "foreign individuals" are included in "foreign corporations."

and relevant regulations). Finally, there should be more active transactions on the stock market (i.e., individual shareholding should be encouraged), rather than the current limited supply of shares, which pushes prices unreasonably higher.

Individual Shareholding

When the American Occupation dissolved the prewar *zaibatsu* that controlled most larger corporations, the intention was to return control to the public. Three methods were used: public tender, underwriting sales, and employee sales (Hadley 1970: 183). Thus, when the stock exchanges were finally reopened in 1949, 68% of all outstanding shares were individually held. However, a decade later institutional investors held the majority of outstanding shares. Today, the proportion is approximately the opposite of what it was in 1949: three-quarters of investors are institutional, one-quarter individual (table 35). Of course, distribution of shareholding varies considerably, depending upon the corporation. Institutional shareholders of banks are mostly nonfinancial institutions; for the trading companies, the majority are financial shareholders. Individual shareholders lost their lead in the shareholding of large corporations for the fundamental reason that individual income could not keep up with the quick expansion of the market. Individual shareholders bought and sold much more frequently than institutions, because for an individual there is no taxation on profit from the sale of securities, provided the number of transactions per year is less than 50 and involves fewer than 200,000 shares (Individual Income Tax Law, Art. 9, and relevant Cabinet Order, Art. 28). In fact, few individuals were able to keep up with the frequent capital increases. Issuing corporations, concerned about increasing control over outstanding shares, also contributed to the trend of declining individual shareholding, for example, by strengthening the position of stable shareholders and allotting new shares on a selective basis.

Until very recently, half of the financial assets of Japanese individuals have been in the form of savings deposits with banks and post offices: between 1981 and 1985, such saving deposits decreased from 51.4% to 48.4%, while investment in securities increased from 16.3% to 19.0% (table 36). Because deposits are channeled into industry, it can be said that Japanese individuals have traditionally preferred indirect to direct investment. In a sense, the individual who makes deposits at a bank entrusts his money to investment specialists, namely the bankers, and thus takes a very conservative risk. His risk is comparable to that of an investment in capital stock with two exceptions: returns on investment take

TABLE 36.

Financial Assets of Individuals (End of 1981 and 1985)

	Amount (billion yen)	Percentage
Currency		
1981	16,162	4.2
1985	20,288	3.5
Current and demand deposits		
1981	30,406	7.8
1985	35,823	6.2
Time deposits		
1981	199,668	51.4
1985	278,169	48.4
Trusts		
1981	24,216	6.2
1985	39,422	6.9
Insurance		
1981	51,997	13.4
1985	88,662	15.4
Securities		
1981	63,480	16.3
1985	109,369	19.0
(Bonds)		
1981	(29,967)	(7.7)
1985	(43,741)	(7.6)
(Stocks)		
1981	(27,488)	(7.1)
1985	(48,587)	(8.5)
(Investment trusts)		
1981	(6,025)	(1.5)
1985	(17,040)	(3.0)
Other		
1981	2,868	0.7
1985	2,476	0.4
TOTAL		
1981	388,796	100.0
1985	574,229	100.0

SOURCE: Tokyo Stock Exchange 1987b: 66.
NOTE: Amounts of stocks are based on market prices.

the form of fixed interest rather than the fixed dividend prevalent in the stock market, and he enjoys the lack of risk of bank closure over the risk of corporate bankruptcy. (In postwar Japan, not a single bank has failed, although the Ministry of Finance has had to arrange several rescues!)

In general, the smaller the capital of the listed companies is, the larger the percentage of shares held by individuals. In 1985 and 1986, on the First Section of the stock exchanges, individuals held less than one-quarter of the shares, but they held well over one-third on the Second

Section, although their percentage decreased in both sections. In contrast, financial institutions increased their shareholding from 41.8% to 44.5% on the First Section but maintained the same 21.9% on the Second Section (table 37).

The position of individual shareholders on the Japanese stock exchanges remains fluid. The 1982 amendments to the Commercial Code were meant, in part, to encourage individual shareholdings. This intention was reflected in the ability to issue no-par stock (with the resultant ease of stock splits), the requirement to credit one-half of proceeds of a public offering to capital, and the ability of corporations to issue stock with detachable warrants. Moreover, the Tokyo Stock Exchange (as of November 1, 1986) revised listing requirements of "floating stock" (*fudō kabu*). For a new listing, at least 1,000 shareholders holding one unit (1,000 shares) or more are required if the number of shares to be listed is less than 10 million, 1,500 if the number of shares ranges between 10 and 20 million, and 2,000 plus 100 per 10 million shares in excess of 20 million shares. In addition, the total number of shares held by "special few" (i.e., ten largest shareholders and persons having a special interest in the issuer) must not exceed 80% at the time of listing. This percentage must be reduced to 70% or less by the end of the first business year after listing. For companies with a capital of less than three billion yen, the percentage of individual shareholding is now set at a minimum of 10%; for larger companies it is less (TSE, Standards for Listing of Stock, Art. 4.2, and Standards for Delisting of Stock, Art. 2.2).

Stock options as prevalent in the United States do not exist in Japan, because allocation of shares at a significantly lower price than the market is prohibited by the Commercial Code (Art. 280.2), and the difference between market price and allocated price is taxable as gift income. An Employee Stock Ownership Plan (ESOP) is, however, sponsored by almost 90% (70% in 1975) of the listed companies, in which 40% of their workforce participate.

> The employee stock ownership plan in Japan is set up and run in the form of a permanent voluntary association of employees participating in the plan of their own volition. The participants put up a certain amount of money regularly (usually withheld from their monthly salaries or wages), and the company itself gives a subsidy to them. The total money—participants' installments and the subsidy—is pooled in the plan and used for the purchase of shares of the company at regular intervals. (Tokyo Stock Exchange 1987a: 47)

Given the current boom of the stock market, securities houses have been looking for new means to attract individual savers.

TABLE 37.

Share Ownership Distribution of Listed Companies (FY 1985 and 1986)

(percentage)

Size of Capital (billion yen)	First Section Total	0.1 to 1	1 to 10	Over 10	Second Section Total	0.1 to 1	1 to 10	Over 10
(Number of companies)								
1985	(1,120)	—	(775)	(345)	(714)	(337)	(369)	(8)
1986	(1,144)	—	(765)	(379)	(738)	(326)	(404)	(8)
Total (No. of billion shares)								
1985	100.0	—	100.0	100.0	100.0	100.0	100.0	100.0
1986	100.0	—	100.0	100.0	100.0	100.0	100.0	100.0
1985	(253)	—	(56)	(196)	(14)	(4)	(9)	(0.6)
1986	(315)	—	(54)	(260)	(15)	(3)	(10)	(0.7)
Government								
1985	0.2	—	0.2	0.2	0.0	0.1	0.0	0.2
1986	0.9	—	0.2	1.1	0.0	0.1	0.0	0.1
Domestic institutions								
1985	68.9	—	66.4	69.6	60.4	56.4	61.9	62.6
1986	70.9	—	67.9	71.5	62.6	58.5	64.3	61.1
Financial								
1985	41.8	—	34.4	43.9	21.9	19.0	22.2	34.0
1986	44.5	—	35.2	46.5	21.9	19.1	22.5	28.6
(Banks)								
1985	(21.5)	—	(19.5)	(22.1)	(12.8)	(10.9)	(13.7)	(12.3)
1986	(23.7)	—	(20.6)	(24.4)	(13.1)	(11.1)	(14.0)	(9.6)
(Life insurance)								
1985	(13.2)	—	(8.0)	(14.6)	(4.6)	(3.6)	(4.4)	(12.8)
1986	(13.7)	—	(8.1)	(14.9)	(4.8)	(3.7)	(4.6)	(12.0)
Securities companies								
1985	2.1	—	3.1	1.9	1.5	2.3	1.1	1.3
1986	2.6	—	2.9	2.5	1.6	2.5	1.3	1.1
Corporations								
1985	24.9	—	28.9	23.8	37.1	35.0	38.6	27.3
1986	23.8	—	29.7	22.5	39.1	36.9	40.5	31.4
Foreigners (corporate and individual)								
1985	6.2	—	4.8	6.7	2.3	1.6	2.6	1.8
1986	4.9	—	4.2	5.0	2.0	1.4	2.3	1.3
Individuals and others								
1985	24.7	—	28.7	23.6	37.3	41.9	35.5	35.3
1986	23.3	—	27.8	22.4	35.3	40.0	33.4	37.6

SOURCE: Zenkoku Shōken Torihiki-jo 1986: 37; and 1987: 37.

For example, Daiwa Securities and Daiwa Investment Trust Management introduced in 1987 a new savings product called "Million." It is an alternate form of employee savings plan and is initiated by the corporation by contracting a securities company. The product was originally targeted at public servants and employees of unlisted companies who are not able to use current employee stock ownership plans. However, because this innovative product offers easy and efficient fund management, a large number of listed companies are joining, bringing the total number of registered participants to more than 1800. Under this system, participants invest a fixed sum (minimum ¥5,000), withheld from the individual employees' monthly salaries. Funds raised by the securities companies in this matter are then turned over to investment trust management firms, which handle the actual management of the fund. In many cases, companies will subsidize their employees' contributions, as is the case in employee stock ownership plans. Prospects for the growing popularity of this product are very good (*Nihon Keizai Shinbun* 1987, June 10).

Other attempts to promote individual shareholding, such as the stepping up of reimbursement to shareholders of premiums earned through public offering, have been advocated. Also, legal restrictions on stockholding by financial companies have been returned to the pre-1953 limit of 5%. There was much ado in 1985, when it was announced that the number of individual shareholders had crossed the 20 million mark (20,468,599 compared to 19,855,198 in 1984) (Zenkoku Shōken Torihiki-jo 1986: 11–12). Despite the apparent increase in the number of individual shareholders, the ratio of shares they hold is steadily decreasing. Between the end of March 1986 and the end of March 1987, distribution in billion shares evolved as follows:

	1986/3	1987/3	Rate of Change
Total	325 (100.0)	337 (100.0)	3.8%
Corporations	224 (69.0)	240 (71.3)	7.3
Individuals	82 (25.3)	80 (23.9)	(−) 1.6
Foreigners	18 (5.7)	16 (4.8)	(−)14.1
(i.e., foreign corporations and foreign individuals)			

(Zenkoku Shōken Torihiki-jo 1987: 116)

This drop in individual shareholding represents the eleventh consecutive year-by-year decline. It is attributed to the increased participation of companies in financial operations (*Nihon Keizai Shinbun* 1987, July 31).

Institutional Shareholding

Through the years, financial institutions steadily increased the percentage of their shareholdings; having financed corporations through debt capital, they began to predominate also as far as equity capital was concerned. At the end of a ten-year grace period in December 1987, they came, however, under the Antimonopoly Law limitation that "no company engaged in financial business shall acquire or hold stock of another company in Japan if, by doing so, it holds in excess of five percent of the total outstanding stock (ten percent in the case of an insurance company)" (Iyori and Uesugi 1983: 83). When a financial institution holds more than 5% of the total outstanding stock, it must obtain approval of the Fair Trade Commission.

Nonfinancial corporations are considered choice shareholders, not only because of the systems of related companies and industrial groupings, but simply because they act as stable shareholders. One method of inflating shareholder structure is the so-called *mochi-ai* (cross-shareholding). Company A owns 5% of company B's shares in return for company B's holding 5% of company A's shares of a similar market value. This practice developed initially to support the market when share prices were depressed. Much of this interlocking shareholding is the result of direct contacts between the executives of the companies involved and securities brokerage firms actively persuading potential shareholder companies to purchase shares of their clients.

> Nisseki House Company's President Horiuchi announced in February 1987 . . . that an agreement had been reached between Nisseki House Co. and Misawa Home Co. to mutually acquire 200,000 shares of each others' stock in March 1987 for the purpose of stable shareholding. (*Nihon Keizai Shinbun* 1987, April 17)

The current result is that stock prices tend to move radically even by small-block transactions, hindering transactions at a fair market price. Corporate capital itself may be jeopardized: a substantial portion of the capital stock account on the credit side may be wiped out if the investment account (in shareholders' shares) on the debit side is offset against capital stock. It is not surprising, then, that pure portfolio investments by institutions is still immature. Most portfolios remain interlocked.

Venture Capital

Although often mentioned in the mass media and business periodicals, venture capital in Japan is yet far from enjoying the popularity it knows in other industrial countries.

> The prohibition on establishing holding companies, on the one hand, and the confiscation of the largest private fortunes under the U.S. Occupation (1945–1952) on the other hand, have prevented individuals from playing a significant role in the postwar financial reconstruction. Moreover, steep progressive taxation and a strict income distribution system have made Japan, along with the Scandinavian countries, one of the most egalitarian industrial nations. The result has been that Japan counts very few extremely wealthy capitalists who can turn themselves into professional individual capitalists. . . . [Furthermore] participating firms [in the venture capital industry] have been established mainly at the initiative of large Japanese banks and securities companies, as a kind of subsidiary of large industrial groups. . . . To banks, venture capital was a promise to turn R&D-oriented ventures into a new clientele of borrowers. Similarly, Japan's "Big Four" securities companies (Nomura, Daiwa, Nikko, and Yamaichi, which account for nearly 80 percent of all Tokyo Stock Exchange transactions) perceived venture capital as a new speculative game and a new means to become the underwriters of venture companies when they went public. (Turpin 1986: 4–6)

Already in 1963, MITI had introduced the Small Business Investment Law that established three Small Business Investment Companies (SBIC) (*Chūshō Kigyō Tōshi Ikusei Kabushiki Kaisha*) in Tokyo, Osaka, and Nagoya. They are considered the forerunners of venture capital in Japan. The capital stock of these investment companies, as of March 31, 1987, was over ¥6 billion in Tokyo and Osaka, and over ¥4 billion in Nagoya. The number of clients and amount invested were 1,556 companies and ¥63 billion (SBIC 1987). In 1972, the Fair Trade Commission promulgated guidelines reminding venture capitalists that Section 9 of the Antimonopoly Law forbids a single financial institution from holding more than 5% of the shares of a single company. It stipulated, among others, that venture capital firms are not allowed to have representatives on the Board of Directors of a company in which they have invested and to hold more than 49% of a company's stock (FTC 1986b). From the mid-1970s on, the government became increasingly involved in the promotion of venture capital as a new instance of its overall support policies of small/medium enterprises. In 1975, MITI established the Venture Enterprise Center, whereby it can guarantee up to 80% of the loans from private banks to small firms with an original project. In November 1983, the OTC markets (Tokyo, Osaka, Nagoya) were drastically reorganized so as to facilitate their access by innovative small enterprises. From the early 1980s on, with MITI's support, regional venture capital funds were established. Their impact on the regional economies is beginning to be noticed.

On the basis of a survey of "venture business" (to use the popular Japanese expression), conducted in December 1986, 26% of these companies were founded after 1975. In the past five years, 64% achieved an increase of 30% or more in sales, and in 41% the number of employees increased by 30% or more. Bankruptcies, however, jumped sharply from 21 cases in 1985 to 64 cases in 1986 (MITI 1987b: 135–136). Venture business is thus a recent buzzword in equity financing. In financial circles, it is still largely limited to encouraging listing on the stock exchange. Such encouragement is forthcoming not only from venture capitalists, but also from financial instances seeking new clients. It was reported that even *kansa hōjin* (audit corporations) are in the fray (*Nihon Keizai Shinbun* 1987, September 7). However, the major constraint on what some observers call the boom of venture capital in Japan comes, apparently, from the reluctance of Japanese entrepreneurs to submit themselves to financial backers aiming solely at a financial profit, a fortiori foreign financial backers. Whether this attitude will change under greater familiarity with the nature of venture capital remains to be seen.

8

INTERNAL SOURCES OF FUNDS

THE SITUATION WITH REGARD to internal sources of funds at the end of the 1960s has been described in macroeconomic terms as follows:

> Gross savings of corporate businesses (provision for capital consumption and retained profits) have been about 37% of total gross domestic savings. If we take retained profits (net savings) only, these account for about 21% of total net domestic savings (average 1960–69). Retained profits have a secular tendency to grow, which reflects the expansion in the scale of the economy, but they show fairly conspicuous ups and downs in the course of a business cycle. On the other hand, provisions for capital consumption (allowances for depreciation) have steadily increased year by year, reflecting the past high growth in fixed investment in plant and equipment. Their proportion to the total gross savings of corporate businesses has come to surpass that of retained profits. (Bank of Japan 1973: 71)

For the same period (1960–1969), however, it was noted that "the volume of internal funds available to corporations moved in the same direction as the availability of external funds," and "total external funds raised by corporations generally followed the same pattern as their credit from financial institutions" (OECD 1972: 46). There was a close relationship between general economic conditions as reflected in tax policies and the way management looked at internal funding.

Tax Policies

Earlier it was stressed that industrialization in Japan was not started through private initiative; it was launched by the government to solve a national emergency (created by the Western powers) that occurred in the mid-1800s when Japan was forced out of its two-century-old isolation. The government has not failed since in its support of industry, expressed in the very tangible form of subsidies and tax breaks, not to speak of protection against foreign control of industry. Especially after World War II, management was mainly concerned with gaining all possible benefits from participation in the general economic development. Companies derived benefits from involvement in related companies and industrial groups and through reliance on financial institutions that shared the same concerns. Once this involvement was guaranteed and with limited help from the stock market, if it cared to be listed, a Japanese company could turn, again with official blessing, to internal sources of funds with an eye to "business" (i.e., expansion) rather than "returns." Tax favors were not meant as incentives to corporate independence; rather, they promoted a sense of responsibility for the national economy whose fate, with proper government encouragement and guidance, was placed in the hands of the private sector.

The last 50 years have seen a radical shift in tax revenue:

> ... in 1934–36 from direct taxes at 34.8% and indirect at 65.2% to 71.1% and 28.9%, respectively, in 1980. The present heavy reliance on direct taxes is inordinately large. . . . Revenues from the corporation tax exceeded those from the [individual] income tax in the 18 years between FY 1957 and FY 1974, except for several years when corporation tax revenues fell due to a business recession. Estimated at 30.9% for FY 1984, the revenues from the corporation tax as a percentage of total national tax revenues are far greater than in other industrialized countries. Comparable figures for 1983 were 9.8% in the United States, 6.9% in the United Kingdom, 6.9% in the Federal Republic of Germany, 9.1% in France, and 4.5% in Italy. The large share of the corporation tax is mainly ascribed to the relative importance of corporate activities in the national economy, and to the accelerated incorporation of individual proprietorships after World War II. (Aoki [Torao] 1986: 104, 112)

Among six industrialized countries, Japan receives the highest percentage of tax revenue from income and profits (table 38).

Generally speaking, fiscal incentives may be classified as exemption- and deferral-type measures (table 39).

> Exemption-type fiscal incentives are prevalent in most countries, especially in developing countries. Japan was no exception at least until the early 1960s. . . . A fact to be noted is that exemption has not been granted to corporations across the board, but only to those in keeping with the objectives of the government, e.g., corporations belonging to infant and export-oriented industries.
>
> Deferral-type incentive policies consist of the allowance for tax-free re-

TABLE 38.

Tax Revenue of Main Headings as Percentage of Total Taxation: International Comparison (1985)

	Japan	U.S.A.	U.K.	F.R.G.	France	Italy
Income and profits	45.8	42.8	38.9	34.8	17.1	36.8
Individual	24.8	35.7	26.0	28.7	12.7	26.7
Corporate	21.0	7.1	12.9	6.1	4.3	9.2
Social security	30.2	29.4	17.5	36.5	43.6	34.7
Payroll	—	—	0.1	—	2.1	0.6
Property	9.7	10.1	12.0	3.0	4.6	2.5
Goods and services	14.0	17.7	31.6	25.6	29.4	25.4
Other	0.3	—	—	—	3.3	—
TOTAL	100.0	100.0	100.0	100.0	100.0	100.0

SOURCE: OECD 1987: 85, 86–87.

serves and accelerated depreciation. Accelerated depreciation writes off the value of fixed assets faster than their actual economic value diminishes and thus lessens the tax levied in the early phase of asset lives. This method has been one of the most widely adopted measures for promoting investment in postwar Japan. . . .

Actually, the most significant characteristic of postwar Japanese fiscal incentive policies is to be observed in the provision for tax-free reserves. Corporations have been allowed to accumulate as reserves a part of their income for a certain period, the reserves being added back to income and taxed only when the period expires. In other words, corporations can delay the payment of taxes levied on a portion of their income. The rate of tax savings, accordingly, becomes larger as the tax-free reserve period is prolonged. (Ikemoto, Tajika, and Yui 1984: 374–376)

The impact on corporate financial reporting has been considerable: financial statements, except those for listing purposes, have been meant largely as documentation for tax returns. (Note that in Japan corporate taxes were directly assessed by tax authorities until 1947.)

Under the Law of Temporary Measures for the Structural Adjustment of Specific Industries (1983–1988), tax provisions are: "1) A special depreciation system for modernization and capacity reduction investment. 2) Extension of period for carry-forward deductions from 5 to 10 years. 3) Reduction of fees for the registration of mergers, investment in kind, and transfer of business, as well as for license tax and real estate acquisition tax" (Peck, Levin, and Goto 1987: 119).

"Temporary Measures," including those of a fiscal nature (mostly entrusted to the Ministry of International Trade and Industry), are a golden opportunity for administrative guidance.

The effectiveness of tax incentives has been a matter of much scholarly debate. A recent study reached the tentative conclusion that they "were

TABLE 39.

Fiscal Incentives in Postwar Japan: Some Examples

Measures	Purposes and Conditions of Application	Effective Period
I. EXEMPTION-TYPE MEASURES		
1. Exemption from corporate tax of income raised by producing certain goods	Applied mostly to petro-chemical products	pre-1966
2. Exemption from corporate tax of income raised by exports	Promotion of export-oriented industries	1953–1963
3. Exemption from corporate tax of income spent for dividends for increased shares	To enhance corporate savings	1954–1957
II. DEFERRAL-TYPE MEASURES		
A. TAX-FREE RESERVES		
1. Reserves for bad debts	For expected losses in the collection of receivables	1950–
2. Reserve for retirement allowances	To let corporations prepare for payments for employees' retirement	1952–
3. Reserves for loss on returned goods	Applicable to publishers, pharmaceutical producers, etc.	1965–
4. Reserves for special repairs	Repairs of vessels, blast furnaces, etc.	1951–
5. Reserve for repairs and guaranteeing of certain products	Applicable to completed construction works, vessels, cars, television sets, etc.	1971–
6. Reserve for price fluctuations	For losses due to the fluctuation of prices of inventories	1951–
7. Overseas market development reserve for small- and medium-sized businesses	For export-oriented small- and medium-sized firms	1964–
8. Reserve for drought	To allow power companies to prepare for seasonal fluctuations in output	1952–
B. ACCELERATED DEPRECIATION		
9. Accelerated depreciation for special equipment	—	1951–1961 (revised)
10. Accelerated depreciation for equipment designated under the modernization promotion act	—	1952–1961 (revised)
11. Accelerated depreciation for equipment suitable for modernization	This unified accelerated depreciation measures 9 and 10	1961–

SOURCE: Ikemoto, Tajika, and Yui 1984: 375.

TABLE 40.

Loss Enterprises and Amount of Loss by Size of Capital (1985)

Capital (million yen)	No. of Enterprises	Of Which Loss Enterprises	
		Number	Amount of Loss (million yen)
Less than 1	186,333	122,598	156,458
1 and more	332,781	209,844	413,121
2 and more	500,598	295,127	799,115
5 and more	311,392	163,529	617,909
10 and more	183,224	77,806	732,069
20 and more	101,376	37,781	717,371
50 and more	24,349	7,810	331,669
100 and more	15,521	5,208	507,643
500 and more	1,566	430	51,566
1,000 and more	2,023	510	189,348
5,000 and more	408	94	78,888
10,000 and more	439	68	165,963
TOTAL	1,660,010	920,805	4,761,120

SOURCE: National Tax Administration 1987: 51.
NOTE: Enterprises closing accounts twice a year, even if they were profitable in only one term, are included in profitable companies.

more effective in promoting the investment of manufacturing industries, especially such growth-promoting industries as the chemical, iron and steel, and machine industries, than of the rest of the industries, and that among growing industries accelerated depreciation was a more effective means than tax-free reserves" (Ikemoto, Tajika, and Yui 1984: 394).

If, however, all these tax advantages are not enough to keep a corporation in the black, there remains a last recourse under tax laws: deferral of corporate income tax by a loss company (*kesson-gaisha*). Under the Corporation Tax Law (Arts. 57 and 81), a company filing the blue-form tax return enjoys the privilege of carry-back and/or carry-forward of loss. The current year's loss can be carried back for one year against the previous year's profit (if any), and a tax refund can be claimed to the extent that the previous year's profit can be offset by the current year's loss. Or, the corporation can carry forward its current loss for the succeeding five years, to be offset against future profit. Thus, until the loss carried forward is exhausted (within these five years), the company is not liable to pay taxes, with the minor exception of a nominal per-capita tax. Between 1975 and 1985, among all companies the number of loss companies increased from 520,139 (43.0%) to 920,265 (55.4%) (National Tax Administration 1987: 14). Of course, the smaller the capitalization, the larger the number of loss companies (table 40).

"Internal Retention of Earnings"

There is no doubt that Japanese business executives are committed to expanding market share, a vital corporate necessity (Abegglen and Stalk 1985). The result is, then, that most Western terminology related to business survival and success, based on the concept of profit, has a peculiar ring in Japan, where the same or almost the same terminology was based on debt, the ransom of rapid expansion. However, the slower economic growth in the 1980s and growing international involvement has begun to affect the Japanese outlook to a certain extent. At stake is *naibu ryūho* (internal retention of earnings).

From the tax viewpoint: Because profits are taxable by more than 50%, as an internal source of funds they are not as attractive as reserves taken before income taxation and profits. It could be said that tax-deductible reserves are a much favored sort of *naibu ryūho*.

From the shareholders' viewpoint: Institutional shareholders are happy with semiannual dividends of at least 10% to 12% on par value. In some extreme cases, the profit is calculated to meet only dividend requirements, after allocating the largest possible amounts to tax-deductible and nondeductible reserves. Between 1965 and 1985, as a percentage of before-tax earnings, dividends were reduced from 25% to 10% (table 41).

From the lenders' viewpoint: In the case of long-term credit for such purposes as acquiring land or building a factory, lenders expect loan repayment mainly from two sources, after-tax profit and depreciation. It naturally follows that repayment committed to bankers is given prefer-

TABLE 41.
Distribution of Before-Tax Earnings (1965–1985)
(percentage)

	1965	1970	1975	1980	1985
Directors' remuneration	4.5	3.7	4.0	2.6	1.9
(in large corporations)	(0.9)	(0.7)	(0.7)	(0.5)	(0.5)
Dividends	24.1	15.7	12.9	9.8	9.6
(in large corporations)	(36.4)	(21.2)	(19.8)	(16.5)	(13.2)
Taxes and other disbursements	41.1	41.8	49.5	51.4	56.0
(in large corporations)	(41.7)	(40.7)	(48.2)	(51.0)	(55.5)
Retained earnings	30.3	38.7	33.6	36.2	32.5
(in large corporations)	(21.0)	(37.4)	(31.3)	(32.0)	(30.8)
TOTAL	100.0	100.0	100.0	100.0	100.0

SOURCES: National Tax Administration, various years. For 1985: National Tax Administration 1987: 15, and "large corporations" calculated from ibid.: 89.
NOTE: "Large corporations" means corporations capitalized at one billion yen or more.

TABLE 42.

Operating Revenue and Earnings (1965–1985)

	1965	1970	1975	1980	1985
All corporations:					
operating revenue	92,417	209,598	399,146	762,099	992,264
Of which profitable corporations:					
Operating revenue (A)	73,985	187,046	317,882	633,296	824,582
Before-tax earnings (B)	2,599	7,500	11,331	22,330	30,285
B/A (percentage)	3.5	4.0	3.6	3.5	3.7

SOURCE: National Tax Administration 1977: 14; 1987: 12.

ence over raising the dividend rate. (Customarily, some borrowers submit a draft of financial statements and appropriation of profits to their main banks before a shareholders' meeting.)

Under these constraints, management faced a situation in which, in spite of large cash operations received and disbursed every month from high sales and successive expansions, the balance remaining as profit was too small to be applied to expansion of facilities. Between 1965 and 1985, before-tax earnings remained between 3% and 4% of operating revenue (table 42). As corporate management felt caught in successive waves of rapid expansion to maintain or improve its market share, profit was applied to the repayment of past borrowings, and, of the new funds required, only 20% to 40% were raised in the securities market by capital increases and/or corporate bonds (for the privileged companies). The remaining 60% to 80% were borrowed from the same banks that were willing to finance this relentless expansion as long as former loans were repaid without delay. The foreign reader of Japanese financial statements had the impression that debt was never refunded but continuously expanded. What differentiated companies amongst themselves was their market share, not so much a "measure" of relative strength as of an elementary drive. It was expressed in simplistic but highly effective terms: the volume of products sold by the manufacturing company, the volume of sales, products and services of the trading company, the volume of deposits received by the bank, and so on. This market share was the ultimate guarantee of corporate survival, and on it Japanese management was expected to concentrate all energies.

Such is the context in which corporations look at the two main sources of internal funds, depreciation and reserves.

Depreciation

The modernization of Japanese industry, especially in the postwar period, owes much to favorable depreciation allowances (deferring income tax payments). Depreciation (*genka shōkyaku*) can be taken on tangible assets, such as building, machinery, and furniture; they are to have a residual value of 10% of the acquisition cost. Companies are required to keep separate records for each item of plant or equipment depreciated. The "official" useful life by type of assets, during which they can be depreciated for tax purposes, is regulated by the Ministry of Finance. For example,

Item	Years
Tangible fixed assets other than machinery and equipment	
Reinforced concrete buildings (for office)	65
Wooden buildings (for office)	26
Elevators	17
Desks, chairs, or cabinets made of metal	15
Electronic computers	6
Trucks (for transport business)	4
Machinery and equipment	
Beer brewery plants	14
Automobile manufacturing plants	10
Intangible fixed assets	
Patent rights	8
Utility model rights	5

(MOF Printing Bureau 1986: 82)

Useful life can be extended, but not shortened, without approval of the tax authorities; the official tables of useful life give only minimum life. There is little to stop a company from extending life and thus depreciation, if profits so require, until the total amount catches up with 95% of the acquisition cost. Whatever the form of depreciation, normal or special, the difference is only in regard to the time span of depreciation; the total amount must remain the same, i.e., the acquisition cost.

Amortization (straight-line method) can be applied to intangible fixed assets, such as copyrights, patents and franchises, and deferred expenses (research and development, and start-up expenses). No residual value is required.

The Corporation Tax Law provides only two methods of normal depreciation for industries other than mining: the straight-line method and the fixed-rate-on-declining-balance method. In order to defer income tax payment (what Japanese businessmen call *setsu-zei* [tax saving]) and to meet short repayment terms of five to ten years, most companies adopt the latter method, which amounts to accelerated depreciation and allows approximately double the amount of depreciation in the early years compared with the first method. However, it is not uncommon to start with accelerated depreciation and change to straight-line, if the profit situation looks unfavorable, and then when company income turns profitable again to switch back to accelerated depreciation! Although this practice is condoned with some reservations in other industrial countries, the problem in Japan is that, in general, financial statements reported to shareholders do not provide comparative data with previous periods. Tax regulations do not permit depreciation not taken in any given year to be carried forward to the following year even though the total depreciable amount remains the same.

In addition to normal depreciation, tax regulations permit certain kinds of special depreciation to companies properly filing the "blue form" of income tax returns. (This is where fiscal policy is periodically adjusted as a result of pressure brought to bear on the government by particular groups.) Special depreciation comes in two categories, increased initial depreciation and normal-plus-given-percentage depreciation.

Increased initial depreciation (*tokubetsu shōkyaku*) allows deducting a portion of an asset's acquisition cost, in addition to normal depreciation, during the first accounting period in which the asset is acquired. It is allowed for certain specified plants and equipment (in underdeveloped areas of the country and in "designated" industries, such as advanced data processing), and rates range from 8% to 36%.

Normal-plus-given-percentage depreciation (*warimashi shōkyaku*) is allowed for a specified period on certain facilities, machinery, and equipment (storage of crude petroleum), and for houses newly built for rent. By Western standards, fixed assets are usually undervalued through this accelerated depreciation. A reserve for special depreciation may cover increased initial depreciation as well as normal-plus-given-percentage depreciation. The Special Taxation Measures Law also allows 14% of acquisition cost for depreciation on equipment purchased by small enterprises. A special depreciation for export promotion was abolished as of March 1974. A tax deduction had been allowed for accelerated depreciation based on export sales made in the immediately preceding year. If, for example, export sales were 25% of total sales, ordinary depreciation could be increased by the same percentage (until March 1971) or by 20% (after that date).

Like other reserves, the reserve for special depreciation is recorded under either the statement of income or the statement of retained earnings, as explained below. Contrary to normal depreciation, special depreciation can be carried forward for a period of one year. However, whatever

TABLE 43.

Depreciation (1975–1985)

(100 million yen)

Year	Depreciation		B/A
	Maximum Amount (A)	Actual Amount (B)	
1975	87,323	81,044	92.8
1976	101,689	93,431	91.9
1977	109,474	101,107	92.4
1978	109,826	104,271	94.9
1979	125,976	120,926	96.0
1980	138,474	131,265	94.8
1981	152,508	145,551	95.4
1982	165,798	155,745	93.9
1983	180,621	169,171	93.7
1984	190,314	179,241	94.2
1985	211,789	200,329	94.6

SOURCE: National Tax Administration 1987: 20.

method is used, the depreciation charge allowable for tax purposes cannot exceed the maximum allowed by tax regulations and the amount recorded in the books of account. It should be noted also that the same method of depreciation must be used for both tax and accounting purposes. (In the U.S. practice, the double-declining method is used for tax purposes and the straight-line method for accounting.)

The aggregate depreciation in industry more than doubled between 1975 and 1985. In 1985, the maximum amount was ¥21 trillion and the actual amount ¥20 trillion (table 43).

By industry, the depreciated amounts in 1973 and 1985 were

Industry	1973	1985
	(billion yen)	
Construction	542	1,016
Chemical	1,082	2,006
Machinery	977	3,485
Wholesale	512	1,295
Finance, insurance	126	653
Transportation	1,468	4,100

(National Tax Administration 1975: 31, and 1987: 21)

It appears that, whatever the size of the company, depreciation as an internal retention of earnings amounts today to one-half of the company's capitalization (in the case of a loss company, however, the larger the company, the smaller its depreciation compared with a profitable company).

Reserves

Reserves are the second major internal source of funds. Their variety as well as the variety of their reporting methods make them a complex accounting procedure. Appropriate English translation of the Japanese terminology only complicates the issue further. For the sake of clarity, the following three aspects are distinguished: reserves under retained earnings, allowances under liabilities, and tax-deductible reserves and allowances.

Reserves under Retained Earnings

The standard Japanese terminology here is *junbi-kin* and *tsumitate-kin*, both translated as "reserves." Two types exist: legal reserve and general reserve.

The Commercial Code (Art. 288) requires appropriation as legal reserve (*hōtei junbi-kin*) of portions of retained earnings in amounts equal to at least 10% of cash dividends paid at each financial period, until the reserve equals 25% of the capital stock amount. This reserve is not available for dividends, but may be used to reduce deficit (by resolution of the shareholders) or may be capitalized (by resolution of the board of directors).

General reserve (*nin-i* or *betto tsumitate-kin*) is a caption summarizing for international reporting purposes a number of reserves found in Japanese statements, where they are often specified as reserve for research and development, reserve for dividend equalization, reserve for directors' retirement benefits, and so forth. They are part of retained earnings but are not available for dividends unless reversed to inappropriate earnings by the shareholders' meeting.

Allowances under Liabilities

The standard Japanese terminology in this case is *hikiate-kin*, translated as "allowance or reserve." Except for tax-deductible allowances reviewed in the following section, all other allowances are not tax-deductible and come under various names that suit the reporting company.

In 1965, when capital liberalization became an issue in Japan, Shiseido, the largest cosmetics maker, carried an "allowance for capital liberalization" of ¥2,137 million. Presumably, management wanted to protect itself against the onslaught of foreign competition on the future "liberalized" domestic market!

One allowance under liabilities that may be given special consideration from the tax viewpoint, is known as "payables estimated." Tax examiners tend, however, to disallow such allowance unless the amount is supported by invoices.

Tax-deductible Reserves and Allowances

Under the Corporation Tax Law and the Special Taxation Measures Law (Arts. 54 to 57-7), several reserves (*junbi-kin*) and allowances (*hikiate-kin*) can be set up; their amounts within prescribed limits are deductible as expenses for tax purposes. They provide tax deferment but not tax exemption. In general, *junbi-kin* is considered to result from some specific economic policy and is dealt with in the Special Taxation Measures Law. These reserves are available only to blue-return taxpayers. Major ones are for overseas market development, overseas investment loss, and structural improvement of small enterprises. On the other hand, *hikiate-kin* is directly concerned with corporate accounting. These allowances are described in the Corporate Income Tax Laws. The major ones are for doubtful accounts, sales returns, seasonal allowances (bonus), employees' retirement benefits, special repair, and product warranty.

Two general principles rule the reporting of reserves and allowances for domestic purposes: (1) All allowances and most reserves must be entered in the profit-and-loss accounts and under liabilities; some reserves can be entered as disposition of profits and under retained earnings; (2) Tax authorities allow them as tax-deductible expenses only within set limits. Any excess above the limit set by the regulations will not be deductible, and the deduction comes into effect only when the loss is actually incurred.

For all tax-deductible reserves, two accounting methods are followed, *rieki shobun keiri* (accounted for as appropriation of retained earnings) and *sonkin keiri* (accounted for as expense). The following major reserves can be appropriated from retained earnings: special depreciation, price fluctuation, overseas market development, overseas investment loss, and small business structural improvement. Any one of these reserves can also be included in liabilities, when the amount is expended in the income statement rather than appropriated from retained earnings.

The National Tax Administration reports annually on allowance for doubtful accounts, allowance for employee bonus, and allowance for employee retirement benefits. The larger the company is, the more common these allowances are (table 44).

An allowance for doubtful accounts (*kashi-daore hikiate-kin*), based

TABLE 44.

Companies Carrying Allowances for Doubtful Accounts, Bonus, and
Retirement Benefits, by Capitalization (1985)

(percentage)

Capitalization (million yen)	Allowance for Doubtful Accounts	Allowance for Bonus	Allowance for Retirement Benefits
Less than 5	19.5	8.8	2.0
More than 5–10	30.4	15.7	6.0
More than 10–100	46.7	29.7	20.6
More than 100–1,000	70.4	61.0	61.6
More than 1,000	87.7	83.8	82.9
TOTAL	27.3	14.6	7.0
(1975)	(26.2)	(13.7)	(7.8)

SOURCE: National Tax Administration 1977: 27; 1987: 19.

on the company's estimation, is required by the Commercial Code (Art. 285.4-2). However, Japanese tax regulations allow a deductible reserve up to the specified percentage of net accounts receivable outstanding at the end of the business year. This percentage has been reduced by half since 1973:

	Percentage	
Business of the Corporation	1973	1986
Retail or wholesale	2.0	1.0
Retail on installment payments	2.5	1.3
Manufacturing	1.5	0.8
Banking and insurance	1.0	0.3
Others	1.2	0.6

The current limit is increased to 116% of each percentage for the corporation whose capital amounts to ¥100 million or less. However, "corporations have the option to choose the experience method (which permits calculation of the amount deductible by an empirical rate based on past records of bad debts) instead of the percentage method above" (MOF Printing Bureau 1986: 87). In usual circumstances, this allowance, set up in accordance with tax regulations, is considered proper. It should, however, be unnecessary where there is little possibility for such a loss, for example, when a subsidiary sells all its products to the parent in good financial position. Experience has shown, however, that the 1.3% (even the previous 2.5%) allowance for installment sales is often inadequate. In any case, the amount reserved in excess of the tax-deductible limit is subject to income tax, and, therefore, in determining the income tax amount per income statement, prepaid income tax should be considered. Whereas in 1975 over 300,000 companies (26.2%) recorded an allow-

TABLE 45.

Allowances for Doubtful Accounts, Bonus, and Employee Retirement Benefits, by Size of Company (1975 and 1985)

Capital[1] (million yen)		Allowance for Doubtful Accounts		Allowance for Bonus[2]		Allowance for Employee Retirement Benefits	
		No. of Companies	Amount (million yen)	No. of Companies	Amount (million yen)	No. of Companies	Amount (million yen)
Less than 1	1975	46,406	10,945			3,141	76,854
	1985	24,204	68,706	11,309	165,400	1,998	227,300
1 and more	1975	148,931	50,636			22,229	49,888
	1985	60,175	23,258	25,797	40,450	5,907	18,179
2 and more	1975						
	1985	114,716	50,838	52,135	83,540	12,489	54,149
5 and more	1975	50,796	36,449			16,431	54,872
	1985	94,814	82,253	48,896	139,523	18,658	114,276
10 and more	1975	60,875	149,488			38,346	320,586
	1985	75,729	146,209	45,396	242,263	25,630	211,604
20 and more	1975						
	1985	53,683	237,321	34,791	409,308	27,429	411,100
50 and more	1975	4,031	32,526			5,117	138,115
	1985	14,928	179,491	11,679	367,470	10,585	384,217
100 and more	1975	4,796	111,938			7,475	731,299
	1985	10,683	318,194	9,179	715,375	9,301	1,102,443
500 and more	1975						
	1985	1,338	101,114	1,238	232,506	1,231	379,023
1,000 and more	1975	746	123,850			1,219	703,740
	1985	1,754	411,536	1,676	672,692	1,635	1,138,790
5,000 and more	1975	133	52,925			204	400,363
	1985	364	235,456	335	343,217	340	665,756
10,000 and more	1975	150	249,603			214	1,728,404
	1985	398	1,270,052	395	1,564,872	403	3,872,986
TOTAL	1975	316,864	818,360	165,607	2,113,448	94,376	4,204,162
	1985	452,786	3,124,429	242,826	4,976,618	115,606	8,579,821

SOURCE: National Tax Administration 1977: 27, 151; 1987: 18, 146.
[1]A slightly different breakdown was used in 1975.
[2]No breakdown given for 1975.

ance for doubtful accounts, in 1985, 450,000 (27.3%) did so; meanwhile, the aggregate amount increased from ¥800 billion to ¥3 trillion (table 45).

Tax authorities report also, since 1969, on the employee bonus allowance (*shōyo hikiate-kin*). For tax purposes, the term "bonus" includes any nonperiodic payment, in cash or kind, or any other sort of economic benefit including release of debts, unless they represent retirement allowances; it cannot include directors' bonuses. A so-called seasonal salary allowance (*kimatsu teate*), popularly called "bonus," is paid to all regular employees twice a year; it usually amounts to roughly two to three times the monthly pay and constitutes a short-term liability as a deferred wage payment. The total provision is deductible as expense, but the amount credited to the allowance in a given accounting period must be added back in full to income in the following period. This allowance was used by 165,000 companies (13.7%) in 1975, and 250,000 companies (14.6%) in 1985; its aggregate amount increased from ¥2.1 trillion to ¥5 trillion (see table 45).

The allowance for employee retirement benefits (*taishoku kyūyo hikiate-kin*) is another deferred wage payment. It would be substantial if it were adequately provided for. When a regular employee quits ("voluntary" retirement) or retires ("involuntary" retirement for reasons of age or death, or for company reasons), he is given a lump-sum retirement benefit (*taishoku-kin*). The calculation of this benefit is related to length of service, and a higher amount is paid for "involuntary" retirement. This liability does not result from law, but from the Rules of Employment (*shūgyō kisoku*) of the company or the collective labor agreement (*rōdō kyōyaku*). It is sometimes combined with or in addition to a pension system (see Murakami 1985).

Although there is no legal obligation for such provision, generally tax authorities approve an allowance amounting to 40% of the obligation incurred under "voluntary" retirement (Corporate Tax Law Enforcement Ordinance 1965, Art. 106). When the benefit is actually paid, it must be debited to the allowance account. Consequently, for international reporting purposes, a substantial adjustment is required, as the liability should be stated in full as if all qualified employees were to retire "involuntarily."

The 1985 Annual Report of Kubota, Ltd., gave the following note: "Up to and including the year ended April 15, 1984, the provisions for severance payments were not funded. Since the year ended April 15, 1985, a portion of the provisions has been funded with an outside trustee. The liability for severance payments is sufficient if all employees voluntarily retired at year end less funds held by the trustee. The Company's policy for its non-contributory trustee pension plan is to fund and charge to operations normal costs and prior service costs over 20 years" (p. 23).

Employee retirement benefit allowances were recorded by only 95,000 companies (7.8%) in 1975 and 115,000 companies (7.2%) in 1985; the aggregate amount thus reserved increased from ¥4.2 trillion to ¥8.5 trillion (see table 45).

Another allowance reported by tax authorities was the price fluctuation reserve (*kakaku hendō junbi-kin*). It was a provision against loss in market price of inventories and securities (including national bonds). This was used by 24% of the companies in 1965 and by 30% in 1973. This allowance was prohibited beginning with the accounting period starting after April 1, 1986.

Obviously, reserves and allowances, including the portion exceeding the tax limit on tax-deductible reserves, could become convenient hiding places for profits. And so they did on a grand scale. The Commercial Code condoned the practice, and under the Securities Exchange Law audit requirements, it was treated as "qualified" (*gentei-tsuki tekisei*, literally, "fair with limitation").

> The most typical of these hiding places for profits is the reserve for exchange-rate fluctuation. At the term ending September 1974, for example, Ishikawajima Harima had ¥15.7 billion in such a reserve, Mitsui Shipbuilding ¥11.4 billion, Mitsui & Co. ¥7.5 billion, and Mitsubishi Corporation ¥5 billion. Under the allowance for research and development, Takeda (pharmaceuticals) had ¥2.4 billion, and Nissan Motors ¥4.3 billion. (*Nihon Keizai Shinbun* 1975, March 24)

However, after the 1974 revision of the Commercial Code, the practice came under close scrutiny. In March 1975, the Japanese Institute of Certified Public Accountants, with the backing of the Ministry of Finance, announced that all profits hidden under the names of reserve for exchange-rate fluctuation, allowance for research and development, and others, would have to be disclosed as of April 1, 1975. Today, tax-deductible reserves under the Special Taxation Measures Law are to be appropriated from retained earnings, except for those that for accounting purposes qualify as expenses or losses during the current year.

9

FUND MANAGEMENT

UNTIL RECENTLY, it would have been appropriate to state that for the vast majority of Japanese corporations fund management was of no immediate concern; financial management consisted of cultivating bank relations, participating in stable shareholding, and having a tax expert on hand. Executives could with effective single-mindedness concentrate all their attention on corporate growth in terms of market share and required levels of profitability. Such was the case until Japanese corporations started to look abroad for sourcing capital and Western investors woke up to the Japanese opportunity.

Sourcing Capital Abroad

In Japan before World War II, surprisingly for a country fully dedicated to industrialization even in a warlike manner, reliance on foreign capital was minimal.

> Japan's [prewar] economic development . . . owed no major debt to the Western investor, although there were two short periods, 1899 to 1913 and 1924 to 1930, of which this conclusion is true only with qualifications. During the first of these periods, however, the motives which led her to borrow abroad were not solely, nor even predominantly, for the purposes of financing industrial expansion; for the chief loans were intended to cover expenditures on war or war-preparation. Even in the second period a substantial part of the capital raised abroad was required for reconstruction after the Great Earthquake. (Allen and Donnithorne 1954: 323)

> Several private bond issues abroad, mostly by electric power concerns, were . . . allowed in Paris and London in the 1920s, but this exceptional

private borrowing abroad dribbled down again to nothing by 1931. The
level of gross foreign indebtness reached about ¥2 billion in 1914 and
¥2.3 billion in 1932. Generally we can say that before World War II the
Japanese maintained throughout a policy of minimal borrowing from
abroad, a policy caused by fear of what might happen to control of Japanese industry if it were unable to pay such debts; also this doubtless
accounts in part for an impeccable Japanese record of repayment. (Henderson 1973: 14)

Postwar reconstruction started with substantial American aid; this was
soon replaced by military procurement needed during the Korean War.
Some large private corporations, such as Yawata Steel, as well as public
corporations, obtained substantial loans from the World Bank and other
international organizations, but even in the 1960s, few Japanese private
corporations sought foreign loans. For the period 1960–1969 foreign
debt as an external source of funds amounted to 4.9%, 2.2% short-term,
and 2.7% long-term (OECD 1972: 16). Whatever foreign loans there
were had little impact on Japanese corporate accounting and auditing as
long as they were obtained with the guarantee of a Japanese bank. Risk
to a foreign lender was practically nil; he would remain screened from
his borrower by the guarantor. In the early 1960s, many foreign banks
provided loans to large Japanese companies in such industries as iron and
steel, electric machinery, chemicals, synthetics, and oil, especially during
periods of tight credit domestically.

This practice continued smoothly until 1965, when the fraudulent
bankruptcy of Sanyo Special Steel Co. jolted the Japanese business community and government authorities.

When Sanyo Special Steel Co., on March 6, 1965, filed for corporate rehabilitation with the Kobe District Court (under the Corporate Reorganization Law), it
had obtained three impact loans (US $5 million from the Banque Lambert, $3
million from BOLSA, and $3 million from the Chartered Bank), guaranteed by
the Bank of Kobe and the Mitsubishi Bank. The Ministry of Finance directed the
Japanese banks to repay the loans; the repayment was effected April 15, 1965.

Meanwhile, steady expansion of the economy had brought several
Japanese companies to consider issuing securities overseas. Unlike foreign
investors, Japanese investors, particularly financial institutions, had so
far largely neglected to provide financial backing on the basis of a corporation's earnings as expressed by its financial statements. After several
well-known companies failed in their attempts to issue securities abroad,
it became clear that a mere translation of Japanese statements was not
enough. There were a few cases in which, after international accounting
and auditing standards were applied, the company turned out to be in-

solvent by U.S. accounting conventions (for example, when the full accrual of employee retirement benefits wiped out capital stock and retained earnings). There were also cases in which, because of a failure to satisfy disclosure requirements abroad, companies switched to an impact loan guaranteed by a Japanese bank, based on parent-only financial statements. Soon, however, some Japanese companies were able to raise funds in the European capital markets with the use of their Japanese financial statements (generally the format of the financial statements had been changed to one more easily understood outside of Japan, and a few additional disclosures were made).

At the same time, several Japanese corporations sold what came to be called "depositary receipts" on American and European capital markets and later in Hong Kong, Singapore, and elsewhere. The first overseas equity financing was the American Depositary Receipts (ADR) issue of Sony Corporation in 1961. Most overseas equity issues took place in the United States until the Interest Equalization Tax (1963) brought them to a halt. Despite a limited number issued in European capital markets, depositary receipts as a means of corporate financing remained insignificant until the Interest Equalization Tax was abolished in 1973. Then they experienced a renewed surge in popularity, peaking in 1981 with a record 24 issues worth $1.2 billion. More recently, however, a growing trend toward the overseas issuance of corporate bonds, notably convertible bonds and bonds with warrants, has led to a sharp decline in the usage of depositary receipts: only two issues were recorded in 1985 for a total of $42 million (Japan Securities Dealers Association 1987: 70).

The result has been that the U.S.-style Generally Accepted Accounting Principles (GAAP) became the source of most subsequent evolution in Japanese accounting and auditing practices. Because Japanese financial statements were not easily presented according to foreign requirements, it had become necessary to produce two sets of financial statements: one for domestic purposes and one for international purposes. Auditors were in a quandary: which set should be certified? In fact, both had to be certified as to correctness and fairness, even though figures under the same item may be different.

From the 1960s on, foreign investors have had a strong influence on the Japanese stock market. Buying Japanese shares in Japan for portfolio purposes, they introduced new concepts that rested on an altogether different perspective on financial results. They stimulated securities companies to popularize, among issuers as well as domestic buyers, the Western concept of earnings per share. Not less than "consolidated financial statements," "earnings per share" was a concept alien to Japanese business executives and investors. It was a major reason why a number of large, traditional corporations had refrained from foreign listing, at least so long as such consolidation was not required in Japan. Some of the less inhibited, growth-oriented companies were thus able to reap the benefits and glamour of raising equity abroad.

A remarkable development since the early 1980s has been the overseas issuance of bonds.

There are a number of general reasons for this increase in fund raising through foreign bonds: (1) increased necessity to hedge forward exchange risk in response to increasing foreign currency-denominated claims and corporate internationalization, which has motivated the holding of foreign-denominated liabilities; (2) the flexible procedures of overseas markets in terms of security, prospectus, etc. (especially the Swiss-franc market); and (3) progress of the diversification of funding in overseas markets, including exchange rate swaps, interest rate swaps, and debt assumptions. (Bank of Japan 1986/10: 15)

Whereas the total amount raised from straight, convertible, and warrant bond issues was only ¥58 billion in 1974, it increased nearly 60-fold to reach ¥3,485 billion by 1985 (see table 32). The main factor behind such a spectacular increase was the restrictive nature of the domestic capital market. As mentioned earlier, corporations wishing to issue bonds in Japan were faced with collateral requirements, unfavorable terms of issue, and restrictive issuing procedures.

In terms of type of issues, straight and convertible bonds were the only types up until 1981, when warrants began to be issued. Although convertible bonds made up only 36% of foreign issues in 1974, by 1976 they were on a par with straight bonds at ¥208 billion each. Their popularity continued to dominate the market until 1985, when once again the percentage of straight bonds took the lead. One of the inherent drawbacks of issuing convertible bonds was illustrated in 1985, when Minebea attempted to acquire Sankyo Seiki with some five million shares it had accumulated through convertible bond issues abroad. (Ironically, Minebea itself became a takeover target when Trafalgar Holdings of the United States attempted a similar move.)

American corporations are not such avid C/B issuers, because of the fear that they could become vulnerable to takeover moves. Their Japanese counterparts have not had to face the danger of hostile takeovers—yet. They think of convertible bond issues only in terms of low-cost fund-raising. (Takahashi 1986: 41)

In addition to wariness toward convertible bond issuance, the increased sophistication of Japanese corporations in foreign fund raising renewed the interest in straight bonds. Many corporations armed with good credit ratings are now able to lower their cost of capital through an array of swaps and multidenominated instruments and therefore tend to favor straight bond issues. Consequently, overseas issuance of straight bonds increased by almost 250% in one year to ¥1.5 trillion in 1985, while convertible bond issues remained constant at ¥1.3 trillion. Warrants on the other hand, have increased sharply every year since their introduction in 1981, and by 1985, their value reached ¥700 billion (see table 32).

> The popularity of warrant bonds rose, however, with many issues being oversubscribed, if not sold out on the grey market well before the actual date of subscription. For foreign investors in the Euromarket, these appeared as an ideal instrument, again because of the equity bait. (Roscoe 1986: 78)

The participation of Japanese corporations in international financial markets as well as the rapid expansion of the domestic financial markets have had deep repercussions. By the mid-1980s, Japanese corporate financing found itself caught on the horns of a dilemma: two schools of thought were confronting each other. Some believed investment should remain focused on real assets; others, in growing numbers, focused on financial assets. The Bank of Japan makes a distinction between real assets (land and other tangible assets, provisional accounts for buildings under construction, and total inventory assets) and financial assets (sum of currency in circulation, deposits, and short- and long-term holdings of marketable securities). Referring to the period since the current easy money policy was initiated in the summer of 1980 as the relaxation period, the Bank stated recently:

> A look at the portfolio of real assets and financial assets of the corporate sector in the current relaxation period shows that the proportion of real assets has consistently fallen and, conversely, that of financial assets has consistently risen. . . . This tendency becomes clearer if land [classified as real assets] is excluded, because as a proportion of total assets it has substantially risen in the current relaxation period. . . . The accumulation of corporate financial assets in the present relaxation period cannot be construed as merely the employment of surplus funds in financial assets commensurate with the decrease in demand for funds associated with the deceleration of business activity; rather, it must represent aggressive financial strategies in both the raising and utilization of funds. (Bank of Japan 1986/10: 6, 10)

The shift of emphasis toward financial assets was a further manifestation of the fundamental change that corporate financial management underwent once the Japanese economy switched to slow growth.

Fund Employment

In the years prior to 1973, Japanese finance had been characterized by excess demand for long-term funds and heavy reliance on indirect financing using banks as intermediaries. After 1973, an excess supply of such funds soon appeared and direct financing rapidly increased in importance.

> The rapid economic growth based upon borrowed technology inevitably results in excess demand for long-term funds. During the postwar high growth period, the financial system was specially tailored to fulfill the aim of creation and allocation of long-term funds. This was attained through rationing of industrial bonds, use of government finances and specialized private financial institutions, along with a complementary but important role played by Bank of Japan credit controls. [With the low economic growth period after 1973] the rapid accumulation of government bonds and concomitant development of bond and money markets drastically increased the liquidity in the financial markets. Coupled with the recent decline in government deficits, this is considered to have reversed the market condition for long-term funds from excess demand to excess supply. Although [the] foreign sector provides a natural outlet for these long-term funds . . . this flow has been quite gradual as institutional investors and corporate sector have been slow to adjust their portfolios on account of government regulations and lack of expertise in international financial dealings. (Teranishi 1986: 133)

The availability of funds had a profound effect on the way banks had behaved since the war. A turn-around took place. Thus, for example, in 1979, the Sumitomo Bank launched a reorientation of its traditional procedures in an effort to get closer to the market by delegating greater responsibility to employees at lower levels. Small teams of four to six employees were assigned to take care of the needs of a single large client, and the Western method of asset/liability management was introduced for domestic operations, replacing the tradition in which funding and lending were performed by unrelated departments in the bank (Bronte 1982: 24). Sumitomo was immediately followed by other major banks. Furthermore, competition among banks was intensified by changes in the management of government bonds and by partial deregulation of interest rates and of banking itself, while innovations in microelectronics and telecommunications lowered the information and management costs of financial transactions (Suzuki 1986: 49–75).

The slower economic growth since the mid-1970s has not affected all companies in the same way. Some industries have been pushed against the wall, if not over the brink altogether, as exemplified by the shipbuilding and the aluminum industries. As mentioned earlier, changes in the domestic financial system as well as in international circumstances are bringing about a shift in the main sources of capital. What has not changed yet is the traditional dividend policy.

> Japan's dividend payout [a dividend/profit after tax] is low and constant. This is different from the stable dividend policy in its actual sense, where the ratio of dividend payment to stock face value is constant. The way to determine whether a certain investment is attractive is based on the amount of dividend payout rather than dividend ratio. Unlike in the United States, where fluctuations of dividend payouts are linked to the level of the company's profit, in Japan quite a few companies adopt the low dividend payout system, disregarding the level of company profit. (Shibakawa 1985: 198)

The ratio of average dividends to the average share price has declined, but the policy of stable dividends meets with the expectations of Japanese shareholders.

> [This ratio] for all listed nonfinancial corporations has declined steadily from more than 5 per cent in the early 1960s to 1.5 per cent in the early 1980s. According to an estimate by the National Tax Agency, the proportion of before-tax profits paid out as dividends by the entire corporate sector has been around 10 per cent in the past several years (10.4 per cent in 1982). The corresponding figure in the United States is estimated at about 40 per cent. However, returns to shareholding are composed of dividend receipts *and* capital gains. Since dividend income is taxed separately at 20 to 35 per cent and capital gains are not taxed in Japan, from the viewpoint of individual shareholders it is rational for companies to reduce dividend payments and retain profits internally, provided that the share price reflects the value of retained profit. In fact, . . . the annual rate of capital gains has been substantial for the past 20 years (averaging 13.1 per cent); during the same period, the one-year deposit rate remained at only 6.0 per cent on average. (Aoki 1987: 276–277)

Undoubtedly, Japanese companies are rapidly increasing their financial sophistication, but the purpose remains wealth creation by their own corporate growth, i.e., investments. Under conditions of slow economic growth as well as under rapid growth, companies have maintained their concern for investment in rationalization of operations and labor-saving equipment. The priority of investment for expansion, however, has been replaced by R&D investment.

The ranking of equipment investment purposes in the 1970s and the 1980s has been contrasted as follows:

	1970s	1980s
Expansion	1	4
Rationalization	2	2
Labor-saving investment	3	3
Pollution prevention	4	8
R&D	5	1
Energy saving	6	5
Introduction of higher-level technology	7	6
Resource-saving investment	8	7

(adapted from Shibakawa 1985: 199)

The contrast is especially clear for high technology industries that benefit from official encouragement and where venture capital makes but slow progress.

High tech R&D is encouraged through tax write-offs, government loans, subsidies, government industrial research labs (mainly under MITI jurisdiction), favorable antitrust provisions, and government funding for joint, cooperative, R&D projects among major corporations. Finance depends on industrial structure. Large firms moving into high tech activities can readily utilize internal funds and borrowing capacity. The major problem has been the provision of risk capital to new, small firms. Venture capital institutions are in their infancy, but that is now rapidly changing. Quite large amounts of Japanese and foreign venture capital funds apparently are becoming readily available; the problem is mainly to develop venture capital markets, and to create an environment in which creative scientists and engineers (usually in large firms) are willing to leave secure positions and become entrepreneurs. (Patrick 1986: 17–18)

Also in the first half of the 1980s, fund employment in the corporate sector shifted away from traditional time deposits into more sophisticated financial instruments (table 46). Two new features of financial management emerged. First, "the weight of securities investment, including foreign securities, is increasing. . . . A conspicuous characteristic is active short-term transactions of securities aiming at capital gains. . . . Corporate investment in securities in the current relaxation period can be termed 'high risk, high return', compared with past periods of monetary relaxation." The second feature was "the emergence of liquid deposits with relatively high interest rates, reflecting the liberalization of interest rates, including the creation and successive liberalization of CDs and MMCs and the liberalization of interest on large-denomination time deposits. These instruments have prompted companies to be aggressive in accumulating financial assets" (Bank of Japan 1986/19: 10, 13). The new features brought about a new aspect of corporate financial behavior, "financial technology."

TABLE 46.

Fund Employment of the Corporate Sector

(percent change during the period or the year)

	Previous Period	Current Period	1983	1984	1985
Increase in financial assets	100.0	100.0	100.0	100.0	100.0
Cash and deposits					
Currency (cash and demand deposits)	35.4	14.8	(−)3.8	15.0	5.8
Time deposits[1]	45.6	25.7	57.2	23.3	0.6
Deposits with liberalized rates[2]	1.1	30.1	20.0	26.1	59.4
(of which foreign currency deposits)	(1.1)	(10.1)	(11.3)	(9.5)	(15.6)
Short-term holdings of securities[3]					
Bonds	12.3	3.8	6.2	5.2	3.2
Stocks	3.8	3.8	2.5	4.3	4.5
Trusts and others	(−)2.4	1.2	2.9	3.2	0.3
Long-term holdings of securities[3]					
Bonds	1.5	1.0	5.1	(−)1.9	1.2
Stocks	4.0	9.7	1.4	8.1	9.3
Trusts and others	(−)1.3	1.1	2.2	0.3	2.2
Foreign securities	0.0	8.8	6.3	16.4	13.5
MEMORANDUM ITEMS					
1. Cash and deposits	82.1	70.6	73.4	64.4	65.8
Securities	17.9	29.4	26.6	35.6	34.2
2. Financial assets with regulated interest rates	81.0	40.5	53.4	38.3	6.4
Financial assets with liberalized interest rates[4]	19.0	59.5	46.6	61.7	93.6
3. Yen	98.9	81.1	82.4	74.1	70.9
Foreign currency	1.1	18.9	17.6	25.9	29.1
4. Short-term	95.8	88.2	91.3	93.5	87.3
Long-term	4.2	11.8	8.7	6.5	12.7

SOURCE: Bank of Japan 1986/10: 12.
[1]Excluding large-denomination time deposits, MMCs, and foreign currency deposits.
[2]Large-denomination time deposits, MMCs, and foreign currency deposits.
[3]Excluding investment in foreign currencies.
[4]Including bonds and stocks.

"Financial Technology"

Investment in financial assets has recently been nicknamed *zai-teku* (financial technology), as a counterpart of *hai-teku* (high tech) in the production field. It is thus the Japanese "high tech" of making money through financial operations, in particular at the international level. Popularly, "financial technology" came to be understood as financial operations by industrial companies that were unrelated to their trading operations. "Large enterprises tried to increase their financial effectiveness and lower various costs by investing their working funds in higher yield activities (so-called Zaitech) and diversifying their ways and means of fund procurement" (EPA 1985: 29). In particular export-oriented companies, such as the automobile and electronics industries and general trading companies, suffered from falling profits and the strong yen. One countermove was to generate income by investing excess cash in financial instruments. The cost of raising external funds has declined because of lower interest rates. As a result, many companies have issued convertible bonds and warrants, even though they did not have an immediate need for cash (in the current slow economy, not much is spent on expansion of production capacity). One estimate has it that 70% to 80% of this additional income is invested in interest-bearing instruments (bank deposits and repurchase agreements) and the rest in stocks and bonds in search of capital gains (*First Boston: Equity Research* 1987).

Such investments were triggered by the new Foreign Exchange Law (1980) that abolished foreign exchange controls. They came into full bloom after April 1984, when the Japanese were permitted to participate in swap transactions.

> Essentially, the corporations borrow in the international markets and have the option to profit by either "relending" in Japan, or re-investing overseas. . . . They are facsimiles of financial intermediaries, or Eurobanks. Their advantage is their ability to borrow less expensively than banks in the capital markets. . . . They have been able to transfer payments from fixed to floating interest rates and from one currency into another on their liabilities. Hence, with the aid of financial intermediaries, they are able to obtain a swap and a matching asset to adapt to almost any instrument they issue in the world's capital markets. . . . In the most common zaiteku operation, a Japanese company will issue a Dollar Eurobond, swap it for floating rate Dollars and then either purchase a floating rate asset or deposit the floating rate Dollars with a Japanese bank in return for inexpensive Yen financing. (Troughton 1986: 72–73)

Zai-teku was pioneered by the general trading companies that established financing subsidiaries overseas. Sumitomo Corporation had already established Sumitomo Corporation Finance in London in October 1983. In 1984, it set up Sumitomo Corporation International Investment in Luxembourg; the following year, it opened financing subsidiaries in three other locations.

> The most sophisticated zaiteku operation in London is Mitsubishi Corporation Finance. Since it started in 1985, it has built up an investment portfolio of more than $1 billion. Mitsubishi buys fixed-rate Eurobonds, floating rates notes (FRNs), Treasury bonds, warrants for equities and

bonds convertible into equity. It trades this portfolio actively. Mitsubishi funds these assets through bank borrowings, the sale of Euro-commercial paper and Eurobond issues which are swapped into floating-rate money. Thanks to the AAA rating of its trading-house parent, Mitsubishi Corporation Finance is often able to raise money at several tenths of a percent cheaper than the income from its investments. (*The Economist* 1986, June 28)

The case of C. Itoh & Co. reveals the changing outlook on *zai-teku*, from an alternative investment to a main goal. Although for the business year ending March 1987, the company ranked number one in sales among the general trading companies, pushing Mitsubishi Corp. out of the top spot for the first time in 18 years, in terms of profitability it only managed to place third. Its poor standing was attributable to the highly profitable *zai-teku* operations of Mitsubishi Corp. and Mitsui & Co., which contributed greatly to recurring profits of ¥79.5 billion and ¥54.6 billion to place them first and second, respectively. In response, C. Itoh is strengthening its own *zai-teku* operations in an attempt to capture the top slots in both sales and profitability. The main purpose of the company's three-year "Plan 88" is to shift from being "sales-oriented" to being "profit-oriented." The plan emphasizes the promotion of new businesses together with the strengthening of the financial department. In addition to implementing Plan 88, C. Itoh is also expanding business in project financing, sales financing, venture capital, and mergers and acquisitions activities. Capitalization will also be boosted to ¥200 billion in a bid to acquire AA rating (*Nihon Keizai Shinbun* 1987, June 14).

Obviously, the greater the funds a corporation controls, the better its potential to benefit from *zai-teku*. This was vividly illustrated when the Toyota Motor Corp. revised its earnings for the business period ending July 1987 from ¥350 billion to ¥380 billion.

Toyota officials attributed the upward revision to massive income resulting from its successful securities investment of surplus funds totaling ¥1.4 trillion. . . . Toyota's sophisticated portfolio management yields about 9 percent of its surplus cash each year. This amounts to about ¥126 billion of annual income. (*The Japan Times* 1987, July 23)

Even the government is benefiting. In July 1987, it was reported that in view of increased receipts from the securities transaction tax, the Ministry of Finance revised its revenue estimates upward by over one billion yen (*Japan Economic Journal* 1987, August 1).

Concern has been expressed that too many Japanese corporations lack the required sophistication and approach *zai-teku* in gambling fashion. Furthermore, it is repeatedly pointed out that some of the funds used by industrial companies for the exercise have been obtained from insurance companies. As stated by a Japanese expert, "the life insurance companies may be happy for money to go abroad via manufacturing industry because they are well aware of the risks of foreign investment. Japanese financial institutions like to buy secured debt—and the *zaiteku* paper issued by Japanese industrial companies gives them that. They think it is very safe to lend to Japanese companies" (*Euromoney* 1986, November).

"Financial technology" thus amounts to flexing the financial muscle of Japanese corporations; it attests to the growing sophistication of financial officers in the management of corporate funds. Speculation is rife, however, concerning the impact of *zai-teku* on corporate behavior. Could it be counterproductive? Caution is sounded by analysts, government, and industry itself.

> The Bank of Japan has recently released a financial report warning against overheated investment in stocks and real estate for capital gains. The report said that firms were reducing their investment in production of goods in favor of speculative investment in land and financial assets. Financial institutions, it said, were meanwhile meeting the needs of these firms by expanding their lending under pressure from reduced margins, triggered by the liberalization of financial markets. (Iwaki 1987)

Industrial leaders are ambivalent. On the one hand, they share the traditional sentiment that elbow grease and brow sweat are what made Japanese industry successful internationally. This is the reason why R&D and diversification are pushed at the top of investment objectives. On the other hand, *zai-teku* is a heaven-sent expedient to help resolve the havoc caused by the yen's extremely rapid appreciation. There is also another side to *zai-teku*—the glamour bestowed on it by the mass media, providing one more opportunity to furbish the corporate image, a facet of business that no Japanese executive is about to neglect.

THREE

ACCOUNTANTS & AUDITORS

10

THE CORPORATE
FINANCIAL FUNCTION

THE FUNDAMENTAL REASON why Japanese corporate financial reporting is often not adequate in the eyes of Western investors is the nature of Japanese employment. The norm, although not necessarily the practice, is that the employment relationship starts when an employee enters a firm at the time of graduation from school and continues until a mandatory age limit between 55 and 60, today commonly 60. Where the norm is also the practice, as in the larger corporations, the beneficiaries, in popular parlance, are not referred to as "employees" (*jūgyō-in*), but as "corporate members" (*sha-in*). The distinction is of the greatest practical importance. The nature of such an employment relationship determines, of course, the style of corporate organization.

Scholars have described Japanese corporate organization in organic terms, pointing out that process rather than structure is dominant, problems are shared and solved by trial and error in an incremental fashion, tasks are overlapping, and, characteristically, an individual job description is not relevant. As a consequence, the functional rather than the divisional approach to corporate structure is preferred (Kagono, Nonaka, Sakakibara, and Okumura 1985: 162–166). The role of the head office and its staff is predominant. There, "sales and marketing" are considered more influential than "control and finance." Positions in finance are ranked first in Europe, second in the United States, but only fifth in Japan (table 47). Only about 5% of all promotions to directorship originate in "finance and accounting" (table 48).

> The educational background of Japanese top managers is high . . . a very high percentage majored in engineering and natural science. The percentage of engineers is even higher—up to 50 per cent—in technology-related product companies. For example, in Hitachi, seventeen out of twenty-five

TABLE 47.

Power Distribution among Departments: International Comparison

	U.S.		Japan		Europe	
	Rank	Score	Rank	Score	Rank	Score
Sales and marketing	1	3.78	1	4.08	2	3.70
Research and development	5	2.71	4	3.29	5	2.51
Production	3	3.20	2	3.66	3	3.50
Control and finance	2	3.61	5	3.27	1	3.85
Personnel and labor relations	6	2.34	7	2.72	6	2.37
Corporate planning staff	4	2.76	3	3.34	4	2.66
Purchasing and procurement	7	1.93	6	2.73	7	1.76

SOURCE: Nonaka and Okumura 1984: 37.
NOTE: Mean scores of influence. 1 point: little or no influence; 2 points: some influence; 3 points: quite a bit of influence; 4 points: a great deal of influence; 5 points: a very great deal of influence. Significant at .001 level of t-test of means.

TABLE 48.

*Departments or Positions from Which Managers
Are Promoted to Director*

(percentage)

Research and development	8.7
Production	6.5
Plant manager	9.6
Marketing and export	18.2
Sales branch office manager	7.6
Personnel	12.1
Finance and accounting	4.8
Material	1.8
Planning	5.8
Division manager	9.9
Regional branch manager	8.3
Other (general management)	6.7
TOTAL	100.0

SOURCE: Adapted from *Diamondo*, July 1981.
NOTE: 1,195 directors promoted from within the company.

directors, in Matsushita twelve out of thirty-two full-time directors . . . in Canon ten out of sixteen directors are engineering and natural science graduates. . . . Once [the graduate] enters the corporation, he will stay for life. Most of the present top executives have been working in one corporation for more than thirty years. He will be transferred from one department to another, within a certain range. . . . The graduate from social science departments will experience marketing, accounting and personnel jobs. None of these jobs are considered as jobs for professionals. Again, he has no experience of any other company, but he has a wide experience within his own company. He has a core expertise, but he has a wider view and a wider human communication network than if he had moved, as a professional, from one company to another. (Kono 1984: 34–35)

For the time being, despite the popularity of *zai-teku*, the prospects for basic reorientation of the Japanese corporate financial function are indeed dim. Both protagonists and adversaries of *zai-teku* are keeping the U.S. experience in mind, the former in terms of an unavoidable direction for progress, the latter as an example of a dangerous weakening of industrial potential. The Japanese implication of "specialization" pervades the argument. In the West, the term is understood in the context of an individual's business career, which evolves independently from any specific company in which it is exercised. Such a view does not fit Japan, where one's business capacities and opportunities are essentially tied to a given company; career is understood as the career of the "corporate member." A financial specialist is thus a corporate member of a financial institution; there is little use (or prospect) for a financial specialist in, say, a manufacturing company.

> It has always been generally held that finance and accounting divisions play a secondary role [in the personnel make-up of corporations]. Accounting divisions have been underestimated and not given enough voice in decision-making. It has then been quite rare for leading companies to have presidents who were originally financial specialists. (Iwaki 1987)

This may be changing. In the politics of business and human relations at corporate headquarters, the managers in the financial function are being allowed greater participation and given greater say in the formulation of corporate policies. The new weight given to financial considerations is not seen as the result of their opinions as "financial specialists;" it is the result of opinions expressed by "corporate members" reflecting the changing business environment.

Financial Officers

Revision of the Commercial Code in 1951 dropped the requirement that directors hold shares in their companies. It was hoped thereby that directorship would be essentially open to talent. However, in the standard employment system, personnel eligible for promotion to directorship come from among senior employees who would otherwise have to retire at the mandatory age limit. They are, not surprisingly, loyal to the company that nurtured them from graduation. There is a great temptation to harbor a proprietary feeling toward the company that is the locale of one's activities, shared with peers. If, then, the company president happens to be also the founder, he and some of the directors close to him may form a clique that considers the company their "property." Colloquially, the Japanese refer to this as a "one-man" company. But, more generally, rather than to hear the "*your* company" with which American shareholders are familiar, the Japanese shareholders hear from the president and his retinue "*my* company" or "*our* company." Accountability to shareholders is often felt by executives to interfere with the company and its management. As a result, despite the legal requirement since 1982 that fuller details be given out by the larger corporations, disclosure is reduced to a minimum: operational and financial information to shareholders is found in business reports presented as small, cut-and-dried, highly stereotyped pamphlets.

The board of directors (*torishimariyaku-kai*) is legally the supreme authority to which the corporation is entrusted; it is directly responsible to the shareholders (Commercial Code, Arts. 254–272). It is rare to find a vice president in charge of finance; but the finance manager will be one of the directors. In larger corporations, some direct financial experience is often provided by one or more directors who formerly worked for a bank. The board must, however, be assisted by one or more *kansa-yaku* (statutory auditors). Formerly, the term of office of the statutory auditor was one year; he could be reelected and frequently was year after year. Rarely did he have an audit staff, and his function as auditor was not comparable to that of an internal auditor and even less like that of an independent auditor. In most cases, he had no professional capacity; he was a former employee appointed to the post upon retirement in recognition for past services.

Generally, the statutory auditor is considered inferior (*shita*, as opposed to *ue*, superior) to the directors. This attitude was implicit in the opposition of businessmen to the original and stricter version of the Commercial Code revision (1974), in which the statutory auditor would have the right to call on the general meeting of shareholders to report directors' irregularities (see Horiguchi 1974).

The 1974 amendment of the Commercial Code brought about a major change. It gave the statutory auditor authority and also responsibility to examine not only accounting but operations as well. As this amendment required also that the financial statements of larger corporations be examined by independent auditors (CPAs), the statutory auditor was expected to concentrate his attention on corporate operations. He could now sit in at meetings of the board of directors, serve the same two-year term as directors, and check the operations of subsidiaries (frequent hiding places for profits and losses of the parent company). He could, and was required to, order directors to cease improper acts; he also became subject to review by the shareholders' meeting. Thus, his responsibility is now to shareholders as well as to management. He must also be given the necessary staff and time to perform his function. As yet, however, no professional training has been required.

The first test of the new legislation came with the closing of accounts in October 1974.

> No change is observed in spite of the revised Code's intention to enlarge the function of internal auditing of accounts to auditing of operations. . . . Unless [the statutory auditor] has enough experience and knowledge to evaluate daily operations properly, the system will result in "An image of Buddha was made, but it has no soul" (*Hotoke tsukutte, tamashii irezu*). (*Nihon Keizai Shinbun* 1974, December 5)

The 1981 amendment of the Commercial Code further required, among other things, that in larger corporations there be two or more statutory auditors and that at least one be full-time. However, the lack of needed professional capacity and, often, past obligations toward top management still interfered with their duties. Although many companies have stated that they look for an experienced and knowledgeable auditor outside the company, it usually remains in the realm of wishful thinking rather than actual implementation. In the light of prevailing practice in 1987, a comment made in connection with the 1974 amendment remains largely valid:

> The independence of the external auditors flows from the independence of the statutory auditor, whose agreement is required for their appointment. The latter's independence is up to the board of directors, that actually controls proxy and agenda of the general meeting of shareholders. As long as the board of directors is controlled by the top management, nothing of substance will come from the revision of the Commercial Code. (Yazawa 1974: 80–85)

In smaller companies, it is common practice to retain as statutory auditor a tax agent (*zeirishi*) or an employee who qualifies as one. Many tax agents are former tax officials who advise on taxes, usually provide bookkeeping services, and prepare tax returns. Japanese law recognizes the *zeirishi* as a specialist in tax matters separate from the lawyer and certified public accountant, who are also authorized to handle such matters. To qualify, the tax agent must pass an examination supervised by a committee appointed by the Ministry of Finance. The first legislation to organize and control *zeirishi* dates from 1942, but it was not until Japan adopted the voluntary assessment system of tax returns in 1947 that the basis was laid for the current practice. This evolution has been embodied in the Tax Agent Law (*Zeirishi-hō*) of 1951. The Tax Agents' Association today has approximately 50,000 members.

Accounting Personnel

In the internal organization of the corporate financial function, human considerations seem to take easy precedence over strict functional responsibilities and the expertise they would entail. Although employees of Japanese companies can be expected to be generally loyal to the company, they are not yet expected to be loyal to their own occupation or skill (Ballon 1969: 63–76; Drucker 1974: 254–258). Thus, companies, in particular major ones traditionally, have adhered to a policy of frequently rotating employees across departments at a national, if not international, level and not within the same function at various locations or levels.

The financial function is usually divided into finance and accounting. The finance department (*zaimu-bu*) manages funds, including daily negotiations with numerous commercial banks, and payments in cash or by promissory notes. Because most purchase contracts do not specify terms—or even if they do, buyers do not observe them—the finance department must adjust payment terms. For example, cash payment may be changed to note payment, or a 60-day note payment once promised may be changed to a 90-day note, depending upon the buyer's monthly cash position. As payment on a fixed day once a month (*shiharai-bi*) is customary, toward the end of the month the finance department is often besieged by vendors trying to negotiate better terms and expedite payments. The finance department manager (*zaimu-buchō*) has the authority to allocate funds to each department according to priority. The authority can be compared with that of the controller in American corporations; it is, however, different in the sense that such allocation as done in Japan is based more on the manager's intuition and on negotiations than on businesslike considerations and meaningfully prepared data, at least in form.

The accounting department (*keiri-bu*), is basically in charge of bookkeeping. Its manager's (*keiri-buchō*) influence in the company comes from working closely with the manager of the finance department and from being first in line to succeed him. Very often, however, the *keiri-buchō* performs both functions, finance and accounting; such a concentration of all financial and accounting authority is convenient for management but most undesirable from the viewpoint of segregation of duties.

The function of controller, as understood in U.S. corporations, was made known in Japan after World War II. (In 1953, the Industry Rationalization Deliberation Board, an advisory organ to the Ministry of International Trade and Industry, issued a report entitled "Procedures for Implementing Internal Control.") The function did not take root, because budgeting and control (by comparison with the budget) of daily or monthly operational results, are not always effectively implemented. Incentives given to managers rarely take into account for performance compared with budget. The incentive is merely that, at some later date, the manager will be promoted to a higher position if his performance deserves such reward. Because the power to allocate scarce funds to operating departments is controlled by the finance manager, the separate position of controller, if established, is usually totally eclipsed.

Neither is there a position truly equivalent to "chief accountant." The function is normally filled by a section chief (*kachō*), who may stay in the position for three or four years. He is probably not promoted from within the section, and upon leaving it, he is usually promoted to a higher position in a different department. Japanese corporations, even the largest, rarely have a *kōnin kaikeishi* (CPA) on their staff, and the *zeirishi* (tax agent) may be only part-time.

Finance and accounting staff are usually without formal technical training, although they may have been encouraged to attend accounting seminars or study bookkeeping at night school. Senior male clerks often stay in the section for a number of years or rotate within the *keiri- bu*. They have a great deal of experience with routine accounting procedures. Junior male staff members are usually college graduates who stay in the section for two or three years as part of their general company training for future executive positions. The female staff members, often more numerous than male, work on average six or seven years.

Internal Control and Trustworthiness

As defined by the American Institute of Certified Public Accountants:

> Internal control comprises the plan of organization and all of the coordinate methods and measures adopted within a business to safeguard its assets, check the accuracy and reliability of its accounting data, promote operational efficiency, and encourage adherence to prescribed managerial policies. (American Institute of CPA 1973: 15)

This definition, used since 1949, is probably broader than the meaning usually attributed to "internal control." It recognizes that a system of internal control extends beyond matters directly related to accounting and financial department functions. This position was officially adopted

TABLE 49.

Percentage of Major Companies Using Planning and Control Systems:
International Comparison (1980)

	U.S.	Japan
Standard cost accounting system	92.0	73.8
Flexible budgetary control system	63.1	51.7
Short-range planning system	86.7	87.2
Middle-range planning system	72.4	80.0
Strategic planning system	78.7	34.8
Fixed assets investment analysis system	68.9	42.8
Cash-flow planning system	86.2	93.8
Capital budgeting system	94.2	33.1
Financial investment analysis system	64.4	24.5
Planning-programming-budgeting system (PPBS)	30.7	3.4
Contingency planning system	42.7	5.9

SOURCE: Kagono, Nonaka, Sakakibara, and Okumura 1985: 37.
NOTE: About 300 major companies in each country.

in Japan in 1953. The report "Procedures for Implementing Internal Control," recognizing the need to modernize Japanese enterprises, stressed the importance of expediting such modernization. It focused attention not only on general internal control, but on controller functions (by establishing a department specifically in charge of budgeting, accounting, statistical data preparation, and internal auditing) and preparation of an internal accounting manual. Implementation has not met the objectives set by the report. Thirty and more years later, even in the largest firms, internal control is still much less formal and the controller function still much less effective than could be expected. Where accounting manuals have been prepared, they are practically never revised and are thus out of date. Even in major corporations where control systems are known, they appear to be significantly less standardized than, say, in the United States (table 44). In Japan, the principle remains: people are the system, people make the organization. It is not a system of inanimate internal controls.

This "human" system, nonetheless, raises the ominous question of trustworthiness. Ronald Dore aptly stated the point when he wrote that Japanese management believes "in original virtue, rather than in original sin" (Dore 1973: 238). Because employees are permanent, they cannot but be loyal to the company, and in order to make them feel loyal, management must feel in turn that employees are trustworthy. Managers share the conviction that errors and fraud are much less frequent in their company than in other companies and, for that matter, less frequent in Japan than in any other country! The result of this belief in "original virtue" is that if there is fraud, it often causes the company more damage than if some control system had been installed to prevent such action. In past years, several embezzlements of hundreds of millions of yen have come to light. But in the tradition of Japanese organization, the human bond comes first.

Throughout this society, and therefore throughout business circles as well as within companies, social values such as *nai-nai ni sumaseru* (to be settled internally) or *tasuke-ai* (to help each other) prevail. Generally, the consequence is that in case of embezzlement, outsiders, such as police, are not called in. (It might be added that companies would naturally be reluctant to open their books to a police investigation.) Loss of face and adverse publicity are good enough reasons for management to settle problems internally. At the same time, superiors, such as top management, are rarely "officially" informed. The same concern for loss of face prevails among sections in a company; again, the problem should be handled internally as much as possible. If a problem cannot be settled on a person-to-person basis, the culprit will be transferred to some other department and then encouraged (if not virtually forced) to "voluntarily" submit his resignation. Any future employment references will be couched in general, noncommittal terms.

Job rotation is one effort to circumvent the danger of embezzlement. This personnel policy produces the generalists Japanese companies nurture; it is also a method for controlling employees, especially where temptations are great and become more difficult to resist as one remains in the job longer. In a second method, each new employee is required to submit a letter (*mimoto hoshō-sho*) signed by one or two guarantors (parent, relatives, school teacher, or parents' friend) who promise recovery of damages caused by the employee. Legally, such a letter is only valid for five years. Morally, the obligation never expires. This recourse is, in fact, open to the culprit as well. When an employee embezzles or loses company money owing to a mistake, he can go to his guarantors to beg rescue. In most minor cases, he will thus return the money to the company. If he fails, he loses social respect, is segregated from the community no matter where he goes, and may be unemployable. The immediate superior is no less caught in this web of obligations. He is afraid of being accused of not properly supervising his subordinate and, thus, of being demoted or transferred to less important functions, jeopardizing his lifetime employment career.

The Westerner steeped in a different social environment will legitimately wonder why the problem of trustworthiness is not "guaranteed" by fidelity bonding, an insurance system that protects the company. Speaking of bonding to a Japanese employee is tantamount to considering him a potential criminal. Bonding of accounting personnel (as well as of independent auditors) remains socially repulsive. And even in the few cases in which bonding is practiced, one can legitimately doubt whether the company would report to an outside agency for recovery of loss.

A direct challenge to internal control is the Japanese tradition of using a seal rather than a signature. To execute a check or promissory note (as well as any other corporate document), it is customary to affix the company (*sha-ban*) and authorized individuals' seals (*in-kan*). (A special understanding must be obtained from Japanese banks, as, for example, by foreign companies, to use a signature rather than a seal. In recent years, however, the signature has become common for personal checking accounts.) Proper custody of seals is thus important but sometimes poorly implemented. Most cases of petty larceny result from the surreptitious use of seals by nonauthorized employees. Such wrongdoings are usually discovered—but often too late.

11

ACCOUNTING PRACTICES

Bookkeeping was already an elaborate and widespread business practice in the Tokugawa Period (1600–1868). However, the form in which it is understood today is one of the innumerable imports that, after the middle of the last century, resulted from Japan's opening to international trade. From the beginning, two characteristics, no less obvious today, marked this particular import: (1) the countries of origin were varied, and (2) government authorities played a key role in implementing the new input. Bookkeeping became an international potpourri.

Probably the first Japanese enterprise to introduce Western bookkeeping was the Yokosuka Shipyard. In 1864, it hired two Frenchmen, one as director, the other as chief accountant and bookkeeper. In 1871, the company sent one of its employees to France to study bookkeeping. From 1872 to 1878, the government engaged the services of an Englishman to give guidance in the dissemination of knowledge about banking; he introduced the methods of bank bookkeeping and bank accounting (Adams 1964: 10). American input was provided by Yukichi Fukuzawa, a scholar who in 1873 translated an American textbook, Bryand and Stratton's *Common School Bookkeeping*, published in 1871. German influence came later through enactment of the German-inspired revised Commercial Code (1899). Mitsubishi Steamship Co. was the first company to promulgate bookkeeping rules for its own use, in July 1877, but it was not until the late 1890s that Western bookkeeping was adopted outside of banking, by industry in general (Emura 1953: 7; Nishikawa 1971: 10–11). In the process of introducing Western accounting practices, the Japanese relied on their abilities to adopt, adapt, and develop whatever methods suited their purposes, even as alien systems, such as the prewar German-inspired Commercial Code and the post–World War II American-inspired Securities Exchange Law, came to be superimposed.

TABLE 50.

Tokyo Clearing House: Monthly Number and Amount of Checks and Promissory Notes/Bills of Exchange (1975–1986)

Year	Checks — Accounts Number (thousand and %)	Checks — Accounts Amount (million yen and %)	Transfers Number (thousand and %)	Transfers Amount (million yen and %)	Promissory Notes and Bills of Exchange Number (thousand and %)	Promissory Notes and Bills of Exchange Amount (million yen and %)
1975 March	8,264 (67.68)	26,365,134 (70.10)	326 (2.67)	1,892,067 (5.03)	2,585 (21.17)	5,039,671 (13.40)
September	8,151 (64.10)	25,974,307 (66.69)	277 (2.18)	1,709,785 (4.39)	3,249 (25.55)	7,002,182 (17.98)
1980 March	8,268 (64.33)	51,515,105 (65.04)	426 (3.31)	3,002,224 (3.79)	3,028 (23.56)	8,887,867 (11.22)
September	8,118 (60.13)	59,461,771 (67.97)	400 (2.96)	2,526,286 (2.89)	3,829 (28.37)	11,800,133 (13.49)
1985 March	7,953 (68.12)	84,064,764 (58.24)	365 (3.12)	5,029,097 (3.48)	2,267 (19.42)	9,179,362 (6.36)
September	7,691 (64.91)	124,305,906 (59.57)	277 (2.33)	4,850,031 (2.32)	2,842 (23.99)	14,103,896 (6.76)
1986 March	8,145 (65.41)	121,776,836 (58.84)	306 (2.46)	5,721,539 (2.76)	2,860 (22.97)	16,781,922 (8.11)
September	8,004 (62.33)	120,964,805 (57.77)	253 (1.97)	6,045,132 (2.89)	3,374 (26.28)	19,958,634 (9.53)

SOURCE: Federation of Bankers' Associations 1987: 12–13.

There is no such thing as Japanese-style bookkeeping. The only difference, but a consequential one, between Western and Japanese bookkeeping is a preference in Japan for given forms. The multicolumn expense journal is not widely used; instead, ledgerless bookkeeping is quite popular, and a number of card methods are available. In order to eliminate posting, a multicopy *denpyō* (slip) is created for each transaction (cash receipt, disbursement, noncash transaction), both for the credit and the debit side of the same transaction. This slip then becomes the journal entry to be distributed to each file by account number and sequence. Copies filed by account number become ledger after weekly or monthly summary is attached; copies filed by sequence become journal.

The method saves time but is undesirable for auditing and internal control, although it is accepted by tax authorities. Unless mechanized, the system does not allow the financial manager a quick visual review of detailed transactions; often, the clerical employee in charge of particular records is the only one able to trace a transaction or prepare an analysis. At present, this system is in almost universal use in smaller companies.

Payment Methods

Four methods of payment are common: cash, bills and checks, credit transfer, and direct debit (table 50).

> Payments from corporations to individuals used to be mainly in cash, but credit transfers to bank accounts have been increasing. Payments of wages, stock dividends, pension benefits, etc. are delivered to payers' banks by slips or magnetic tapes. . . . On the other hand, collection of accounts receivable by corporations from individuals is increasingly switching from the cash collection method of visiting the homes of individuals to direct debiting of the billed amount from the deposit accounts of individuals. The direct debit method is being applied to many items of collection, such as public utility bills, monthly payment of loans, and payment of credit card bills. . . . Fund settlement between corporations was traditionally done by the use of bills or checks. Even at present a considerable number of bills and checks is employed. . . . However, a recent tendency is to shift to the utilization of direct credit to the accounts of receiving parties. (Federation of Bankers Associations of Japan 1985: 26)

Bank checks, bills, and promissory notes represent about 20% of the volume of cashless payments but 84% of their value; interbank transfers account for about 15% of total value (table 51). The Japanese concept of *tegata* (note) covers not only promissory notes but also drafts and acceptances. These notes often pose a major problem of safekeeping when they

TABLE 51.

Relative Importance of Cashless Payment Instruments (End of 1983)

(estimates)

Cashless Payment Instruments	Volume of Trans- actions (million)	Percent of Total	Value of Trans- actions (billion dollars)	Percent of Total
Checks issued by deposit-taking institutions[1]	418	18.7	11,466	84.0
Postal checks issued	1	0.0	21	0.2
Payments by credit cards	230	10.3	59	0.4
Paper-based giro payments	33	1.5	9	0.1
Paperless giro payments	8	0.4	3	0.0
Direct debit	1,260	56.3	16	0.1
Interbank transfers[2]	288	12.9	2,071	15.2
TOTAL[3]	2,238	100.0	13,644	100.0

SOURCE: Bank for International Settlements 1985: 60.
[1]Including bank checks, bills, and promissory notes.
[2]Including remittances, transfers, and direct credits but excluding transactions between the Bank of Japan and banks.
[3]Number of cashless payments per inhabitant: 19.

are accumulated in the company's safe until discount is needed. It therefore is a duty of the independent auditors to inspect and count (physically) these notes on closing date. They advise delivery of all promissory notes to the banks for custody until discounted or due date and substitution of the physical check by the safer certificates of custody issued by the banks.

Sales Accounting

Sales accounting is an example that provides direct insight into the accounting operations of Japanese corporations. A typical sequence is illustrated below:

1. The salesman visits a potential customer, with or without previous appointment or introduction, chats for half an hour without even touching on business (the purpose is to get acquainted).

2. After repeated visits, the salesman may receive a small order. He must negotiate price, delivery terms, payment terms, and product specifications. A price list is available, but frequently a discount price is offered, which may differ from customer to customer.

3. The customer often does not want the product delivered at once; he prefers piecemeal delivery at bulk price, using the seller's warehouse and delivery services free of charge.

4. Payment terms are usually by promissory note (*yakusoku te-gata*) issued at the end of the month after delivery; notes can mature in 60 to 180 days. Notes must be picked up by hand; mail is seldom used. Several phone calls are necessary to confirm the issuance of notes. Sometimes notes may not be issued until the following month.

5. Often notes are often not issued on the grounds that the product delivered is pending "inspection" (*kenshū*) or does not meet a minor detail of the buyer's specification. When the product is delivered toward the end of the month, owing to the rushed delivery of many sellers, inspection is delayed several days, and payment of notes, therefore, is delayed one month.

6. Promissory notes are delivered to the seller's banks for discount. If the seller is a small company, negotiations with the lending department of a bank are necessary to obtain cash upon delivery of the notes. Finally, the seller gets cash after deducting interest and compensating balance. (If such a company has to borrow even a relatively small amount, it must sometimes do so by calling on several banks. For instance, instead of borrowing ¥30 million from one bank, it borrows ¥10 million from each of three banks. Such allocation is planned in order for the company to maintain a smooth relationship not only with its main bank but also with other banks. The practice also reduces the banks' credit risk, especially when the customer is in a poor financial position.)

Accounting operations start from accrual of sales, when delivery is made and before inspection by the buyer has taken place. Small quantities and small yen-amounts are recorded daily. These sales are customarily accumulated once a month, usually on the twentieth or twenty-fifth, for a one-month transaction, and one invoice is created and delivered to the customer. There usually are two or three phone calls by the sales or accounting department to expedite or confirm payment on a regular monthly payment date, for example on the last day of the month or the fifth or tenth day of the succeeding month.

Cost Accounting

A comparison of about 300 major firms in each the U.S. and Japan revealed that the standard cost accounting system was in use at 92.0% of the American companies and 73.8% of the Japanese companies (Kagono, Nonaka, Sakakibara, and Okumura 1985: 37). The method of distributing direct and indirect costs to each product or each group of products and comparing them with standard cost is little appreciated in Japan. If standard cost is used at all, it is rather a "best-effort" target (like the budget) and often unrealistic. The fundamental reason for this lack of cost-consciousness lies in the fact that most costs are considered to be fixed. Most important, labor cost is to a very large extent considered a fixed cost. An hourly wage rate is practically nonexistent; salaries are paid by the month even to blue-collar workers. Following the pattern of lifetime employment, a substantial portion of the salary is determined by the years of service in the company (Ballon 1985a). Of course, overhead expenses on plant and administration are fixed as well, as are depreciation charges and interest expenses.

Fixed costs, when allocated, become high when the production level is low and low when the production level is high. Pricing, then, should be based on an optimum level of production over the period of depreciable plant assets. But, strapped by their fixed costs, companies must keep production high and engage in fierce competition. Sales managers have little control over pricing, which is largely left to the discretion of the salesman who "adjusts" it to the customer. Cost accounting is used only to determine the cost of inventories shown on financial statements. Progress is expected, but not yet apparent, from automation of the standard cost system and the daily-cost allocation system.

Cash Management

In part 1 of this book, it was indicated that overwhelming attention to relationships pervades Japan's society and economy. Currently, computerization is turning out to be a handy, but still limited, way to get around this cultural hurdle as far as collection and disbursement are concerned. At the same time, treasury management is beginning to benefit from the growing variety of financial instruments, especially those of a short-term nature. Broadly speaking, however, for Japanese firms, bank relations outweigh the maximization of cash management gains, "because bank loans replace the more normal equity accounts of Western companies" (Prindl 1981: 95). It would not be much of an exaggeration to state that a company does not handle its own liquidity; its banks do. The financial department of most corporations, even the larger ones, apparently fulfills at best a bookkeeping function, the true management of its finances being entrusted to the banks. Most companies cannot survive without month-to-month financing through bank loans and discount of notes. It is standard practice, instead of opening a line of credit, to negotiate loans each month for the coming month, essentially as discounted notes instead of straight loans, because notes are self-liquidating. The amount of notes receivable is reported so that each bank can prepare its monthly quota (*waku*) of note discount for the coming month.

For several decades, banks, depending upon their cash position, requested that their borrowers adjust the amount of their loans and discounts every month. When money supply was abundant, as in 1971, they requested that companies borrow more than actually needed and use the surplus to purchase real estate or securities or even to corner (*kaishime*) the entire rice crop of a certain area (Baldwin 1973: 396–409). The result was, of course, inflationary pressure on the entire economy. Then, for example, under the very tight money conditions that prevailed throughout 1974, banks requested that their borrowers reduce loans and discounts and increase notes payable (meaning longer maturity) or that they liquidate inventories at below-normal prices and sell unused assets, such as idle property or company housing.

The interdependence between company and lender is a month-to-month phenomenon in which there are both good and bad months. Deferred payments expressed in promissory notes have become a common occurrence throughout the economy. As a matter of fact, deferred payment is not only characteristic of business transactions; it also characterizes wage payments. The Japanese salary system includes at least two major deferred payments: the seasonal allowance (*kimatsu teate*, or bonus), paid twice a year and often averaging one-third or more of the annual income of regular employees, and the retirement benefit (*taishoku-kin*), paid whenever a regular employee retires or quits, its amount roughly equal to one month's salary for each year of service (Ballon 1985). It is accepted practice among employees and labor unions, in hard times and particularly for the seasonal allowances, to let companies manipulate this payment in a way reminiscent of the promissory notes, with the cooperation, if not upon the request, of the banks. Deferred wage payments were used on a grand scale immediately after the first oil shock when the economic growth rate turned negative.

It is also a fairly common custom for regular employees in large firms to deposit savings with the company, usually at the plant (establishment) level. The practice comes under the Labor Standards Law (Art. 18) and is surveyed annually by the Ministry of Labor. According to the latest survey, total employees' savings with their company (in a total of about 8,000 companies) increased from ¥1,200 billion in 1970 to ¥3,500 billion in 1986, although the number of savers decreased from 5.3 to 4.5 million (Ministry of Labor 1986: 2). Such savings may be tied to a housing loan scheme, and interest paid often depends on the nature of the deposit (table 52). Listed companies have such employee deposits (*jūgyō-in azukari-kin*) itemized in their balance sheets. Surprisingly, however,

TABLE 52.

Employee In-Company Deposits: Type and Interest Rate (1970–1986)

(percentage)

	Ordinary Deposit	Time Deposit	Installment Deposit		Other
			Housing	Other	
Percentage of all in-company deposits					
1970	68.7	10.0	16.2	4.2	0.9
1975	65.7	11.5	17.9	3.7	1.1
1980	71.5	8.0	15.3	3.9	1.2
1986	77.0	6.3	12.7	2.8	1.2
Interest rate (average)					
1970	7.27	8.10	8.57	7.68	7.69
1975	7.56	8.21	8.68	7.89	8.13
1980	6.61	7.29	7.41	7.17	7.09
1986	6.59	7.33	7.15	7.00	6.97
Interest rates by size of company (1986)					
1 to 29 employees	6.51	7.34	6.98	6.87	6.92
30 to 299 employees	6.65	7.28	7.27	7.12	6.94
300 employees and over	6.93	7.52	7.97	7.24	7.41

SOURCE: Ministry of Labor 1986: 16, 19, 21.

they are not funded; the only protection of the employee is the survival of the company and his own dedication to its survival. Employee saving schemes are one more contribution to the dynamic combination of security and motivation so characteristic of Japan's regular employment.

The banks provide a Cash Management Service (CMS) that connects a bank's computer with that of an enterprise to send funds transfer instructions on-line. It includes an accounting information service through the supply and receipt of documents by telephone, telex, magnetic tape, and so on. Almost all banks participate. However, as the Federation of Bankers' Associations readily acknowledges, "full-scale cash management service is yet to emerge in the future" (1985: 27).

Lag in Centralization

Generally, the weakness of accounting operations in Japanese companies, especially of small and medium size, is traceable to a lag in centralization in at least three areas—money management, sales management, and inventory control—the steady progress in electronic data processing notwithstanding.

In its survey of manufacturing companies listed on the Stock Exchanges over the period from 1975 to 1984, MITI reported that the percentage of companies using computers in accounting increased from 72.5% to 86.4%; in cost accounting from 66.3% to 83.8%; in economic accounting for equipment investment from 11.5% to 19.8% (table 53).

Lag in Centralized Money Management

Some major companies still authorize branch offices to borrow locally (with compensating balances locally and often aggregate overborrowing) and to issue promissory notes (misuse of cash and notes is an inherent danger here). This is done for several reasons. In the days when money supply was tight, the banks encouraged borrowers to tap all possible sources throughout the country (including local branches of the same bank, local banks, credit unions, and agricultural cooperatives). This lender/borrower relationship has perdured even after the money market has become a borrowers' market. Other reasons are the traditional preference in Japanese banking for frequent personal visits to customers

TABLE 53.

Computerization in Listed Manufacturing Companies (1975 and 1984)

(percentage)

Type of Computerization	1975			1984		
	Total	First Section	Second Section	Total	First Section	Second Section
Production process control	29.9	40.6	13.8	73.5	83.3	53.4
Quality control	21.7	31.3	7.4	56.6	66.0	36.9
Inventory control	79.3	88.6	65.4	93.4	95.2	89.7
Client-transaction information	45.6	54.8	31.9	75.3	79.4	66.9
Accounting and delivery notes	72.5	80.4	60.6	86.4	88.1	82.7
Salary calculation	90.0	95.4	81.9	97.4	97.9	96.4
Production cost calculation	66.3	78.6	47.9	83.8	87.5	76.4
Economic calculation of investment in facilities	11.5	16.7	3.7	19.8	24.2	10.6
Personnel information control	35.6	47.0	18.6	63.8	74.7	41.0
Demand forecasting and market research	16.8	25.3	4.3	25.9	31.5	13.8
Measurement of advertising effectiveness	0.9	1.4	0	2.6	3.0	1.9
Scientific and technical calculations	39.9	54.8	17.6	57.0	68.4	33.1
Information for strategic decision making	12.4	21.6	4.3	20.2	24.7	10.6
Miscellaneous	—	—	—	18.8	21.3	15.5
AVERAGE	40.2	49.0	27.5	58.1	63.4	47.2

SOURCE: MITI 1985a: 76–77.

rather than the mailing of data and the fact that local banks and smaller financial institutions compete to establish a direct relationship with well-known companies.

In the decade from 1975 to 1984, among listed manufacturing companies, the percentage of firms dealing with only a few banks increased from 13.2% to 29.7%, and the percentage of companies dealing with many banks decreased from 18.5% to 16.2%, but for companies listed on the Second Section, it decreased to 11.4%. The trend was interpreted as a strengthening of the main bank's role (MITI 1985a: 146, 275).

Lag in Centralized Sales Management

Products are generally sold directly or through multilayer wholesalers with local and customer-to-customer adjustments of the list price by sales offices throughout Japan. Cash or notes are collected and stored in a safe (at least overnight for cash, usually a few days for notes). This again is traditional; it implies customer-by-customer negotiations on product specifications, delivery date, sales discount, payment means, and date. For example, each of the four largest securities companies maintains nearly a hundred sales offices throughout the country. Salesmen as well as customers see in this proliferation of sales offices a sign of the importance of the company, but foreign competitors consider it a sign of inefficient sales management. Among listed manufacturing companies the percentage of firms with computerization of so-called client-transaction information increased over the last ten years from 45.6% to 75.3% (see table 53).

Lag in Centralized Inventory Control

Centralized inventory control using EDP (electronic data processing) systems is popular among nationwide retailers and large-scale distributors of daily commodities. In other industries, however, inventories are still stored at each sales office, their volume far exceeding an optimum, scientifically calculated level (operations research is more a topic of study than of application). The reasons include the tradition of customer-oriented delivery that still prevails, for example, in use of telephone request for immediate delivery and in the reluctance of customers to maintain their own inventories (often simply for sheer lack of space). Furthermore, an integrated inventory control system throughout a company is still rare, even though computerized inventory control has progressed among listed manufacturing companies from 79.3% in 1975 to 93.4% in 1984 (see table 53).

Obviously, considerable progress has taken place over the last decade. But the average score of computerization in listed manufacturing companies, representative of Japanese industry in general, is still low and remains a drag on the needed sophistication of accounting practices. The weaknesses in Japanese accounting practices should not be blamed on corporate management alone, however. Most reflect the resilience of tradition in the Japanese distribution system.

12

INDEPENDENT AUDIT

THE FIRST GROUP of professional accountants in Japan was organized in the late 1890s; it provided general accounting services and taught bookkeeping. In 1909, the government recommended that the accounting profession be organized like the British systems of chartered accountants, but it failed to formulate the recommendation into a law. Not until 1927 was the Registered Public Accountant Law (*Keirishi-hō*) finally enforced. By that time, there were 200 to 300 practitioners. However, institutionalization of the profession waited until after World War II. The Certified Public Accountant Law (*Kōnin Kaikeishi-hō*) was passed in June 1948 as a result of enactment of the Securities Exchange Law (April 1948). Services of certified public accountants developed largely in conjunction with the auditing required by this law (Art. 193.2).

Administrative Guidance

In 1965, after some 15 years of relatively uneventful practice, the Japanese CPA profession met its first ordeal when the fraudulent bankruptcy of Sanyo Special Steel Co. (often compared with the famous 1940 McKesson and Robbins case in the United States) shocked the Japanese community.

Under the direction of an aggressive president, Sanyo Special Steel Co., a listed company with capital stock of ¥7.4 billion, had grown to the level of a major special steel manufacturer with 3,700 employees. On March 3, 1965, it suddenly applied for corporate reorganization on grounds of insolvency. Investigation revealed that the company had created fictitious earnings since 1959, for a total of about ¥7 billion, paid dividends of 10% to 12% out of overstated profits, and remunerated management more than three times as much as indicated in the financial statements. The independent auditor (CPA) of the company, a retired official of the National Tax Bureau, knowingly reported these fictitious statements as "presented fairly." The prosecutor indicted the president, and the Ministry of Finance temporarily suspended the auditor from practice.

Public outcry was overwhelming. Supported by the pronouncements of the Business Accounting Deliberation Board, the Ministry of Finance initiated legislative revision and administrative guidance. The Securities Bureau of the Ministry became the pivot of the campaign. First, the Securities Bureau was allowed to expand: its Corporate Finance Division became two separate divisions. In 1972, both divisions were further reorganized, the former as the Capital Market Division (*Shihon-shijō-ka*), the latter as the Corporate Finance Division (*Kigyō-zaimu-ka*). Administrative guidance by these divisions became increasingly severe. Staff reviewing registration statements and annual (securities) reports came mostly from the Tax Administration Bureau, which began by compiling a "blacklist" of some 100 listed companies considered enough of a problem to have their financial statements closely scrutinized. It was soon apparent that some window dressing was taking place in one out of two cases. Managers and external accountants were questioned, and in a number of cases these auditors were reprimanded, if not suspended (such suspension is officially only temporary; practically, it is final because the practitioner has lost his integrity). Officials even suggested that companies change external auditors when the latter could not explain why they approved statements that should have been qualified or rejected.

The filing with the Ministry of Finance of audited annual (securities) reports and semiannual reports reviewed by CPAs had been done on a routine basis. By the end of the 1960s, however, any disclaimer or adverse opinion by the external auditor was made public. In most cases, the threat of publicity by the auditor was sufficient to convince management to heed his recommendations. Once newspapers issued such a report, a company's public image would plummet, and in some extreme cases the stock exchanges would take action to delist the stock. Banks would also be moved to act and might reduce the outstanding loan balance by not extending renewal, partly or fully. Stock exchanges, at least those of Tokyo and Osaka, now publish audit reports of their listed corporations every month.

Further administrative guidance came in revised legislation directly affecting the auditing profession. The Certified Public Accountant Law was revised in 1966 to strengthen the Japanese Institute of Certified Public Accountants and create audit corporations (*kansa hōjin*). These audit corporations were looked upon as a refuge by older CPAs, who had long seen their livelihood guaranteed by a few traditional auditing jobs and who were now alarmed by the questioning and disciplinary actions taken by the Ministry of Finance. The Ministry reported that during the ten years 1966–1975, 4 CPAs had licenses revoked, 48 were suspended, and 7 were disciplined; the last revocation of license was in 1978.

All of these legal changes, promoted under the jurisdiction of the Ministry of Finance, had direct repercussions on the Commercial Code, which is under the Ministry of Justice. A major revision of the Code was finally made in March 1974. Among other things, it strengthened the general function of the statutory auditor by assigning to him the duty of management audit and by requiring independent audit for all stock companies with capital of one billion yen or more. Objection came from various sectors, including small and large companies (the latter represented by *Keidanren*, the Federation of Economic Organizations). The original draft of the revision spoke of independent audit for all stock companies with ¥100 million or more capital. The lower limit was later raised to ¥300 million, then ¥500 million. Then, in view of the small number of CPAs, objections by smaller companies, and lobbying by the *zeirishi* (tax agents), who insisted on being equal with professional accountants, an addendum (*fusoku*) to the law was promulgated deciding on one billion yen for the time being. However, this addendum was revoked by the revision of the Commercial Code in 1982, effective 1984.

An expansion of the scope of independent audit covering small corporations is under discussion (1987). It is expected that tax agents will have to be satisfied with being independent auditors of smaller companies as well as being encouraged to become their statutory auditors.

The Profession

Major difficulties in the auditing profession in Japan stem from its relative youth. Certified public accountants still number only slightly more than 8,000, and the necessary professional prestige is slow in coming. (By contrast, the United States counts over 250,000 CPAs, of whom 80% are practicing their profession in the strict sense; the United Kingdom counts 65,000 chartered accountants.)

The Japanese Institute of Certified Public Accountants

The Japanese Institute of Certified Public Accountants (JICPA) started in 1949 as a voluntary association but soon developed into a *shadan hōjin* (incorporated association) under the Civil Code. The 1966 amendment of the CPA Law established the Institute as a *tokushu hōjin* (special juridical entity) under Article 43 of the amended law and made membership mandatory. The institute is patterned after the American Institute of Certified Public Accountants, with the difference that it is closely supervised and guided by government authorities, i.e., the Securities Bureau of the Ministry of Finance. Generally speaking, the Institute follows the ministerial lead, for example, when taking disciplinary action or engaging in the revision of accounting principles and auditing standards. In fact, the Business Accounting Deliberation Board attached to the ministry determines principles and standards; the JICPA issues rules and guidelines paraphrasing those standards. It establishes rules of conduct prohibiting, among other things, solicitation of services and advertising, any business or occupation incompatible with the profession, and services for a fee contingent upon results. It also does research and professional publishing.

Since the Securities Exchange Law (Art. 21) was amended in 1971, an independent auditor (or underwriter) can be sued for malpractice. However,

On December 9, 1974, the Yokohama District Court announced that fraudulent manipulation in the case of Tokyo Tokei Seizo amounted to ¥1.6 billion in past years. On the following day, the Osaka prefectural police reported fraudulent manipulation in the case of Nippon Netsugaku amounting to about ¥3.5 billion.

The securities underwriters voiced dismay at the JICPA, but no legal action was started against the independent auditors in these two (or other similar) cases. In fact, the Institute's role is far from comparable to that played by similar institutes in other countries. In Japan, the thrust for improving accounting and auditing standards comes from the government and from audit corporations.

The Individual Practitioner

Qualification as *kōnin kaikeishi* (certified public accountant) requires three examinations (CPA Law, Arts. 10–12).

The *preliminary examination* is automatically waived for any graduate of a four-year college.

The *intermediate examination*, given once a year, covers seven subjects: bookkeeping, accounting theory, cost accounting, auditing, business administration, economics, and commercial law. It grants the status of Junior CPA.

The *final examination* can be presented three years after the intermediate one. These three years must include two years of internship under the direction of a qualified CPA. A candidate must become a member of the Japan Institute of Certified Public Accountants before engaging in actual practice.

TABLE 54.
Certified Public Accountants in Japan (1955–1986)

Year	Intermediate Examination		Final Examination		JICPA Registered Members
	Number of Applicants	Number Who Passed	Number of Applicants	Number Who Passed	
1955	2,372	194 (8.2%)	897	95 (10.6%)	1,121
1960	2,427	196 (8.1)	863	83 (9.6)	1,508
1965	2,612	174 (6.7)	934	221 (23.7)	2,494
1970	4,634	244 (5.3)	548	164 (29.9)	4,208
1975	5,597	465 (8.3)	964	267 (27.7)	5,047
1980	4,357	252 (5.8)	1,990	458 (23.0)	6,035
1985	3,969	317 (8.0)	580	273 (47.1)	7,690
1986	4,282	452 (10.6)	481	240 (49.9)	7,885
TOTAL[1]	130,337	9,083 (7.0)	33,345	7,073 (21.2)	

SOURCE: JICPA, News, various years.
[1]Total since the establishment of the JICPA in 1949.

From 1949 to 1986, of the 130,000 applicants for the intermediate examination, 7% passed; of the 33,000 applicants for the final examination, 21% passed (table 54). Only a handful of teachers of courses related to accounting, even in universities, have passed the final examination for CPA.

Auditing is not the only service CPAs perform. Even today, many practitioners act individually to provide other services. A CPA is given by law the qualification of tax agent (*zeirishi*); as an individual, he can thus provide tax service to his clients. However, following a regulation newly added to the enforcement rules of the revised Commercial Code, contrary to practice in other countries, if one director of an audit corporation is retained as tax advisor by a client, the audit corporation cannot accept an audit engagement with this client (this was the result of lobbying by tax agents hard-pressed to protect themselves).

Before the 1966 amendment of the CPA Law, there were about 3,800 fully qualified individual practitioners, but only approximately one-third were engaged in auditing (the remaining were largely active in tax services or as consultants to smaller companies). Each CPA had a small office with, at most, ten assistants and clerical help. Many undertook the audit of such giant corporations as Mitsui & Co., Mitsubishi Corp., Hitachi, and Matsushita. Obviously, the true capacity and, therefore, independence of these individual practitioners was questionable. This dismal situation was corrected by the creation of *kansa hōjin* (audit corporations). These days, the majority of audits are conducted by these audit corporations; the remainder are conducted either by CPAs on a joint basis, which may involve an audit corporation, or by individual practitioners (table 55). (Because it is increasingly difficult for an individual CPA, even with assistance, to audit a large company, two or three CPAs may establish a joint office and all sign the audit report. Such is often the case in areas outside the major cities).

Audit Corporations

In addition to seeking to control the profession by making membership in the Institute of Certified Public Accountants mandatory, the 1966 amendment of the CPA Law encouraged and facilitated the incorporation of individual practitioners. Because Japanese law does not provide the form of partnership common in the West for accounting partnerships, the concept of *hōjin* (juridical entity) was used. A *kansa hōjin* is thus a *gomei kaisha* (unlimited partnership) performing an audit (*kansa*). It groups together a number of qualified accountants, who are legally not regarded as partners but as directors sharing unlimited liability. (Hence,

TABLE 55.

Types of Audit (December 31, 1982 and 1986)

Types	Listed Companies	Unlisted Companies	Total	
AUDITED BY *KANSA HŌJIN*				
1982	1,303	627	1,930	(70.7%)
1986	1,501	697	2,198	(76.3)
AUDITED ON JOINT BASIS				
Kansa Hōjin involved				
1982	57	35	92	(3.9)
1986	78	47	125	(4.3)
Kansa Hōjin not involved				
1982	355	180	535	(19.5)
1986	236	146	382	(13.3)
Audited by individual practitioners				
1982	20	167	187	(6.8)
1986	19	156	175	(6.1)
TOTAL				
1982	1,735	1,009	2,744	(100.0)
1986	1,834	1,046	2,880	(100.0)

SOURCE: JICPA, *News,* July 1983 and July 1987.
NOTE: For companies submitting financial statements to the Ministry of Finance concerning their fiscal periods ending during the 12 months ended December 31.

most of these organizations are not named after their partners as is customary in the West.) The main requisites for such an entity are as follows:

1. Membership is limited to certified public accountants.

2. It must consist of five or more members.

3. All have the right and duty to participate in the practice.

4. None can be under suspension of practice or have contravened certain other provisions of the law.

5. The audit corporation must be provided with organization, personnel, and facilities to ensure adequate conduct of practice. (CPA Law, Art. 34)

What is attractive to individual practitioners is that each director (equivalent to "partner" in Western practice) of an audit corporation can retain, at least for the time being, his own clients (usually those he had while he was still acting as an individual practitioner) and conduct an audit in his own capacity, calling however on the staff of the audit corporation in a sort of stand-by capacity. But the audit report to be issued must be signed and endorsed by the *kansa hōjin,* not by the individual director. New clients become direct clients of the audit corporation.

The Ministry of Finance has also revised the Securities Exchange Law (1971, Art. 21) since the 1970s to enumerate the legal responsibility of underwriters and independent auditors, and the relationship between the two. It promoted the merger of smaller audit corporations into larger ones (specially in preparation for bank audits to start in 1976). As of June 1987, 92 audit corporations were in operation. Three or four with offices in major cities in Japan and overseas audited each some 300 listed companies, the largest counting close to 1,000 directors and staff. Of the remainder, 78 counted fewer than 50 directors and staff, and audited each fewer than 50 listed companies. Already by 1982, roughly three-fourths of the audit reports submitted to the Ministry of Finance were the work of *kansa hōjin*.

It is recognized that the legal status of audit corporations needs further improvement. For example, at present, audit corporations are prohibited from engaging in tax practices under their own names; this activity remains the domain of the CPA as an individual practitioner.

Foreign Auditors

In the early postwar years, foreign accounting partnerships, mostly based in the United States, set up offices in Japan to serve foreign corporations. Their clientele was suddenly broadened to Japanese corporations in 1961 with the advent of American Depositary Receipts (ADRs).

In that year, Sony offered, for the first time, a new stock issue for sale in the United States and had to engage an American accounting firm to certify its financial statements for filing with the U.S. Securities and Exchange Commission.

Sony's example was followed by an ever-increasing number of Japanese companies, who offered stocks and bonds in the United States as well as in various European countries. The need for an international audit of these companies grew at the same pace.

The legal status of foreign accounting firms in Japan is a peculiar one. All are Japanese branches of foreign partnerships and as such are not organized under Japanese law. Foreign CPAs, however, can apply for qualification as individual practitioners (CPA Law, Art. 16.2). This opportunity for foreign professionals was inaugurated by the military occupation after World War II. Of 107 non-Japanese CPAs who applied to take such an examination, 74 passed. Examinations were last held in December 1975, when 11 of 27 applicants succeeded (a brief written examination in English and an oral examination in Japanese, with the help of an interpreter, if needed, were required).

The audit of a Japanese corporation by a foreign accounting partnership used to present the following pattern:

1. Audit for domestic purposes was not performed.

2. Audit for international purposes started from the company books, all written in Japanese. Bilingual accountants were employed to prepare working papers in English under the direction of foreign CPAs.

3. These working papers were then used by the foreign CPAs, statements were prepared in English for exclusive use outside of Japan, and an opinion was issued under the name of the auditing partnership.

4. When, in rare cases, statements for domestic use were requested, they would be signed by an individual Japanese practitioner who was a member of the accounting partnership.

The change from individual to collective practice, implemented in the *kansa hōjin*, was a turning point: it meant the end of foreign exclusivity over international audits. As would be expected, the "Big Eight" in international accounting have different policies regarding Japan. Cooperation with major Japanese audit corporations is active and takes many forms, from subcontracting to joint audit. Touche Ross, a latecomer to the Japanese market, decided in 1975, ahead of other Big Eight accounting firms operating in Japan, to "integrate" (transfer its professionals and business) with Tohmatsu Awoki & Co., the first and largest multioffice audit corporation, established in 1968. Soon, integration took place between another latecomer, Coopers Lybrand, and the Chuo Audit Corporation by the establishment of a one-firm operation. The integration of Ernst & Whinney with the Ota Audit Corporation took the form of a two-firm operation in one legal entity. Other Big Eight firms are affiliated with one or more Japanese audit corporations mainly for mutual assistance in business referral, without entering the areas of quality control, standard procedures of auditing, and management cooperation (exchange of management personnel).

It is openly acknowledged in Japan that the work of these foreign auditors has been and is contributing immensely to the improvement of the profession and practices here.

Independent Audit

Unless so required by law, it is rare in Japan for a company to engage independent accountants to perform an audit. The term "external audit" (*gaibu kansa*) is usually understood to mean an audit required by the Securities Exchange Law or by the Commercial Code and performed by qualified independent accountants, such as a CPA or an audit corporation. This narrow understanding of the external audit prevails among CPAs as well as laymen, including management, because the concept goes back no further than the Securities Exchange Law of 1948; it expresses a legal requirement, not a business need. Before 1948, audit, as testimony to the credibility of financial statements issued to the public or to a third party, was considered only in the rare cases where it was ordered by the courts in relation to a criminal case.

Under current provisions of laws and regulations, the following organizations are required to be audited by a CPA or an audit corporation:

1. Corporations capitalized at ¥500 million or more
2. Corporations with liabilities of ¥20 billion or more
3. Corporations applying for listing or already listed on the stock exchanges
4. Corporations seeking registration for qualification as over-the-counter stock
5. Corporations that plan to offer or sell stocks or debentures publicly
6. Companies applying for a loan from the Small Business Investment Company
7. Private educational juridical entities when seeking official recognition or permission to expand, and in order to obtain government subsidies
8. Labor unions under certain circumstances (see Trade Union Law, Art. 5)

As distinct from the mandatory audit, the profession coined the term "voluntary audit" (*nin-i kansa*). When CPAs try to persuade management to have such a voluntary independent audit, say, to promote the reputation of the company or help it obtain some additional line of credit from the banks, the suggestion is usually denied. One reason is that management trusts its employees more than outsiders, such as auditors, lawyers, and consultants; another is that banks themselves do not yet fully recognize the responsibility of the auditors.

Cases in which voluntary audit is conducted are few indeed. The company planning to go public will have one, because at the time of application for listing it must submit accounts independently audited for three preceding years. International joint ventures more commonly use voluntary audit. When such a venture is established in Japan between Japanese and American partners, for example, the joint venture agreement usually includes a provision requiring an audit of the annual financial statements, to be performed by an independent firm of public accountants of international reputation. In other words, the financial statements as prepared should be based on the Generally Accepted Accounting Principles (GAAP). The Japanese partner will agree with the provision requiring independent audit only because his American partner insists on its necessity. He feels, rather that financial statements prepared by the internal accounting staff are reliable and that an independent audit is superfluous and an unnecessary expense. Japanese management often insists, and its wish prevails, that such auditing expense be borne by the foreign parent company, but not by the joint venture.

The Japanese position has merit, however. Financial statements that are prepared by independent auditors based on international accounting practices are useless to Japanese management because a number of adjustments and reclassifications must be made to the initial Japanese statements. Although these adjustments are necessary to reflect fair presentation based on U.S. accounting practices, Japanese management is often totally indifferent to them, if it understands them at all; only financial statements based on Japanese accounting principles are meaningful!

Accountants' services are best appreciated when an audit is wanted by management and management willingly pays for what it wants. Too many companies regard the external audit as a necessary evil; it is not surprising, then, that audit services are rarely taken advantage of to improve the accounting system and internal control.

Japanese companies seldom change external auditors. In many cases, the auditor engaged has some private connection with a friend or director of the company or is a former employee of the company. In the early days of the profession, the company treated its external auditor as an employee and expected him to protect the interests of management and staff rather than those of the shareholders or investing public. The concept of employee relationship exists to a lesser degree today, particularly when the auditor is an individual practitioner. Where such a relationship exists, company management usually tells the auditor how to formulate the audit opinion. If the auditor has knowledge of window dressing, he must disclose the matter and qualify his audit opinion. This is not easy when an employee relationship exists. In most cases of window dressing, which are publicized by a company's failure, the external auditor's position has been so weak that he probably has not been able to disclaim or qualify the audit opinion (see Audit Reports below), although he might have known the facts for years before the company finally became insolvent. The company that manipulates accounts usually seeks agreement from its auditor not to disclose this manipulation on the grounds that if it becomes public knowledge, the company will be forced out of business. It may argue with its auditor that he is an employee who can be fired and replaced by someone willing to obey the "request."

Audit Reports

The 1966 Auditing Standards, as revised by the Business Accounting Deliberation Board, determine the proper terminology to be used in audit reports. Opinions of external auditors may be in one of four forms:

1. Unqualified opinion (*mu-gentei iken*), expressed as "The financial statements present fairly financial conditions and results of operations in conformity with accounting principles."

2. Qualified opinions (*gentei iken*), expressed as "Although such exceptions as mentioned exist, the financial statements present fairly. . . ." Such opinions are classified as:

First category (*ichi-go gentei*), for not conforming to accounting principles.

Second category (*ni-go gentei*), for not being consistent.

Third category (*san-go gentei*), for disclosure not being in full compliance with laws and regulations.

3. Adverse opinion (*futekisei iken*), expressed as " . . . do not present fairly."

4. Disclaimer of opinion (*iken sashi-hikae*), expressed as "We are not in a position to express our opinion due to limited scope of examination."

Previously, it was common to use the expression "almost fairly" (*ōmune tekisei*), which, on the one hand, stood for "fairly" when the auditor presented his opinion to management and, on the other hand, stood for "not fairly" if shareholders or outsiders questioned the auditor's responsibility. Since 1966, the Ministry of Finance has discouraged such wording; it is rarely encountered nowadays.

According to a survey of financial statements submitted yearly to the Ministry of Finance between 1966 and 1982, the percentage of unqualified opinions grew from 55% to 87%; qualified opinions were almost all of the first category, i.e., expressing lack of conformity with accounting principles. The Tokyo Stock Exchange reports monthly on the audit reports of listed companies. Of the 1,497 listed companies (First and Second Sections) whose accounting year ended during the year 1986, 1,331 received an unqualified opinion and the remaining 166 a qualified opinion of the second category for not being consistent (Tokyo Stock Exchange 1986c).

FOUR

FINANCIAL
REPORTING

13

DISCLOSURE & FINANCIAL STATEMENTS

A POPULAR SLOGAN at the time of the introduction of Western bookkeeping in the nineteenth century was *wakon yōsai* (Japanese spirit, Western techniques). Western bookkeeping was merely a set of techniques to be learned in some objective fashion (*yōsai*). Financial reporting, i.e., reporting on these techniques, was altogether another matter. It assumes a degree of subjectivity in the sense that reporter and reportee must share a common understanding of the social and economic circumstances surrounding them. It, then, came under *wakon* (Japanese spirit). Subjectivity was and still is a vital ingredient of Japanese society and thus of Japanese business.

Several factors, external and internal to the corporation, affect financial reporting. External factors are related to the business environment, itself determined by the social dynamics of contemporary Japan. Of particular importance are the close cooperation, if not partnership, between government agencies and business, as expressed in administrative guidance, and a similarly close cooperation among the various sectors of private business of which the rule is interdependence. These two factors, among others, tend to squeeze out the investing public, as exemplified by the standard debt/equity ratio, the predominance of institutional investors on the capital market, and, more fundamentally, a reluctant acceptance of the accounting profession. Two internal factors directly affect financial reporting as well: directors are often also operations managers, and personnel administration stresses mutual commitment to the organization. These factors preclude the kind of internal control necessary for financial reporting to make sense. More fundamentally, they tend to preclude proper audit of financial statements.

Besides the Commercial Code, the Securities Exchange Law (*Shōken Torihiki-hō*) is the principal legal source for disclosure. The title of this law is translated variously as Securities Transactions Law, Securities Exchange Act, Securities and Exchange Act, and others. The law was first approved in the Diet in March 1947 and later revised and enacted on March 7, 1948. It was modeled after the United States Securities Act (1933) and Securities Exchange Act (1934); its reporting requirements are similar to those found in the two U.S. acts. It should be noted that, already in 1874, the Meiji government promulgated "Stock Exchange Regulations" (*Kabushiki Torihiki Jōrei*), supposedly modeled on rules of the London Stock Exchange. This was the first time that the term *torihiki* (exchange) was officially used, and it has been standard terminology ever since. At the end of the nineteenth century (1893), a new "Exchange Law" (*Torihikisho-hō*) was enacted such that exchanges could be organized on either a membership or joint-stock principle. (Misleadingly, the two earlier laws are sometimes referred to as "Securities Exchange Law.")

Articles in the Commercial Code and the Securities Exchange Law together with directives of the Securities Bureau of the Ministry of Finance, supplemented by directives issued by the stock exchanges, stipulate disclosure requirements for reporting to the Ministry of Finance and for listing on the Japanese stock exchanges. The regulation enforcing requirements of the Securities Exchange Law, true to the origin of this law, was modeled after Regulation S-X in the United States. In 1963, the regulation applying Commercial Code requirements was adjusted to the Securities Exchange Law, leaving, however, significant discrepancies. Both regulations were finally revised in 1974. As a result, Japanese financial statements look similar to U.S. financial statements, but their terminology is more stereotyped, and the substance of each account differs owing to differences in accounting principles and practices. In fact, the terminology standardized by official regulations is for the convenience of official reviewers; it is not descriptive and often does not detail what is actually involved.

Board of Directors

Under pressure during the military occupation after World War II, Japanese corporations were to be democratized. The board of directors was to be composed essentially of representatives of interests other than capital, i.e., other than the major shareholders as in prewar major corporations. Thus, the practice evolved that directors were selected from among the employees, thereby enforcing the lifetime employment principle all the way to the top of the management hierarchy. Thus, in postwar Japan there is no real distinction at the top of the corporation between policy making and the executive function. The result is twofold. First, most corporate directors, being executive managers, have no interest in adopting a split personality: they continue in the same role on the board as on the factory floor, representing internal executive responsibilities rather than external responsibilities to shareholders. Second, very few members of the board are outside directors, and when they are, it would seem to indicate that their function is to "internalize" some outside circumstance.

In 1974, a survey of 131 large corporations revealed that as against 1,928 inside directors, there were only 218 outside directors. The reasons for calling on the latter were:

To reflect surrounding circumstances	41.9%
As a result of strengthening ties	20.9
As a result of joining a *keiretsu* or a group	18.6
For financial reasons	14.0
Other	5.6

(Kudo 1974: 111)

In 1985, MITI published the report of its Committee on Management Ability. It surveyed 505 manufacturing companies listed in Tokyo and Osaka: 40% of these firms had no outside director; in the retail industry, among 202 major retailers of which 40 were listed, over 55% had no outside director (table 56). This characteristic is confirmed by the origin of the company president: for the manufacturing companies surveyed over the period 1974–1984, the percentage of presidents coming in from outside the company decreased from 40% to 31% (table 57).

Given such composition of the board of directors, what are then the

TABLE 56.

Outside Directors (1984)

(percentage)

Number of Outside Directors	Manufacturing[1]			Retail[2]		
	Total	First Section	Second Section	Total	Listed Firms	Not Listed
None	39.2	43.5	30.7	56.8	30.3	61.3
Fewer than 1/8	30.1	32.4	25.3	20.1	51.5	16.3
1/8–fewer than 1/4	16.9	14.6	21.7	12.6	10.2	13.1
1/4 and more	13.8	9.5	22.3	10.5	15.4	9.4

SOURCE: MITI 1985a: 49; MITI 1985b: 40.
[1]505 companies listed on Tokyo and Osaka stock exchanges.
[2]202 major retailers, of which 40 were listed.

TABLE 57.

Manufacturing: Company Presidents' Origin (1974–1984)

(percentage)

Year	Founder	Second Generation	Through the Ranks	From Outside
1974	13.6	17.4	28.4	40.6
1975	11.5	23.6	30.4	34.6
1976	10.7	20.8	36.1	32.5
1977	9.8	21.1	34.6	34.6
1978	10.9	21.5	35.7	31.9
1979	9.1	19.6	37.6	33.7
1981	8.3	23.4	34.9	33.4
1982	6.8	23.3	35.9	34.0
1983	5.6	25.2	35.0	34.2
1984	6.0	22.2	40.1	31.7

SOURCE: MITI 1985a: 45.
NOTE: 505 companies listed on Tokyo and Osaka stock exchanges.

TABLE 58.

Top Management in Manufacturing: Views of Most Important Financial Indicators (1978–1984)

(percentage)

Indicator	1978	1979	1981	1982	1983	1984
Rate of sales growth	9.8	10.2	12.5	13.8	14.9	16.1
Rate of profit growth	9.3	8.2	10.0	11.9	10.5	11.5
Profits	42.6	45.3	40.5	40.4	44.6	43.8
Ratio of profits to sales	22.3	21.4	17.5	19.8	18.4	18.1
Ratio of profits to equity	1.1	1.3	1.3	1.7	0.2	1.0
Ratio of profits to total liabilities and net worth	11.2	9.9	13.7	9.6	10.0	6.7
Net worth ratio	1.7	2.6	2.5	2.6	0.8	1.0
Receipt and outlay of funds	1.1	0.2	1.0	0.2	0.2	0.2
Stock prices	0	0	0	0.2	0	0
Dividend rate	0.4	0	0.4	0	0	1.0
Other	0.4	0.9	0.6	0.2	0.4	0.6

SOURCE: MITI 1985a: 153.
NOTE: Companies listed on the First and Second Sections of Tokyo and Osaka stock exchanges.

financial indicators they consider most important? At one extreme of the spectrum are profits (43.8%). At the other extreme are stock prices (0%) and dividend rate (1.0%), two criteria that would be of immediate interest to shareholders (table 58). Commenting on the style of decision making of top management, the head of the MITI Committee on Management Ability wrote as follows:

Top management's decision making in Japanese companies is characterized by . . . (among others) long-range business concept. . . . The long-range business concept results from the Japanese business management aiming at long-term survival and growth of the firm itself, rather than at benefiting stockholders; even when there is a drop in profits and stock prices due to a large-scale equipment investment for the purpose of rationalizing and labor-saving, or due to a large investment for basic research, the top management are not held responsible for it. Many business executives in Japan cite sales increase rates and earnings as important financial indicators, while less than one percent of Japanese top management quote stock prices and dividend ratios. (Shimizu 1986: 12)

Shareholders' General Meeting

The shareholders' general meeting (*kabunushi sōkai*) was the object of great expectations according to the Commercial Code (Arts. 230–253), but the 1974 and subsequent revisions of the code concentrated, rather, on disclosure requirements and methods. The main functions of the shareholders' general meeting, other than election of directors, are approval of the balance sheet and income statement as well as determination of dividends. These functions require considerable technical knowledge about accounting that is hardly found among individual shareholders even if they were interested in performing the functions. However, they are not much interested, and the mechanism of the stock market, in particular the fixed dividend rate, satisfies them without requiring them to be concerned about the financial statements. Institutional investors, who are essentially lenders and/or stable shareholders, have little need to participate in the general meeting.

The organizational structure of the corporation also precludes a truly distinctive role of the general meeting. Directors are usually nominated by current management, with the result that the board is not so much a superior organ of policy making, accountable to shareholders, as simply a management forum. The general meeting is then a legal formality to be handled with great dispatch. Japanese executives are concerned that no embarrassing questions be asked, private matters revealed, or public disturbances occur with shareholders present. Most general meetings are adjourned after only a few minutes.

In a survey of 1,131 companies that closed their accounts between March 20 and April 20, 1987, the length of their shareholders' general meeting was reported as follows:

Length of Meeting	Number of Companies
30 minutes or less	840 (74.2%)
30 minutes to 1 hour	268 (23.7%)
1 to 2 hours	16 (1.4%)
2 to 3 hours	4 (0.4%)
3 to 4 hours	1 (0.1%)

For the remaining two companies, the length was more than 5 hours (*Shōji Hōmu*, Special Issue, 1987/7).

Japan has its own "yellow press," represented mostly by weekly magazines that compete among themselves by exposing private scandals and, in particular, corporations' internal struggles (*nai-fun*). As a rule, such struggles should not surface at the shareholders' meeting; they should be resolved internally and only unanimous resolutions presented at the meeting. Ironically, the shareholders' meeting functions as a deadline for resolving such struggles.

One kind of disturbance given wide press coverage in Japan is that of the *sōkai-ya* (general-meeting specialists), a type of racketeering that specializes in blackmail of corporate executives. Many *sōkai-ya* are either the head or sole representative of an "economic research institute," a "political research center," or a publication house, positions that are used as a cover. Shortly before a general meeting is called, they visit executives and threaten to divulge mistakes of the company or scandals of its officers. For a "fee" these *sōkai-ya* will not show up at a meeting. However,

An unprecedented police crackdown has put the sokaiya on the defensive and largely cut them off from their former corporate patrons. . . . And companies themselves are feeling the heat now that police are actively enforcing a 1982 revision to the Commercial Code prohibiting payments to sokaiya. In five cases brought since June 1986, police arrested a total of 19 company officials and 21 sokaiya for violations of the code. (Only two such cases had been brought in the previous four years.) Scores of sokaiya have been arrested on blackmail charges. . . . Last Friday (June 26, 1987), more than 6,000 police fanned out to keep vigil over 1,067 general meetings, all held at approximately the same hour at the peak of the so-called shareholder meeting season. (Schoenberger 1987)

In some cases, the *sōkai-ya* ingratiate themselves to management, which turns to them for help to stop, sometimes by strong-arm tactics, disturbances by antipollution and consumer groups, as occurred in the Chisso Corporation, Showa Denko, and Mitsui Metal Mining cases in 1971. Although police have requested cooperation from companies in uncovering information on *sōkai-ya* threats and blackmail, few details have come forth. Tax examiners themselves are not actively investigating them either; apparently such investigation takes place only when *sōkai-ya* are indicted. Auditors often find expenditures supported by a list of names of known *sōkai-ya*; receipts are usually missing.

Sōkai-ya back up their threats to show up at shareholders' meetings by ownership of a few shares. (In the mid-1960s a "one-share share-holder" movement was also started by groups in opposition to the armament industry and in connection with some major cases of industrial pollution, but it did not develop to any appreciable extent.) Supposedly as a tactic of management to forestall possible embarrassment by *sōkai-ya*, most companies have their general shareholders' meetings on the same day and keep them as short as possible.

1,131 companies closed their accounts between March 20 and April 20, 1987. Shareholders' meetings were held on June 24: 18 companies (1.6%); June 25: 71 companies (6.3%); June 26: 976 companies (86.3%); June 29: 32 companies (2.8%); other: 34 companies (3.0%) (*Shōji Hōmu*, Special Issue, 1987/7).

Financial Statements According to the Commercial Code

Until 1974, when "net income" according to the Commercial Code was adopted for reporting also under the Securities Exchange Law, financial reporting suffered from a legal dichotomy between the precepts of the Commercial Code, administered by the Ministry of Justice, and those of the Securities Exchange Law and tax legislation administered by the Ministry of Finance. Currently, following the 1981 and 1984 amendments of the Commercial Code, matters are more uniform.

All companies incorporated under the Commercial Code are required (Arts. 282 and 293) to print and make available at their main office to any interested shareholder and creditor the following:

1. Balance sheet (*taishaku taishō-hyō*)
2. Income statement (*son-eki keisan-sho*)
3. Business report (*eigyō hōkoku-sho*)
4. Proposal for disposition of earnings (*rieki no shobun matawa sonshitsu no shori ni kansuru gi-an*)
5. Supporting schedules (*fuzoku meisai-sho*)

So-called financial statements (*zaimu shohyō*, i.e., balance sheet, income statement, and proposal for disposition of earnings) must be approved by the shareholders' meeting within three months of the end of the accounting period. For the large corporations (with ¥500 million or more capital and/or total liabilities of over ¥20 billion) that are to be audited under the Commercial Code, balance sheet and income statement do not have to be approved by the shareholders' meeting; reporting suffices. However, if there is discrepancy between the opinions of external and statutory auditors, approval by shareholders is required (Law Related to the Special Case of the Commercial Code Concerning Reporting by Large Corporations 1974, Art. 16).

All statements must be certified as to correctness by the statutory auditor or auditors (*kansa-yaku*), who do not have to be certified public accountants. No external audit was required until 1974, when amendment of the Commercial Code made it mandatory for corporations capitalized at ¥1 billion or more (capital stock excluding capital surplus) to have their financial statements audited by an independent CPA or an audit corporation. However, this size requirement was lowered under the newly amended provisions of the Commercial Code effective in 1984 to ¥500 million capital or liabilities of ¥20 billion or more. Under the previous amendment (1981), for the company subject to audit by independent CPAs or audit corporation, approval of the balance sheet and income statement is no longer required, provided that the CPAs express an unqualified opinion and the statutory auditors agree to the result of the independent audit; however, the proposal for disposition of earnings has to be approved by shareholders. Financial statements with the attached reports by CPAs and statutory auditors are printed and mailed to shareholders two weeks before the date of the shareholders' meeting.

The Commercial Code (Art. 283.3) requires public notice (*kōkoku*): the balance sheet must be reported in the public media, either in the Official Gazette (*Kanpō*) or in a daily newspaper. From the year ending on or after October 1, 1982, companies subjected to independent audit have been required to report their income statement in the media. Closed companies rarely comply with the public notice requirement. The Commercial Code has no requirement for filing financial statements with public authorities; however, such statements must accompany corporate income tax returns.

Following the 1974 and 1981 revisions of the Commercial Code, all stock corporations were required to present to their shareholders, in addition to the documents mentioned above, supporting schedules covering the following financial information:

1. Changes in capital stock, and capital and legal reserve
2. Changes in bonds and other long- and short-term borrowings
3. Details of changes in fixed assets and accumulated depreciation

4. Details of assets subject to lien

5. Details of debt guarantees

6. Purpose and method of computing the amount of reserves and allowances

7. Details of amounts due from/to controlling shareholder

8. Details of equity ownership in subsidiaries and the number of shares of stock held by these subsidiaries

9. Details of amounts due from subsidiaries

10. Details of transactions with directors, statutory auditors, and controlling shareholder and those with third parties with whom conflict of interest exists

11. Remuneration to directors and statutory auditors (Ministry of Justice 1982: chapter 5).

In addition, if there is a change in the method of significant accounting policies, the reason for the change must be disclosed in the schedules. Further, additional supporting schedules are prescribed for companies with outstanding capital stock of ¥100 million or more. Such schedules include a schedule of equity ownership in more than 25%-owned investee companies and a schedule of selling, general, and administrative expenses.

Prior to the 1981 amendment, no requirements for the Business Report had been provided. Accordingly, the contents and scope of the report were simple and uninteresting, and provided uninformative details for outside readers! Now, however, the following are required:

1. Major business, branch offices and factories, conditions of stock, employees, and other company affairs

2. Progress and results of operations by industry segment (including financing and capital expenditures) in the current year

3. Relationship with parent company, condition of significant subsidiaries, and other significant business combination

4. Result of operations and financial condition for more than three recent years and their explanation

5. Company's task for the future

6. Name of directors and statutory auditor(s) and their positions in the company and other occupations

7. Number of shares held by at least the seven largest shareholders, and the company's investments in these shareholders

8. Major lending banks and other financial institutions, amounts of borrowing from such lenders, and number of shares held by such lenders

9. Major subsequent events. (Ministry of Justice 1982: chapter 4)

Notes to financial statements required by the regulations are normally listed at the foot of the balance sheet and income statement. Aside from items that are not otherwise required if shown separately in the statements (for example, amounts receivable from subsidiaries, allowance for doubtful accounts, accumulated depreciation, depletion and amortization of tangible fixed assets, and amount payable to controlling shareholder), the notes should include the following:

1. Summary of significant accounting policies, such as asset valuation methods, depreciation methods, and methods for recognizing significant reserves

2. Changes in accounting principles and their effect

3. The market value of a significant current asset item that is substantially lower than the carrying amount stated at cost

4. Total amount of receivables from directors and statutory auditors, and total amounts of payables to them

5. Material assets or liabilities denominated in foreign currencies

6. Assets subject to lien

7. Debt guarantees, notes receivable discounted or endorsed with recourse, material litigations and other contingent liabilities

8. Certain reserves that are not shown under the special reserves account in the balance sheet

9. Net income (loss) per share data

10. In connection with computing the limit of earnings available for dividend distribution, the amount of excess of the sum of certain deferred charges (such as start-up costs, research and development costs, expenditures for procurement of resources, and market development costs) over the amount of legal reserves

11. Amounts of revenue earned and costs and expenses incurred from transactions with subsidiaries and the controlling shareholder. (Ministry of Justice 1982: chapters 1–3)

No comparative data for the previous year is required to accompany the current year's financial statements. Generally speaking, the financial statements presented to shareholders are supposed to show the income that can be appropriated by resolution of the shareholders' meeting; they are not so much concerned with current business income. Any accounting change approved by the tax authorities is accepted without reservation, and methods may be changed as often as the tax authorities agree to the change.

For example, installment sales may be changed from cash basis to accrual basis; the depreciation method may be changed from the declining-balance to the straight-line method; the inventory valuation method may be changed from first-in-first-out (FIFO) to last-in-first-out (LIFO).

For comparative purposes, when such changes are made, financial statements of prior periods should be restated based on the newly adopted principles and methods. This creates a problem because financial statements, once approved by the shareholders' meeting as of a certain date, cannot lawfully be changed at will. A strict legal interpretation virtually wipes out the possibility of retroactive restatement of financial statements. Thus, depending on the company, such disclosure ranges from complete lack of notes to (rarely) lengthy explanations.

Tax Returns and Accompanying Financial Statements

Income tax returns (*hōjin-zei shinkoku-sho*) must be filed within two months (or three months, subject to approval by the tax authorities) of the closing of accounts, and figures must be on an actual basis.

Normally, companies are subjected to three kinds of income taxes. In 1987, the breakdown was as follows: (1) national corporation tax, principally 42%; local income taxes: (2) enterprise tax, principally 13.2%, (3) inhabitants tax, 8.7% (20.7% of corporate tax). Aggregate income tax rate thus amounts to approximately 63.9%. However, since the enterprise tax is deductible when paid, the effective income tax rate is approximately 56%.

Corporate income taxes are based on the fiscal period (which cannot exceed 12 months) of a corporation. When a corporation uses a 12 month period, it must pay an estimated amount equivalent to 50% of the preceding year's tax dues or, alternatively, payments based on the actual results of operations during the initial six months of the current fiscal year (*chūkan shinkoku-sho*, interim return). The tax is levied on the difference between total income and total expenses for each accounting period. Expenses, which may be deducted, include allowance for tax purposes and losses of the preceding five years brought forward. Capital gains are taxable income except where stipulated otherwise by the Special Taxation Measures Law. Where discrepancies exist between the Commercial Code and tax accounting requirements, in practice, in order to obtain the maximum tax deduction, these discrepancies are reconciled in one way or another in favor of the tax requirements.

The financial statements prepared for, reported to, and approved by the shareholders in accordance with the Commercial Code are the mandatory basis on which tax returns are prepared, and these statements must accompany tax returns (Corporation Tax Law, Art. 74). This particular requirement had led to a series of accounting practices that are not relevant, and are sometimes contrary, to fair financial reporting. For example,

1. Special tax reserves must be booked in order to claim tax deduction, whether or not such reserves are really needed for financial accounting purposes. Since the year ending on or after October 1, 1982, special tax reserves must be transferred from the liability section to the shareholders' equity section. New provision can be made only by retained earnings appropriation (Ministry of Justice 1982, Transitional Rule, Art. 2).

2. Many companies account for depreciation by the declining-balance method merely because it allows a larger tax deduction and corresponding tax deferral.

3. The reserve for doubtful accounts is recorded at the maximum amount allowable in order to claim the tax benefit. Whether or not that amount is actually needed is not seriously considered.

4. Reserve for employee retirement benefits is allowed as a deduction for tax purposes only to the extent of 40% of the liability at year end arising from services of employees up to that date.

There is always the danger, therefore, that when companies encounter financial difficulties, they will not provide for any such benefit or that they will even reverse the amount reserved in the past to show more generated income.

Tax returns are usually prepared by the accounting clerks of the company with the help of the *zeirishi* (tax agent). In smaller companies, the entire task is turned over to the tax agent hired for that purpose. The returns do not have to be certified by the *zeirishi*, although at the bottom of the tax form a space is provided for his name and seal; the top space is reserved for the company representative primarily responsible for the returns.

It is usually taken for granted that tax returns will be filed on the "blue form" (*ao-iro shinkoku-sho*) because of its advantages. (Two forms are available to the individual taxpayer as well as to the corporation, [Corporation Tax Law, Art. 121]). The most important advantage of the blue form over the white form is the carry-back and/or carry-forward of loss (Corporation Tax Law, Arts. 57 and 81). Other significant advantages of the blue form include a number of reserves and deductions for tax purposes. The corporation wishing to file a blue return must submit an application to the district tax office prior to the beginning of the accounting period (a requirement too often neglected by foreign firms operating in Japan). For newly incorporated firms, application must be made within three months after the date of incorporation or by the end of the first accounting period, whichever is earlier (Corporation Tax Law, Art. 122).

The blue form is granted on the condition, among others, that the corporation maintain a proper set of account books. The privilege may be revoked if there is sufficient evidence of malpractice; a heavy penalty ensues, because revocation is retroactive to the time of such malpractice.

Financial Statements According to the Securities Exchange Law

Financial statements prepared in accordance with the Securities Exchange Law should be included in the *yūka shōken hōkoku-sho* (securities report). They must be prepared annually by corporations listed on the stock exchanges and corporations that have raised capital through public offering of bonds or stock either as new (*boshū*) or outstanding shares (*uridashi*).

These statements must be audited and certified by a certified public accountant or an audit corporation (Article 193-2) before they are filed with the Ministry of Finance, and copies must be sent to the stock exchange (Article 24). Before 1974 independent auditors had been performing audits without reference to the shareholders' meeting, often simply *after* the meeting. Under the 1974 amendment of the Commercial Code, this audit must now take place *before* the shareholders' meeting. The requirement that the meeting be held within three months (previously two months) of the closing of the accounts is intended to allow enough time to complete the audit and to print and mail the financial statements before the meeting.

The Securities Exchange Law dictates that the form and contents of financial statements must conform with the "Regulation Concerning the Terminology, Form, and Preparation Methods of Financial Statements" (*Zaimu Shohyō Kisoku*). The following are required in report form and must be covered by the independent auditor's opinion:

1. Balance sheet
2. Statement of income (multiple-step form), accompanied by the production-cost schedule
3. Statement of disposition of retained earnings
4. Fourteen schedules
    Investment securities
    Tangible fixed assets
    Intangible fixed assets
    Investment in stock of affiliates
    Capital contribution to affiliates
    Loans to affiliates

Bonds
Long-term debt
Borrowing from affiliates
Capital stock
Capital surplus
Legal reserve and voluntary reserve
Depreciation and amortization
Allowances and reserves

In addition, other information, such as cash flow statement, not to be certified by the independent auditors, are required.

Filing of all these statements with the Ministry of Finance becomes mandatory from the first accounting period that follows the filing of the registration statement at the time of new issue or secondary issue of stock to the public. Later, ongoing filing must be made at the close of each accounting period. Thus, financial statements filed in the required format are available for review by interested parties at the Ministry of Finance and the stock exchange where a company is listed. A copy of any part of a statement can be obtained on request. The Ministry printing office also reproduces it in book form for sale about two months after filing.

The Securities Exchange Law requires comparative statements for only two years, the current and the immediately previous year. The stock exchanges require five-year comparative statements only for listing application; the latest three years' financial statements are also to be audited by CPAs or an audit corporation. Notes are also legally required to disclose the following:

1. Significant accounting policies
   Valuation of marketable and investment securities
   Valuation of inventory
   Depreciation of fixed assets
   Amortization of deferred charges
   Translation of foreign currencies
   Provision for allowances or reserves
   Recognition of revenue or expenses
   Other
2. Changes in accounting policies (including presentation method)
3. Subsequent events
4. Other explanations of accounts due from/to associated companies (*kankei-gaisha*), contingent liabilities, etc.
5. Additional information to provide readers with more meaningful information

14

BALANCE SHEET & CONSOLIDATION

$\mathbf{B}$ECAUSE TWO DIFFERENT LAWS are involved, listed companies make public two different forms of financial statements. The balance sheet under the Commercial Code (Art. 283) is usually in account form and rather condensed; under the Securities Exchange Law (Art. 25), it is in report form and contains a wealth of details, some superfluous. It is sometimes assumed that the latter can be derived from the former with additional elaboration. This is not so. The required financial document flows from two very different sources of law: the Commercial Code legislation attempts to protect creditors, the Securities Exchange Law to protect investors. Under the former concept, assets are valued at cost and should be stated more conservatively, and liabilities should include all items legally liable. Under the latter concept, the balance sheet is the connecting link between two successive income statements. Balances of costs or charges not currently reflected in the income statement of a given period are carried forward as assets in the balance sheet. Still, this difference in underlying concept does not affect the general items of the respective balance sheets. Balance sheets of privately held companies, which come under the Commercial Code only, will only be available in rudimentary form.

Three major points (in the eyes of Japanese management) regarding assets and liabilities, which have not been discussed in previous chapters, are debt, current ratio, and investment in securities.

Debt

During the decades of high growth, given the prevailing heavy debt, "liquidity" in the Western sense was a luxury enjoyed by only a few Japanese companies that were well established and not currently engaged in major expansion. Most companies sought month-to-month assistance from the banks in order to raise the cash needed for meeting accounts and notes payable. Cash became available from the banks and from collection of receivables. Debt came essentially in the form of credit between buyer and supplier, notes discount, and loans.

Notes (*shiharai tegata*) and accounts payable (*kaikake-kin*) stand for intercompany credit. It has been mentioned that most Japanese companies issue promissory notes to settle accounts payable. From the standpoint of the recipient, they are recorded as notes receivable, which are discounted by banks to meet current cash flow needs at a rate slightly lower than that of short-term bank loans or sometimes endorsed to vendors in settlement of accounts payable to the vendors. Such discounted notes and endorsed notes are deducted from notes receivable and shown in explanatory notes to the balance sheet as notes receivable discounted or endorsed (contingent liabilities). In Japan, therefore, the settlement of accounts comes in two steps: issuance of the promissory note and settlement of the note by cash on the due date. Most companies carry large amounts in notes payable.

Nissan Motor Co., Ltd., carried notes payable to the amount of ¥152 billion, whereas it had accounts payable of ¥222 billion (March 31, 1986). Mitsubishi Corporation had notes payable of ¥790 billion and accounts payable of ¥1,359 billion (March 31, 1986).

Notes and accounts payable to affiliated companies are shown separately on the balance sheet.

Notes receivable discounted are loan from the bank's viewpoint. From the borrower's viewpoint they are also loan, but they are shown as contingent liabilities outside of the body of the financial statements. Thus, they must be included when total loan is considered. They are disclosed in footnotes (required both by the Commercial Code and by the Securities Exchange Law). Because of settling accounts by promissory notes (*yakusoku tegata*), the amount of notes receivable (*uketori tegata*), including notes discounted, in many cases, is larger than that of accounts receivable (*urikake-kin*).

As of March 31, 1987, Nissan Motor Co., Ltd., had notes receivable for a total of ¥427,848 million (in addition to ¥21,786 million in export bills discounted) and accounts receivable for a total of ¥72,401 million. At the same date, Mitsubishi Corporation had ¥638,990 million in notes receivable (in addition to ¥127,894 million in notes discounted) and ¥1,720,421 million in accounts receivable (Securities Reports).

These various notes usually bear no interest. The distinction between short-term and long-term accounts receivable is usually based on the one-year rule rather than the normal operating cycle. Installment sales are also based on the one-year rule, although the normal operating cycle would be better practice.

A peculiar practice with regard to discount usually brings companies to increase their intercompany credit. Bank policy demands that receivables and payables be balanced. A bank may point out that accounts payable are too small compared with accounts receivable and therefore that a loan will be extended only after the borrower has sufficiently utilized financing through accounts payable.

Most companies in Japan adopt the policy of classifying loans (*kari-ire-kin*) as short-term if the original repayment term is within one year and as long-term if this term is more than one year. Current maturity of long-term loans is shown as such in current liabilities. Short-term loans (*tanki kari-ire-kin*) are usually for three months; although they are renewable almost automatically, they are always treated as short-term. They are supposedly given as working capital (*unten shikin*) but are used for long-term investment as well. Three main advantages are thereby sought: (1) short-term loans carry a lower interest rate than long-term loans, (2) they are renewable (and thus require no repayment), whereas long-term loans are repayable in monthly installments, and (3) collateral requirements are less stringent than for long-term loans. There is no way to distinguish which are long and which are short except by tracing the history of each individual loan. (This presents a problem when financial statements are prepared for international purposes. The current solution is to state in a footnote that in the case of the reporting entity, the banks have, for years, never refused renewal of a short-term loan.)

As explained earlier, many companies rely largely on outside sources, mainly banks, to finance their investment in capital equipment. As a result, long-term debt (*chōki fusai*) assumes 19.6% of total liabilities and shareholders' equity in the larger companies. Of total borrowing, approximately 70% comes from banks and 10% from governmental organizations; the remaining 20% comes from other sources, such as insurance companies. Recently, bonds have become common, but they account for only 16.6% of total liabilities and shareholders' equity. Long-term debt is generally secured by mortgage on property. A fairly common Japanese practice is *kōjō zaidan teitō*, an aggregate mortgage on all facilities of a given factory or plant based on going-concern value. Any facilities acquired later will be added to the list and automatically included in the aggregate mortgage.

As of March 31, 1986 and 1987, Nippon Steel had issued bonds to the amount of ¥270 billion and ¥244 billion, and its long-term loans amounted to ¥656 billion and ¥706 billion, respectively.

The debt position of the corporation is, of course, also reflected in "cash" (*genkin-yokin*) mainly through the compensating balances (*kō-soku yokin*). Banks request most companies financed by notes discount and (later) bank loans to retain a certain percentage of the loan (including notes discount) as deposit. (Because the Ministry of Finance objects to this practice, it is customary to deny it even in writing, although it is actually applied.) As a result, relatively large amounts are carried in bank accounts, mostly as time deposits. They may be regarded as "compensating balance," even though in practice they are merely shown as "cash" in the current assets. Bank deposits maturing after more than one year are shown as investment. Restricted cash is almost never reported as such, not even if it is related to a government contract.

Current Ratio

A commonly accepted indicator of corporate health is the current ratio—the ratio of current assets to current liabilities: the higher the ratio, the healthier the company. Whereas in Western companies a normal current ratio would be 2 : 1 or 3 : 1, in Japan the norm is 1 : 1, and Japanese banks are usually willing to provide long-term loans in order to maintain this ratio. In other words, banks grant short-term loans as long as the 100% ratio is maintained; should the current ratio fall below 100%, say to 90%, the banks will supply the difference of 10% as a long-term loan and thus restore the 1 : 1 ratio.

Foreigners who read a typical Japanese balance sheet get the impression that cash is overstated by the amount of compensating balance in the banks and that notes discounted as well as accounts and notes receivable could have been substantially reduced if cash payments were made immediately after sales accrued. Accounts and notes payable also could have been substantially reduced if cash were available for immediate payment. It is true that large amounts of compensating balance and receivables and payables would disappear from the balance sheet, while maintaining the current ratio of 1 : 1 with the day-to-day assistance of the banks. However, in Japan, it is a long-standing business custom, apparently not about to change, not to pay cash immediately upon receipt of an invoice.

Accounts and notes receivable as well as inventories are financed by accounts and notes payable and bank loans. By extending the maturity of notes payable, some companies finance inventories until they are converted, after being sold, to notes receivable. Accounts and notes payable are further used for the purchase of fixed assets until long-term loans for such purchase are granted by the banks.

Inventories (*tana-oroshi shisan*) are a tricky matter in Japanese accounting, because, given the inflexibility of lifetime employment, even in times of business downturn production continues and inventories rapidly accumulate. On balance sheets inventories are stated at cost. Obsolete and unsalable inventories are rarely recorded at their net realizable value on a timely basis. Write-down to market value is required only when the market price is significantly lower than cost and there is no expectation for recovery of the market price. It is, therefore, understood that in normal times no write-down is required, and few companies recognize losses from obsolescence and such. These losses are deferred until the inventory in question is actually disposed of.

On the current liabilities side, accrued liabilities (*miharai hiyō*) are generally recognized. However, tax regulations stipulate the allowed limit for accrual of certain expense items (accrued employee bonus) or stipulate conditions under which such accrual is allowed (accrued commission or rebate payable). The tendency has been for Japanese companies to accrue expenses only to the extent allowable for tax purposes; this often leads to insufficient accrual for financial reporting purposes of such expenses as: employee seasonal allowances (bonus), employee retirement benefits, accrued commission, accrued sales returns, rebate and discounts, estimated loss on guarantee (lawsuit), and estimated loss on loss contracts.

Investment in Securities

In Japan, a company is usually persuaded by banks, securities companies, and customers to buy and hold other companies' shares in order to assure a stable business relationship. Large companies, therefore, carry large amounts of investment securities (*tōshi yūka shōken*). On average, investment securities would probably amount to 10% of total assets.

On May 20, 1985, and November 20, 1986, Matsushita Electric Industrial Co. carried investment securities to the amount of ¥581 billion, 28% of its total assets, and ¥639 billion, the same percentage of its total assets, respectively. On March 31, 1986, Nissan Motor carried an amount of ¥118 billion in investment securities, 4.7% of its total assets.

These securities are generally carried at cost. Although the market price of securities traded on the stock market has increased considerably, such increment is seldom reflected in the carrying value of investments. This practice may amount to substantial hidden assets. Many companies sell a portion of such securities in bad years to generate profit and meet dividend payment or cover loss. It also happens that a company will sell securities at a profit to an affiliate when it needs such profit to report the level of earnings that the company must show in order to maintain its prestige. The effect of such a transaction is that securities are revalued at current market price with a corresponding revaluation recognized as income, although Japanese accounting principles require investments to be stated at cost. This practice prevails on the grounds that such buy-and-sell transactions have been lawfully consummated.

As of September 30, 1986, Japan's five leading banks held a summarized unrealized capital gain related to investment securities as follows:

	(billion yen)
Daiichi Kangyo Bank	2,746
Mitsubishi Bank	2,696
Fuji Bank	2,335
Sumitomo Bank	2,299
Sanwa Bank	2,118

(*Nihon Keizai Shinbun*, March 2, 1987)

Corporations other than banking and financial institutions account for investment securities as current assets or long-term assets according to negotiability and liquidity. Under Japanese accounting practices, the gain on sale of marketable securities shown on current assets is generally included in nonoperating income. To the contrary, the gain on sale of investment securities shown as long-term assets is special income (*tokubetsu rieki*). When the economic situation is deteriorating, corporations tend to reclassify investment securities from long-term assets to current assets before sale, and such gain is included in ordinary profit (*keijō rieki*). Many executives are willing to maintain a stable level of ordinary profit for outside reporting purpose, and outside readers also have deeper concern with ordinary profit than with net income.

For the years ended March 31, 1986 and 1987, Nippon Steel Corporation recorded a gain on sale of securities of ¥13.6 billion and ¥99.7 billion, respectively, shown as nonoperating revenue. For the year ended March 31, 1987, it also reclassified ¥71,266 million of investment securities (noncurrent) as marketable securities (current assets section).

Corporations also carry investments in subsidiaries and affiliated companies. In Japan, investments in subsidiaries and affiliated companies (*kankei-gaisha tōshi*) are generally stated at cost, except for a certain write-off that is made when the investee has suffered substantial losses deemed to be of a permanent nature. The equity method is applied to consolidated financial statements, namely the investor initially records at cost an investment in the stock of an investee, then adjusts the carrying amount of the investment in order to recognize the investor's share in the earnings or losses of the investee after the date of acquisition. The equity method is, however, not permitted in the preparation of parent-only financial statements.

Shareholders' Equity

In Japan, practically all shares are common stock; preferred stock is rare. The structure of capital accounts in a Japanese balance sheet is simple compared to that in Western countries, where a variety of shares are used.

Treasury Stock

The Commercial Code (Art. 210) permits treasury stock (*jiko-kabushiki*) in only four cases, none of which allows for it to be paid out of earned surplus.

1. Acquisition for reduction of capital stock
2. Acquisition through merger or purchase of an entire business
3. Acquisition when necessary for the execution of corporate right
4. Acquisition when a shareholder exercises his right of appraising management policies, whereby he is, for example, opposed to the transfer of all or part of the business of the company or the takeover bid of another business

The 1981 amendment added a fifth exception: acquisition in pledge transaction at maximum 5% of total shares. Three other exceptions may be noted in practice: gratis acquisition; a trust company's acquisition of its own shares as its own trustee; and acquisition by a brokerage company of its own shares on behalf of its customer.

The 1950 revision of the Commercial Code (Art. 206) allowed the establishment of a registrar (*tōroku kikan*) for all share certificates to be issued and for reserve share certificates (*yobi kabu-ken*). The 1981 amendment of the Commercial Code explicitly prohibited the acquisition of stock in the parent company by its subsidiaries, with certain limited exceptions (Arts. 211–212). A subsidiary holding stock of its parent company on October 1, 1982, was required to sell it within a reasonable period.

For accounting purposes, treasury stock as well as other marketable securities are shown separately in the current assets section, and the gain on sale of these shares is included in income and taxed as income.

As of November 20, 1985 and 1986, Matsushita Electric Industrial Co., Ltd., had ¥12 million (10,806 shares) and ¥44 million (54,165 shares) of treasury stock, respectively. As of March 31, 1986 and 1987, Hitachi Ltd. had ¥50 million (64,757 shares) and ¥17 million (19,471 shares) of treasury stock, respectively.

Stated Capital

Before the 1981 amendment, the amount of stated capital (*shihon-kin*) had to be in agreement with the par value multiplied by issued shares of common stock. After the amendment, at the time of issuance of common stock it was required that at least one-half of the issued amount of shares be shown as common stock. Accordingly, the relationship between amount of common stock and par value has disappeared.

Additional Paid-in Capital

Until around 1970, the item "capital in excess of par value" (*shihon junbi-kin*) was rare and minor in the balance sheet. As a result of the current practice of issuing stock at market price, some companies now carry a considerable amount of capital in excess of par value.

As of October 31, 1986, Sony carried capital in excess of par value of ¥91,694 million, while its capital stock was only ¥11,974 million. As of September 30, 1986, Pioneer carried capital in excess of par value of ¥47,902 million, while its capital stock was only ¥15,778 million.

Because dividends have been customarily determined at some standard percentage of par value of common stock (usually 10% to 15%), return on investment is not sufficient for shareholders who purchase or subscribe at market price. There has been much argument about how the large amount of capital in excess of par value should be treated. One way has been to make a free distribution of shares (such free distribution is, of course, tax free). In accounting for free distribution, Japanese companies are bound by the Commercial Code (Art. 293.3), which requires transfer, at par value of stock issued, from capital in excess of par value to capital stock.

In 1981, a significant revision was made to the Commercial Code in regard to the treatment of additional paid-in capital in the case of issuance of stock in excess of par value. Prior to the effective date of October 1, 1982, when issuing par value stock, an amount equal to the total par value of the stock issued had to be credited to capital stock, and the amount in excess of par value was credited to capital reserve. When issuing non-par value, the total issue had, in principle, to be credited to capital stock, provided, however, that up to one-fourth of the issue price need not thus be credited. Since October 1, 1982, the total amount of the issue price of new stock, whether par or non-par, is, in principle, credited to capital stock. However, upon resolution of the Board of Directors, an amount not exceeding one-half of the issue price may be credited to additional paid-in capital (capital surplus). In the case where half of the issue price of par-value stock is less than its par value, or half of the issue price of non-par-value stock at the time of incorporation is less than ¥50,000, at least the amount equal to the par value or ¥50,000 shall be credited to common stock. Because most corporate executives have customarily determined dividends at some standard percentage of par value of common stock, they believed that the 1981 Commercial Code amendment would result in a heavy burden on dividend. Many corporations had planned, before this amendment, to issue stock at market price.

The Commercial Code (Art. 293.2) permits stock dividend upon approval by shareholders. In such cases, shareholders receive stock newly issued as dividend in lieu of cash dividend. Similar to free distribution, stock dividend is accounted for by transferring, at par value of stock issued, from retained earnings (not from capital in excess of par value) to capital stock. The practice is controversial when reporting for international purposes, at least in the United States.

Under the postwar Assets Revaluation Law, companies were permitted in 1951, 1952, and 1954 to revalue upward their older assets to reflect the effects of immediate postwar inflation; the amount of such increases was to be carried as a revaluation surplus account (*sai-hyōka tsumitate-kin*). This revaluation was subsequently reduced by the amounts of revaluation taxes paid, loss on sales of revalued properties, and transfers to common stock account in connection with the free distribution of par value and subscription offerings (made at a price less than the par value of common stock for the excess of par value over the issue price). Pursuant to the terms of the law, the balance of revaluation surplus existing at the end of the accounting period immediately preceding the period that included March 31, 1973, was deemed transferred to capital surplus.

Reserves

Under the Japanese Commercial Code, companies are required to appropriate as legal reserve (*rieki junbi-kin*) portions of retained earnings in amounts equal to at least 10% of cash dividends paid until the reserve equals 25% of the amount of stated capital. The legal reserve is not available for dividends but may be used to capitalize (by resolution of the board of directors) or to reduce a deficit (by resolution of the share-holders' meeting). Japanese companies may also have voluntary reserves (*nin-itsumitate-kin*) appropriated for various purposes including general contingency. Voluntary reserves are regarded merely as a means to retain part of the earnings and are available for dividends upon approval by shareholders.

Legal and voluntary reserves are listed in the capital accounts. In addition, special reserves that are allowed under the Special Taxation Measures Law are classified in the capital accounts. (Before the 1981 amendment, such reserves had been classified in the liability section). Special reserves are, in essence, deferral of taxes to the succeeding years: some portion is retained earnings and the remaining portion is deferred taxes. However, income tax allocation is not applied under Japanese accounting principles: the capital accounts in the balance sheet include both after-tax retained earnings and retained earnings to be taxed later. Nonapplication of income tax allocation will, therefore, mislead the reader of the financial statements.

At March 31, 1987, Takeda Chemical Industries Ltd. (Takeda Yakuhin) and Toshiba Corporation reported voluntary reserves as follows (million yen):

Takeda Yakuhin

Retirement benefits	5,000
Reserve for dividends	11,000
Research and development	2,400
Expansion of facilities	1,054
Export promotion	438
Overseas investment losses	95
Special depreciation	187
Deferred gains on sales of fixed assets	728
No specified purpose	151,500

Toshiba Corporation

Research funds	3,760
Interim dividends	12,000
Price fluctuation	10
Deferred gains on sales of fixed assets	5,248
No specified purpose	218,055

(Securities Reports)

Consolidation

When, in the early 1960s, Japanese companies appeared on international capital markets with depositary receipts (American Depositary Receipts and European Depositary Receipts) and bonds, it became clear that Japanese accounting practices were not acceptable overseas. Consolidated financial statements (*renketsu zaimu-shohyō*) had to be presented at most foreign exchanges and for international reporting. By 1973, some 60 Japanese corporations had produced consolidated financial statements in order to publicly offer their securities abroad. The Japanese stock exchanges requested each of these companies to submit (in English) copies of these statements. In 1972, for the first time in the history of Japan's stock market, several foreign companies considered raising equity capital in Japan and quotation on the Tokyo Stock Exchange. Their registration statement had to be filed, as it would for Japanese companies, according to the Securities Exchange Law. In May 1973, the Ministry of Finance and the Tokyo Stock Exchange announced jointly that the Exchange would accept application for listing by foreign companies only if applicants agreed to disclose their financial position and results of operations in the form of parent-only financial statements. It was also made clear that consolidated statements could not be accepted then but would be made acceptable in the near future.

By the end of 1973, six foreign companies had applied for and obtained listing on the Tokyo Stock Exchange. Apparently, the lack of substantial subsidiaries or of wide diversification in business allowed them to comply with Japanese requirements. However, a number of multinational corporations raised strong objections and were discouraged from pursuing listing. Confronted with these objections as well as criticism by Japanese accountants, the Ministry of Finance issued an ordinance effective in August 1974, stating that all companies seeking listing on the stock exchanges could file financial statements in accordance with listing practices in the country of origin.

Consolidation raised several problems, one of which concerned the closing date. According to the Commercial Code (Art. 234), companies must close accounts at least once a year. Closing is required, however, whenever dividends are paid. Before 1974 large publicly held companies had usually paid dividends twice a year and thus closed their accounts every six months. The introduction in 1974 of independent audit requirements fundamentally changed the practice. Shareholder registers were closed during the three months allowed for this audit. If the six-month term were to be maintained, these registers would thus remain closed half of the year. Thus, most companies switched to the one-year accounting term.

Adoption of the one-year period raised yet another problem. Most companies were expected to select March as year-end, because the fiscal year adopted by government institutions ends in March. The demand for funds to pay dividends, taxes, and other settlements would then be abnormally heavy in June and July, dangerously straining the cash position of the banks. Trust banks and other agencies that handle stock-title transfers would be swamped in March as new shareholders rushed to register to claim dividends. Nonetheless, most Japanese companies are quite nervous about the shareholders' meeting and prefer to hold it almost simultaneously.

Recently, some leading industrial companies have changed their accounting term to March as follows: Sony: from October 31, 1986, to March 31, 1987; Matsushita: from November 20, 1986, to March 31, 1987; Honda: from February 28, 1987, to September 30, 1987 (transitionally), and then to March 31, 1988.

Before 1983, neither equity method for 20% to 50% owned affiliates and unconsolidated subsidiaries nor criteria of significance in regard to net income had been made mandatory. From 1977 to 1983, if the company intended to transfer a portion of the shares of a subsidiary that had suffered a substantial loss and switch it to a 20% to 50% owned affiliate, it could choose not to reflect the financial position or results of operations of the investee in its own consolidated financial statements (*renketsu nogare*). Because the test of significant subsidiary had not been included in the criteria of net income, the users of the consolidated statements urged the Ministry of Finance to reconsider the regulation. Effective from the accounting year beginning on or after April 1, 1983, the equity method and the criteria of net income have been mandated, with the result that consolidation finally approximates the level of international reporting.

For example, in the automobile industry, the situation among major makers is as follows:

	Consolidated subsidiaries	Unconsolidated subsidiaries and affiliates (equity method)
Toyota Motor (6/30/86)	16	10
Nissan Motor (3/31/86)	41	28
Honda Motor (1/28/86)	119	190

Compared to its two rivals, Honda has aggressively promoted its overseas strategy for a long time and taken a positive stand on consolidating disclosures. Furthermore, Honda's shares have been listed on overseas stock exchanges (New York, London, and Paris).

The Commercial Code does not prohibit accrual of intercompany sales and profit, and dividend payout from intercompany profit. In an extreme case, a parent company can record, at balance-sheet date, sales to or purchases from its subsidiary without physical transfer of products, thus adjusting the profit of either parent or subsidiary.

Fuji Sashi Kogyo (maker) and Fuji Sashi Hanbai (sales company) had indulged in window dressing using intercompany transactions for several years until 1977. The amounts of overstatement were ¥33.4 billion and ¥9.6 billion, respectively (*Nihon Keizai Shinbun*, May 29, 1978).

Japanese executives generally consider it perfectly justifiable to equalize profit from year to year in order to maintain a steady dividend payment. In fact, they believe that a steady increase in profit should be reported at each closing of accounts (a universal feeling among business executives). The matter is complicated when accounts are closed every six months because it is felt they should not reflect seasonal fluctuations.

In 1985, more than 800 industrial companies listed on the Tokyo Stock Exchange provided consolidated financial statements (*Japan Economic Journal*, May 17, 1986). However, even though consolidated financial statements have become the norm, more attention is still paid to the unconsolidated statements. There are some compelling reasons for this.

In the United States, consolidated financial statements are regarded as primary statements. Accordingly, the disclosure of parent-only financial statements occurs in rare cases, when a certain portion of the funds or income of the subsidiaries are restricted in their transfer to the parent company. In Japan, to the contrary, parent-only statements still remain the primary statements under the Commercial Code and for income tax purposes, and consolidated statements are a supplement to parent-only statements under the Securities Exchange Law and regulations. Even though a company may suffer a deficit on the consolidation basis, it can pay dividends and must pay income tax on parent-only statements' recorded income.

With companies apparently belonging to a group, consolidated financial statements present more meaningful information than parent-only statements, but their usefulness is still limited.

At first glance, the Seibu Railway Company, Ltd., appears to promote Seibu department stores and Seiyu "superstores" along its major railway line and at its terminals. However, according to shareholders' ownership, the railway company has no relationship with the Seibu Department Stores, Ltd., and the Seiyu Stores, Ltd., both belonging to the Seibu Saison Group, a group composed of close to 100 companies. Seibu Railway is substantially owned by Kokudo Keikaku Co. (48.31%), which promotes hotel chains and recreation centers in Japan and overseas. This company is unlisted and has never disclosed consolidated statements. The only consolidated financial statements available are those of Seibu Railway as a parent company. On the other hand, Seibu Department Stores, Ltd., is also an unlisted company; it owns 16.7% of Seiyu Stores. Financial data, therefore, do not reveal the nature of the Seibu Group.

The same may be stated about the Tokyu Group. Tokyu Corp. (a railway company) has consistently disclosed consolidated statements, but the consolidated subsidiaries are limited to local transportation operations, hotel chains, and so forth. The following companies are generally regarded as members of the group, but because ownership by Tokyu Corp. is less than 50% they are not included in its consolidation: Tokyu Department Store (11.2% ownership), Tokyu Construction (11.2%), Tokyu Real Estate (15.3%), Tokyu Vehicles (18.1%) (*Kaisha Shiki-hō*, Spring 1987).

Consolidation by itself is not the ultimate development in financial reporting in a country where the dynamics of industrial grouping are what they are in Japan. There is, in fact, a spectrum of problems in financial reporting stretching between what could be considered two extreme cases, that of the general trading company and that of the so-called one-man company.

Japan's large trading companies are unique in terms of size, worldwide operations, diversification, and integration of product lines. Consolidation is not enough to provide truly meaningful statements. It would be necessary in addition, for financial statements of the parent and main subsidiaries to be presented individually as well as by line of business—a herculean task, indeed! And even if all these statements were prepared, who among the investors, especially among the general investing public, would have the time, the energy, or the expertise to read such statements?

The other end of the business spectrum to be affected by consolidation is the not unusual case of a representative director or officer (usually the founder or chief executive of a so-called one-man company) who holds in his own name a majority interest in another company with which his company has significant transactions. Article 265 of the Commercial Code requires such intercompany transactions to be approved by the board of directors, but in many cases the "strongman" has his own way. The problem is, then, when and how to combine these companies and still avoid the full disclosure required in the financial statements. Thus, the delay, in Japan, in regard to implementing consolidated financial statements is partly due to the large and extremely complex world that lies before or beyond consolidation.

15

STATEMENT OF INCOME & OTHER DOCUMENTATION

THE TWO BASIC LAWS regulating financial reporting, the Commercial Code and the Securities Exchange Law, express greatly differing business philosophies, even more so in the statement of income (*son-eki keisan-sho*) than in the balance sheet. The discrepancy between net income according to the Commercial Code and net income according to the Securities Exchange Law, for example, was finally eliminated as of October 1, 1974, when the version of net income set forth in the Commercial Code was adopted by the Securities Exchange Law. Income (*son-eki*) comprises revenue (*shū-eki*) and expenses (*hiyō*).

Revenue

The statement of income in Japanese companies usually begins with net sales. In most types of business in which delivery of merchandise or services is involved, the standard used in recognizing sales revenue is time of shipping. Where no such delivery takes place, for example in long-term construction contracts, revenue is recognized on completion or percentage of completion. (Because of the certainty of computed revenue and related costs as well as the advantage from the viewpoint of income tax deferral, Japanese companies tend to prefer to use completion as a basis rather than percentage of completion.) For companies that sell products on an installment basis, cash as well as the accrual basis are allowed in recognizing sales revenue and related costs; however, the former is preferred for reasons of certainty and tax deferral.

In determining cost of sales, both standard and estimated cost are allowed by tax regulations, provided that resultant cost variances are properly allocated. (Cost variances are computed and allocated between inventories and cost of sales in order to state year-end inventory and cost of sales for the period at actual cost.) Such allocation can be omitted if the amount of variance is less than 1% of total production costs for the applicable period. Duplicate cost is one reason why standard cost (which frequently differs by more than 1%) is not popular.

Generally, sales returns and discounts are deducted from gross sales but not recorded on the statement of income as a separate item. Such return and discount are recognized for accounting purposes when they are actually incurred, which is usually some time later than when sales are made. Theoretically, it is considered adequate to set up a reserve for future sales returns and discounts; this reserve would result in better matching between cost and related revenue. This theory is not generally implemented on the grounds that most sales returns and discounts recur at almost the same level if sales do not grow (if sales increase, there is a time lag and overstatement of profits due to understatement of sales returns and discounts), as well as on the grounds that estimation of future cost tends to be arbitrary. Furthermore, accrual is generally disallowed by the tax laws except (by certain fixed percentages) for specified businesses, such as companies manufacturing and selling medicines, cosmetics, or ready-made suits, or companies publishing books, magazines, or records, where products are returned more frequently than in other businesses.

Nonoperating revenue comprises interest and dividend income. Companies earn interest income on bank deposits and loans to others. As mentioned, they must maintain a certain deposit as compensating balance, although it is not stated as such. Because corporate financing depends largely on these bank loans, the compensating balance and its interest income represent large amounts.

For the years ending March 31, 1986 and 1987, Nippon Steel reported interest income of ¥35 and ¥27 billion and interest expense of ¥150 and ¥113 billion, respectively. For the same years, Nissan Motor Co., Ltd., reported ¥70 and ¥59 billion interest income, and ¥42 and ¥38 billion interest expense, respectively.

This interest income, like rent and other such transactions, is in some cases accounted for on a cash basis, a practice acceptable to tax authorities.

Holding shares of other companies, common among large corporations, achieves the important effect of stable shareholding. Thus, carrying substantial investment securities in turn creates substantial dividend income.

For the years ending March 31, 1986 and 1987, Nippon Steel reported ¥11 and ¥9 billion dividend income, respectively. Nissan Motor reported ¥30 and ¥17 billion, respectively.

Dividend income is recorded when it is received or declared (three months after closing at the paying company). All income arising from investment is recognized as dividend and treated as tax-free income (for domestic investment) after deducting interest expense incurred for loans allocated to investments (Corporation Tax Law, Art. 23). If stock dividend is received, it is recorded as dividend income at par received with a corresponding debit to investments.

Gain on sale of securities is frequently shown as nonoperating income, although gain on sale of investment securities (long-term investments) is, in principle, shown as special income. However, a not uncommon practice is to first reclassify investment securities to current assets and then to show them as sales so as to realize an ordinary profit. Thus, management achieves its strong desire to maintain a stable level of ordinary profit (*keijō rieki*). Readers of financial statements and press releases also express concern for the magnitude of ordinary profit rather than net profit.

Expenses

Tax laws and regulations set limits on the amount of deductible expenses (e.g., provision for doubtful accounts, depreciation, provision for employee bonus, retirement benefit). Most companies provide these expenses up to the tax-deductible limit. However, since the limits themselves do not necessarily provide an adequate basis for financial reporting, in specific cases reporting of tax deductible expenses may be considerably distorted.

Income Taxes (*hōjin-zei tō*)

Companies are subject to taxes based on income: corporation, inhabitants', and enterprise taxes. They account for the corporation and inhabitants' tax on an accrual basis. Some account for the enterprise tax on a cash basis, because such tax is deductible in the next period even though the amount payable at year-end has been determined; in this case, after-tax earnings will be distorted.

A reduction (approximately 10%) in the tax rate is applicable to earnings of the period that are paid out as dividends. Dividends received from domestic companies, minus a portion of interest accrued on borrowed funds, is not taxed twice. Some expense items (e.g., penalty tax, director's bonus) are not deductible for tax purposes. Profit on the sale of fixed assets is income subject to normal taxation. When fixed assets are acquired with proceeds from expropriation of old fixed assets, the new assets are stated at acquisition cost less deferred capital gain (or reserve for deferred capital gain), thus enabling deferred tax payment through reduced depreciation charges (except on land).

It is noteworthy that income tax allocation between accounting years is not practiced and that as of 1987 the matter had never been discussed by the Business Accounting Deliberation Board. Companies include many items in financial statements that, in the case of expenses (employee bonuses or retirement benefits provided in excess of the tax-deductible limit), are not currently deductible or in the case of income (installment sales), are not currently taxable. Financial statements reflect only those income taxes that are currently payable and fail to account for the timing differences of expense and income items in reporting those taxes.

Interest (*rishi*)

The interest rates that banks charge companies represent, in a sense, the credit standing of these companies. Banks classify companies according to their credit, and interest rates are determined accordingly. However, rates are also affected by the amount of bank deposits (the largest part of these deposits may be deemed compensating balance); interest rates decrease as bank deposits increase. The financial department of a large Japanese company usually calculates the effective interest rate after considering the interest income on deposits in each bank and negotiating interest rates with each bank.

Foreign investors consider the fact that Japanese companies carry a large amount of bank deposits, on the one hand, and a large amount of bank loans, on the other, a sign of inefficient financing. This practice is unavoidable for smaller companies, which do not have enough bargaining power with the banks. It may also be unavoidable, but to a much lesser degree, for large companies. In general, there is no meaningful alternative to the recourse to banks. Furthermore, because compensating balance requirements are unenforceable and thus informal, disclosure requirements become more difficult.

Because many corporations rely largely on bank loans for their financing, the interest expense constitutes a large portion of total expenses.

For the year ending March 31, 1986, Nippon Steel paid interest to the amount of ¥150 billion, approximately 5.6% of total sales. For the same period, Nissan Motor paid interest expense of ¥42 billion, approximately 1.1% of total sales.

Remuneration of Directors (*yaku-in hōshū*)

According to the Commercial Code, directors' regular remuneration must be determined either in the articles of incorporation or by the shareholders' meeting (Art. 269). Directors' remuneration is a tax-deductible expense, provided that the amount is set as prescribed in the code and that it is reasonable in view of services performed or compared to the amount of remuneration in other similar companies. But the treatment of directors' bonuses is very different. Although in the spirit of the Commercial Code, such a bonus is the director's share of profits, in postwar Japan it has come to be treated, like the bonus paid regular employees, as a standard component of the salary system. However, whereas employee bonuses are tax deductible as expense, directors' bonuses are not. The tendency is thus to increase monthly compensation and reduce the bonus. Finally, the retirement benefit for directors must be approved by the shareholders' meeting; it is usually determined individually upon actual retirement. Few companies provide a reserve; rather, the amount is charged to operations when paid. Tax laws would not allow such reserve, but the amount is deductible when paid, provided that it appears reasonable.

Remuneration of statutory auditors is treated in the same way as that of directors. The amount limit must be set either by the articles of incorporation or by the shareholders' meeting, and is determined separately from the renumeration of directors (Art. 279).

Entertainment Expenses (*kōsai-hi*)

Entertainment is a very colorful aspect of Japanese business. It is sometimes incorrectly assumed, because of the vogue of business entertainment, that all such expenses are deductible. Entertainment expenses must be supported by a vouchers or receipts that substantiate that they were incurred for business purposes. If such evidence is not available, an expense is not deductible for corporate income tax purposes. In some cases in which there is no evidence that payment was made for company purposes, the amount may be regarded as part of salary and included in the taxable income of the individual who incurred the expense. (Some entertainment places are willing to "sell" receipts!) For corporate directors unable to provide evidence of an expense the amount will be credited to their own bonus and therefore be taxed twice: it is not deductible for corporate purposes and is further taxed as individual income.

As a result of progressive tightening of the relevant tax regulation, none of the tax allowance on entertainment expenses is permitted for

TABLE 59.

Entertainment Expenses versus Corporation Income Tax
(1975–1985)

(billion yen)

Year	Entertainment Expenses (A)	Not Deductible (B)	B/A (percentage)
1975	2,031	592	29.1
1976	2,274	715	31.4
1977	2,409	830	34.5
1978	2,614	957	36.6
1979	2,906	1,090	37.5
1980	3,115	1,322	42.4
1981	3,306	1,401	42.4
1982	3,484	1,491	42.8
1983	3,523	1,793	50.9
1984	3,620	1,887	52.1
1985	3,850	2,026	52.6

SOURCE: National Tax Administration 1987: 16.

corporations whose capital stock is ¥100 million or more. Only small companies can enjoy the tax allowance, which is limited on two scores: the total amount for the year and the increase over the previous period. From the low level of 13.0% in 1965, the percentage of nondeductible entertainment expenses increased, between 1975 and 1985, from 29.1% to 52.6% (table 59). Progressive tightening of the relevant tax regulation notwithstanding, amounts spent keep increasing every year. Between 1975 and 1985, the total amount of entertainment expenses for all enterprises jumped from ¥2,031 billion to ¥3,850 billion (although per ¥1,000 of operating revenue, they dropped from ¥4.56 to ¥3.93). The rule appears to be the smaller the company, the higher its entertainment ratio per ¥1,000 operating revenues. When the capital is less than ¥10 million, the rate is ¥7.99 per thousand yen of sales, whereas it is only ¥2.11 in corporations with capital over one billion yen. But this rate varies widely among industries; in 1985, the largest spenders were construction (¥8.61), printing (¥8.33), and services (¥7.97) (National Tax Administration 1987: 17).

Donations (*kifu-kin*)

Donations as an item of operating expense requires explanation. Tax regulations for corporate donations (and, incidentally, also for individual donations) are definitely restrictive. Between 1975 and 1985, the aggregate total of corporate donations increased from ¥136 billion to ¥285 billion (National Tax Administration 1987: 16). Types of deductible donation are specified (i.e., donations to national or local government or donations to public welfare organizations designated by the Ministry of Finance and to be used for the promotion of science, education, and so forth) but are discouraged by the government, as they limit its power to allocate resources. Direct contributions by corporations (or individuals) to schools or for religious purposes are not deductible per se. Corporate donations are tax deductible up to half of the amount of 2.5% of profits plus 0.25% of capital.

Disposition of Retained Earnings

Three particular items disposed of from retained earnings are to be mentioned: dividends, directors' bonuses, and special reserves. In good years, the shareholders naturally demand higher dividends (usually specified as percentage of par value per annum). Management then presents two kinds of dividends: the normal dividend expected by shareholders and the "special" dividend rate or special anniversary payment, say an additional 5%, reflecting the current prosperous situation. In bad years, the special dividend is, of course, dropped, and only the normal dividend rate is maintained; if profit is not sufficient, general and/or specific reserves are added back to distributable earnings in order to pay out dividends at the normal rate. According to the Special Taxation Measures Law (1987), the dividend portion of taxable income is subject to a lower corporate income tax rate (32% as against 42%). Consequently, a substantial tax savings arises when dividends (cash or stock) are paid out of current profit. In several instances when this potential savings was brought to the attention of the management of international joint ventures, the Japanese directors to take advantage of it objected on the grounds that an "equalized" dividend rate should be maintained year after year.

In Japan, directors' bonuses are not determined by individual contracts between the company and each director. Individual amounts are not disclosed to shareholders, who appropriate the total amount to be distributed among directors, usually at the discretion of the company president, and to statutory auditors as a result of separate negotiations.

Since the year ending October 1, 1982, in line with the 1981 amendment of the Commercial Code, special reserves under the Special Taxation Measures Law are, in principle, to be provided by retained earnings appropriation. (Previously, such reserves had been provided as special expenses in the income statement and shown as a component of liabilities on the balance sheet.)

Supplementary Documentation

In the securities report required under the Securities Exchange Law for filing with the Ministry of Finance, supplementary documentation to be provided comprises (1) 14 supplementary schedules, which together with the balance sheet, the statement of income, and disposition of retained earnings, are covered by the independent auditor's opinion, and (2) additional information pertinent to the corporation and its operations on which, however, the external auditor is not expected to express an opinion. The company must also disclose the following:

1. *Capital stock*: Amount, changes, number of shares, number of shareholders, number of shares held by major shareholders, dividend, stock price, and volume of trading, biography of the directors, and shares held by each director.

2. *Workforce*: Number of employees, sex distribution, average age, average years of service, average pay, number of part-time employees, relations with the labor union.

3. *Outline of the business*: Description of type(s) of business conducted, types of product, sales by divisions and percentage of total sales, technological licensing agreements, important changes in business. (An amendment to the Regulations, in February 1987, added description of research and development activities.)

4. *Business operations*: Production capacity and actual level of operations, production performance, raw materials (purchases and price, amount put into production, and stock on hand), orders received and production planned, subcontractors and their contribution to production, sales performance by major products, sales prices of major products, sales channels, exports by principal export products and ratio of exports to total sales, countries to which exported.

5. *Production facilities*: Capital invested in production facilities and in other types of facilities, total area or floor space for each place of production and business center, machines and equipment by major segments of manufacturing, number of units and their capacities, expansion plan, amount of budget funded and expended, how the funds were raised, sale, disposal, and loss by accident of fixed assets.

6. *Principal assets, liabilities, revenues, and expenditures*:

Notes and trade accounts receivable: amounts by major customers or by line of business of major customers, schedule of maturities of notes, overdue accounts.

Breakdown of each inventory item, such as finished products, semifinished products, raw materials, work in process.

Notes and trade accounts payable: amounts by major suppliers or by line of business of suppliers, schedule of maturities of notes.

Short-term loans (liability): classification by purposes of capital investment and working funds, use of proceeds, terms of loans, loans secured, loans without interest, rate of interest where a lower rate is specially arranged.

Special profit and loss items involving large amounts.

7. *Cash flow*: Cash revenue and disbursement for each quarter, cash flow plan for the next six months.

It is clear from this lengthy enumeration (which omits certain insignificant items), that the information required is not only comprehensive but sometimes redundant, at the cost of a tremendous amount of time and labor. Some of the information involves trade secrets; many companies are legitimately reluctant to or simply cannot divulge it. Nonetheless, strict compliance is expected. The result is that information is more often than not filed pro forma; accurate information is covered up, if not falsified. According to Article 25 of the Securities Exchange Law, the company that wishes to withhold from public inspection some information relating to business secrets can apply to the Ministry of Finance for approval. Such special treatment is usually granted where secret business information relating to some "important" contract is involved, such as merger, transfer of part of the business, or technical license. The amount of disclosure is at the discretion of the administrative agency.

In the early 1970s, the requirement of supplementary documentation invited severe criticism from foreign companies wishing to sell securities in Japan or seeking quotation on Japanese stock exchanges. The required information may be difficult for Japanese companies to provide, it is even more impractical for larger foreign corporations to produce on a consolidated basis. The criticism had some effect. In March 1974, a special ruling waived the requirement of supplementary documentation for foreign corporations and accepted the "form, terminology, and method of presentation" of the home country. Meanwhile, Japanese companies must continue to comply in full and thus continue, willfully or unintentionally, to confuse the uninformed reader.

16

READING FINANCIAL STATEMENTS

SLOWER ECONOMIC GROWTH following the 1973 oil shock, the accompanying restructuring of industry, and the "liberalization" of the capital markets have all contributed to bring Japanese financial reporting closer to the generally accepted accounting principles in Western economies. Nonetheless, "true and fair" presentation of accounts is also determined by the business environment, in Japan no less than elsewhere. Earlier in this volume, the attention of the foreign reader of Japanese financial statements has been drawn to local peculiarities that are not readily translated into figures and even less so into English! In statements to be used abroad, many of these peculiarities should be pointed out in the notes; however, this is not always done when statements are merely translated into English for informational purposes. Reading Japanese financial statements appears to be an "art" that requires more than know!-edge of the techniques of corporate accounting!

Securities Analysis

Institutional factors in Japan, such as stock market behavior and the role assigned to securities companies (a postwar innovation), are apparent deterrents to proper securities analysis. What analysis there is suffers from two major defects, one concerning the analysts, the other the data.

Professionalism is sorely missing among so-called analysts. Analysis is mostly conducted by employees in the research department of financial institutions, in particular securities companies. More often than not, these people have been transferred from sales, accounting, or other departments to the research department for perhaps a two- or three-year assignment. Very few have been trained to be or will become professional securities analysts. The same is true of the underwriting department of some of the securities companies and of the stock exchanges as well.

In connection with the bankruptcy of Nippon Netsugaku (May 1974), the following statement by an executive of the underwriter was reported in the daily press: "Our scrutiny of Nippon Netsugaku's financial position was based primarily on a financial report endorsed by two individual CPAs. Since the latest report available to us covers the air conditioner maker's business performance during a limited period of last year, it was very difficult to discover the company's actual financial condition" (*Mainichi Daily News*, June 18, 1974). At best, this was a very lame defense. The report in question was available in mid-March, the underwriter (and the stock exchange) could have requested an additional report from the auditors on the January–March interval and could have looked for the previous reports on file.

The shortcoming of expertise is little alleviated by the extensive use of computerized data, because there is often a major problem with the data itself. Quality varies depending upon the quality of company accountants, the system of internal control, the competence and professional attitude of independent auditors, and the adequacy of accounting principles followed.

Another problem with relying on Japanese securities analysis is that the method of evaluation is not necessarily similar to Western practice. Profit before income tax is generally used as an auxiliary indicator of share price in Japan. However, it is generally assumed that stock market price is determined not by earnings per share but by the semiannual dividend rate and, especially, popularity or speculation. This practice is illogical in many respects. Thus, if a growth company does not pay dividends in Japan, the share price will be depressed, whereas in the United States, even if dividends are not paid, stock price will continue to rise. In the traditional Japanese environment, fair calculation of after-tax profit is not really expected.

Commercial inquiry agencies (*kōshinjo*) are frequently used for credit investigation. There are fewer than ten such agencies in Japan, and their service is limited to reports based on information obtained by direct inquiry at the company being investigated. Indirect sources (banks, customers) are seldom consulted. Moreover, the financial information forwarded to clients is never checked by professional accountants.

Banks tend to provide more reliable information than *kōshinjo*. Inquiries made at a bank on securities analysis or other financial information will not be replied to in any formal written report, but such information will be given to familiar acquaintances as a private verbal communiqué. The analysis made by bank personnel is more reliable because of the sources the bank has at hand and their position in an industrial grouping. The main bank, in particular, obtains more detailed financial information from a borrowing company than a *kōshinjo* is able to research. Because banks risk outstanding loans, they are more up to date on certain key information, even though they rely mostly on personal relationship with and confidence in the borrower rather than on financial information. Therefore, bank officers frequently visit executives of client companies to learn about their business.

This rather dismal picture of securities analysis and credit investigation in Japan is the result of historical circumstances. "Prewar securities regulation was a European system grafted onto traditional Japanese practices. Postwar legislation began as a carbon copy of the U.S. securities acts. Subsequent amendments have represented, in a sense, a reaction to achieve better harmony with Japanese society" (Tatsuta 1970: 111).

In all fairness, it must be stated that the frequency and depth of legal amendments is steadily increasing. Progress is taking place simultaneously on two levels: the professional outlook of all concerned with financial data is being strengthened, and the quality of data is being improved. Last but not least, the environment has been changed drastically by the emergence of Tokyo as an international capital market and the inflow of foreign expertise.

The Japanese Reader

Three fundamental characteristics appear to distinguish the Japanese reader from his counterpart in the West: he is neither an outsider, nor an individual, nor particularly concerned about the short term. The Western reader of financial statements *is* essentially an outsider and an individual looking for short-term results.

Historically, much of the progress in accounting and financial reporting in the West has been intended to protect the investing public. These improvements have followed the expansion of the stock markets and subsequent requests by regulatory bodies for issuing companies to give a "fair presentation" (U.S. terminology) or a "true and fair view" (U.K. terminology) of financial position and performance. Fairness is thus a criterion imposed on the reporter from the outside, for the assumed purpose, simply stated, of allowing the reportee to ascertain the basis and measurement of his share in current operational results. The individual rather than the institutional reportee is the standard.

In contrast, the Japanese reportee is assumed to be an insider and an institution looking for long-term results. Prewar Japan did not care much about the investing public, because most stocks were controlled by the *zaibatsu*. In postwar Japan, even though former *zaibatsu* shares were initially distributed among the public, institutional investors, who provided the corporate debt, soon dominated the market. The need for publicly oriented reporting has, thus, largely been lost again; institutions buy and hold shares as a mere modification of their creditor position.

Can it be said, then, that "fairness" is an ingredient not found in Japanese financial statements? Can fairness be reconciled with subjectivity? Or, more specifically, how does one be fair to an insider?

If stock market demands are strong incentives for progress in financial reporting, predominance of the par-value concept has for many years been a clever device to keep outside investors at bay. When at last, in the 1970s, public offering became common, the practice of stable shareholding remained determined by subjective considerations, not by objective financial statements. More recently, Japanese corporations raising capital abroad and foreign corporations raising capital in Japan have provided the needed incentive for better reporting. More internationally comparable financial information is definitely wanted, particularly by the Ministry of Finance.

The foreign investor requesting fairness would be mistaken, however, to expect it on his own terms. Fairness does not necessarily require changing an existing relationship. The standard of fairness could well be fairness to a commitment, not fairness to an abstraction. In Japanese eyes, the investing public is an abstraction, the industrial structure of Japan a commitment. The internationalization of this structure demands constant development in financial reporting.

In the mid-1960s, corporate financial reporting for domestic purposes started to be scrutinized and questioned. Currently many changes are resulting from raising capital abroad and developing Tokyo as an international capital market. The Ministry of Finance has provided much-needed guidance, pushing the internationalization of financial reporting as well. Somewhat to the dismay of foreign-based accounting partnerships, the Ministry has offered strong support to Japanese audit corporations, although there is no prospect yet for a rapid increase in the number of certified public accountants. As a result of the mergers of the larger accounting firms, there is now talk of the Japanese "Big Four" approaching the level of the U.S. Big Eight. The large accounting firms are cooperating with the Ministry of Justice on further revisions of the Commercial Code. At the official as well as the private level, it is expected that the developments witnessed in the financial markets will have a deep impact on the Japanese style of business, to be reflected both in financing and in financial reporting.

In the eyes of the Japanese executive, however, the order of priorities does not favor financial reporting; market share, technological progress, and human relations within the company are more important. But these business executives, so sensitive to domestic interdependence, are also undergoing the traumatic experience of international interdependence, which acts as an impetus for change. An often quoted slogan since the 1970s has been *kokusaika*, internationalization. Looking over the shoulder of the domestic reader of financial statements is an increasing number of foreign readers as well. Internationalization is a two-way proposition: the reporting entity must take into account the viewpoint of the foreign reader, but the foreign reader must also adjust his sight to the environment of the reporting entity.

Hidden Assets and Liabilities

Land, buildings, and plant and equipment are all items of financial reporting in which the gap between book and current values widens annually. Only once, between 1950 and 1954, were asset revaluations allowed. In the 1960s, Japanese corporations complained that the tax-free depreciation funds they can set aside within statutory limits were too small to replace outstanding assets. Following the 1973 oil shock, prices in both consumer and industrial goods exploded. In May 1978, the Ministry of Finance instructed the Business Accounting Deliberation Board to study the disclosure of information on the effect of changing prices. An opinion was issued in May 1980, but meanwhile prices had stabilized. The problem of disclosure was shelved.

Land

Japan has traditionally attached great value to land, because only 16% of its total land is arable.

> An estimate made by the Government's Economic Planning Agency at the end of 1983 shows that land accounts for as much as 57% (¥941 trillion) of Japan's entire national wealth totaling ¥1,639 trillion. The comparable figures for the United States and France stand at 32% and 10% respectively. Moreover, the total price of all land in Japan easily exceeds that of [the] U.S. (*Japan Economic Journal* 1987, May 23: 8)

Companies also value land highly—but not in their financial reporting! The principle is that land (as well as buildings and investment) is carried at historical cost from year to year, and accrual from its sale is reported as windfall profit.

Already in 1974, an estimate covering the 1,375 companies listed on the Tokyo Stock Exchange contended that these firms owned land worth four times the national budget. The book value totaled over ¥4 trillion, only one-seventeenth of the market value. If this added value were recorded, the value of net assets per share (at ¥50 par) would increase from the 1974 average of ¥124 to ¥535. The same study further analyzed 1,286 of the listed companies (excluding financial institutions and insurance companies). If the added value of land were recorded, it would increase the ratio of owned capital to total liabilities and net worth from 16.04% to 48.10% (Wakō 1974: 10–15).

Lately, the attention of the investing public has been attracted by corporations' "latent assets" (*fukumi shisan*), namely, land and equity holdings that are recorded at acquisition cost and, therefore, highly undervalued. Latent assets are part and parcel of "inside" information about these companies. Foreign securities houses have picked up the matter and conducted detailed and comprehensive computer analyses on companies with latent assets (e.g., Vickers da Costa 1986). The result has been that such assets became one of the main "themes" during 1986, with stocks of real estate, railroad, warehouse, and paper manufacturing companies experiencing a sharp increase.

> Japan's stock trade press is ignoring p/e ratios because earnings or net profits disregard the net worth or asset-backing of many companies. Thus, investors are searching out companies with "latent assets," such as land and portfolio holdings, which appear on the balance-sheet at their purchase price or par value. . . . Net assets per share according to the balance-sheets of Japan's top city banks in 1984 ranged from ¥250–280, yet if latent assets were added, the average would have exceeded ¥1,000. (Roscoe 1986: 111)

Buildings

In Japanese accounts, the term "buildings" covers not only plant and office buildings, but also a large number of others, such as employee housing, dormitories, and resort facilities. These buildings are leased at a nominal rent and justified on the basis that they facilitate employee transfer from one location to another and represent a substantial fringe benefit. The practice is common among large corporations, but outside the reach of smaller ones.

In Japan, if a person or a corporation leases land in order to construct a building and makes a lump-sum payment (*kenri-kin*), a leasehold right (*shakuchi-ken*) is recognized as an intangible asset. If subsequently the market value of this land increases, the value of the leasehold right is proportionately increased. However, such appreciation is not realized nor recognized until the building is removed or the land returned to the lessor. Generally speaking, depending on the location, the value of the leasehold right is 70% (maximum 90%) of the market value of the land, assuming that there is no occupancy.

Investment Securities

Another reporting item that is likely to contain hidden assets (to be realized when sold) is investment securities. It was mentioned earlier that large companies often hold substantial amounts of such securities, carried mostly at cost but sometimes at lower than cost or, if the securities are traded on the exchange, at lower than market. In most cases, these securities were purchased several years back and added to considerably by subscription to subsequent capital increases at par value.

As of November 20, 1985 and 1986, Matsushita Electric Industrial Co., Ltd., had marketable (current) and investment securities for a total carrying value of ¥765,842 million and ¥828,366 million, of which the aggregate market value on a consolidated basis was ¥1,159,901 million and ¥1,373,515 million, respectively.

The investment account can also affect "true and fair" presentation in another way. Although both the Commercial Code and Japanese accounting principles require devaluing securities if the invested company is in a loss position and recovery is considered difficult, the precept is rarely applied. Hence, investments in profitable subsidiaries and affiliated companies are stated at cost (which is lower than the underlying value), and, conversely, in case of loss operations, the losses tend to be overlooked.

The Sanko Steamship Co., Ltd., applied for corporate reorganization procedures in August 1985. According to its Securities Report and Consolidated Financial Statements for the year ended on March 31, 1985, the Company had investments in subsidiaries and affiliates (mostly paper companies) of ¥15,752 million, net, of investment loss allowance, and accumulated deficit of ¥162,489 million on parent-only financial statements basis. On a consolidated basis, the Company had an accumulated deficit of ¥212,004 million.

Hidden liabilities, may also result from some of the accounting practices described earlier, if not from outright malpractice.

Employee Retirement Benefits

Employee retirement benefits are not fully accrued because of the limit on the tax-deductible amount. The unaccrued balance is thus a hidden liability. However, it is never questioned, not even by regulatory authorities. Retirement benefits should be accrued every year-end and also when special benefits, payable upon layoff, are determined. The proper accounting of this liability is especially meaningful in bad years, when companies attempt what has come to be called the "Japanese-style layoff," in which the employer sets a time limit for voluntary retirement with premium benefits. Employee retirement benefits should be accrued based on sound estimates; otherwise a hidden liability arises.

According to their Securities Reports for the years ending March 31, 1986 and 1987, respectively, Hitachi recorded employee retirement benefits of ¥168,420 million and ¥186,534 million on a 100% basis for the requirement at year end, whereas Toshiba recorded ¥52,414 million and ¥57,358 million on the basis of 50% of the amount if all employees terminated voluntarily their employment at year end.

Guarantee of Loans

Corporate financing is very heavily dependent upon bank loans; however, the financial position of subsidiaries is usually not sound enough for independent borrowing. In such cases, banks will request the parent company's guarantee on a loan; the amount of loan is determined by negotiation between the banks and the parent. Japanese accounting principles require—with little success—disclosure of such guarantees in the financial statements of the guarantor, but they do not require it of the debtor. The reader of financial statements alone would find the subsidiary company in poor financial position still enjoying large bank loans. The guarantee constitutes a hidden liability, if adequate allowance is not provided. The practice traces back to weakness in accounting as well as in auditing.

In December 1976, Ataka filed an amended Securities Report to include the guarantee liabilities for loans to Ataka America. It had guaranteed liabilities of ¥257,375 million, including ¥136,700 million to the New Foundland Refining Co. (*Nihon Keizai Shinbun*, December 10, 1976).

As of March 31, 1979, the Taiko Sogo Bank had not disclosed the guarantee liabilities of ¥76,833 million, most of which had been loans to family corporations of the owner of the bank and had become doubtful accounts. Faced with this problem, the Ministry of Finance supported the reconstruction of the bank (*Nihon Keizai Shinbun*, September 29, 1979).

Peculiar Practices

Some of the major items of financial statements, may be worth a second look.

Accounts Payable

It has been the general practice to settle payments for purchases of goods and services, or liabilities incurred, only once a month. This does not mean, however, that payment is made in the same month that purchase is made; often it is made only two or three months later. Because tax examiners often argue about payables not supported by invoices, the tendency is to understate them.

Notes Payable

Another peculiar custom in Japan is to issue promissory notes to raise money. A company often requests a customer or vendor with whom it has a continuous business relationship to exchange promissory notes of the same amount and nearly the same due date. This note is taken to the bank for discount, as if it were a trade note receivable. Cash obtained from the bank may be recorded as a result of sales; the note issued is not recorded.

Notes Receivable Discounted

Notes receivable discounted by a bank with recourse also constitute hidden liabilities if the reserve for bad debts is not enough to cover such loss.

Allowances for Bad Debts, Returns, and Rebates

Especially in installment sales or long-term receivables, it is not unusual for allowances for bad debts, sales returns, product warranty, and rebates not to cover possible future losses or expenses.

Goodwill

Under the Commercial Code and income tax regulations, goodwill may be written off when purchased, or it may be amortized at least equally within five years. When the company's profit is not sufficient, there is a tendency to treat goodwill and deferred charges as assets. When profit is considered sufficient, goodwill and deferred charges will be written off when purchased or incurred. (Under U.S. accounting principles and practices, goodwill is amortized over 40 years.)

The Sumitomo Bank wrote off goodwill of an amount of ¥105 billion incurred with respect to the merger with Heiwa Sogo Bank on October 1, 1986 (*Nihon Keizai Shinbun*, May 20, 1987).

Statement of Assets

Assets overstated as deferred may be questioned. Such assets may actually be expenses incurred in the past in expectation of future revenue, such as new product development cost related to a project research and development program or preoperating expenses incurred before new business revenue comes in; they are not tangible assets to be matched against past costs. There is a tendency to treat such expenses as deferred assets rather than expenses when the company's profit is not sufficient, in fact using them as another means of profit equalization.

Transactions with Related Companies

Another particularly common practice concerns sale and purchase of capital assets between related companies. As described earlier, many Japanese companies carry large amounts of hidden value in their capital assets, especially land and investment securities. Their carrying value is normally kept well below their fair value. As accounting principles preclude upward revaluation, profits are recognized when these assets are actually sold. However, land is used by the company for its business (plant site) as well as for employee housing or the like; securities are kept, among other reasons, to maintain interdependence within the group or to stabilize shareholders. These capital assets are, therefore, not considered assets subject to sale. Nevertheless, in some cases, especially when profit is needed for maintaining dividends and prestige, these assets are sold to members of the industrial grouping. The seller may subsequently want to buy them back. If a company repurchases these assets within a short period or sells them with a repurchasing agreement, such assets will be restated at market value when reacquired. If the transaction is one-sided (sale without repurchase), the profit arising from the transaction is regarded as real profit, because Japanese accounting principles have not yet adopted the method under which unrealized profit from a transaction within a business grouping is to be eliminated. Such asset transactions within the group, in order to maintain a desired level of profit, become prevalent in periods of business downturn. The practice is less questionable than some others, however, because it generally does not result in fictitious assets or hidden liabilities.

Income Tax Allocation

The 1982 Commercial Code amendment required, that any addition to or deduction from special tax allowances (e.g., special depreciation, inventory price fluctuation reserve) be excluded from the determination of net income. Thus, significant discrepancies between financial statements following Japanese accounting practices and statements following U.S. practices were eliminated. However, the accounting concept of income tax allocation has not yet been adopted in Japanese practice. Furthermore, the requirement for restatement of prior years' financial statements in certain cases of accounting changes is still confusing for Japanese management.

Deceptive Presentation

Financial statements are not only difficult to read, they may also be deceptively written. Although intercompany sales and purchases may be disclosed in a footnote attached to the balance sheet, the effects on profit and loss remain undisclosed. Other intercompany transactions, such as dividends, rent, sale, and subsequent depreciation of fixed assets, also may not be disclosed. As a result, shareholders and creditors are at the mercy of the company and its manipulation of intercompany profit and loss. Even without consolidated financial statements, it would be technically possible to calculate intercompany (and therefore unrealized) profit and disclose it in the notes to the financial statements. This matter is especially urgent among smaller firms, where the president or a company officer often owns controlling interest in another company with which transactions occur. It is commonly observed in postwar Japan that the man who becomes president in a fast-growing company through his own efforts and ingenuity (contrary to the person who is promoted over a lengthier period of time through seniority) tends to create his own companies, through which he benefits in trade with the main company.

In the prospectus announcing issue of depositary shares by the Omron Tateisi Electronics Co. dated January 9, 1970, the following was stated under "Basis of preparation of financial statements:"

> Omron Tateisi Electronics Co. (Tateisi) has no majority-owned subsidiaries. However Tateisi exercises management control over four electronics manufacturers. . . . Between 52% and 87% of the capital stock of these affiliates is held by the family of the president of Tateisi, while the remaining shares are held by Tateisi, certain directors and employees of Tateisi and/or its affiliates, and third parties. Condensed financial statements of these affiliates [as a group] is given below.

Such conduct, when not disclosed, is without doubt unethical; yet it is still by and large condoned. Banks are concerned but often afraid to lose clients. The stock exchanges, when they review the listing application of a company, successfully control the practice of deceptive reporting, but only at the time of application. Independent CPAs advise against deceptive presentation of financial statements with little success. Some legal provisions have come to the rescue. According to the 1974 revision of the Commercial Code (Art. 274.3) and the Special Law Concerning Audit of Corporations (Art. 7), internal and/or external auditors of the parent company have the right to investigate business financial reports of subsidiaries. Subsidiaries may refuse such an investigation for "justifiable reasons" (what is "justifiable" is a matter to be determined by the courts or by a regulation or notification issued by government authorities).

Foreign Readers' Expectations

Many further refinements would be needed in order to make Japanese financial statements more meaningful to foreign readers.

1. In addition to or in replacement of reserves and allowances created for tax purposes (bad debts, sales returns, sales warranty, etc.), accounts matching sales with related costs and expenses should be reported, to avoid over- or understatement of sales and profit.

2. Inventories should be written down to market value, if the market value is lower than cost. However, such write-downs in most cases would be disallowed for tax purposes, unless actual sales experience is given.

3. Investment securities should be written down to equity value, if there is permanent impairment of their value. Such a write-down, however, would be disallowed for tax purposes until securities are sold at loss.

4. Deferred charges should be written down, if they are a mere deferment of losses, as is often and legitimately the case.

5. In installment sales, accrued sales and cost of sales (and resulting gross profit) should be disclosed. (Most companies record cash receipts and related cost of sales for tax purposes.) Also, allowances for bad debts, sales returns, sales warranty, and so forth related to accrued sales should be estimated and provided for.

6. The estimated loss to be incurred upon delivery of products and other accrued losses should be disclosed. (Such loss is not deductible until realized, and Japanese accounting principles do not strictly require recognition of accrued loss until realized.)

7. Accrued liabilities, for example, unbilled payables, employee bonuses, and employee retirement benefits, need adequate disclosure,

because they tend to be accrued only to the extent allowable for tax purposes.

8. Foreign exchange gain or loss should be adequately disclosed, because long-term receivables and payables are often stated at historical cost in order to avoid tax exposure.

9. The tax effect (deferred or prepaid income taxes) related to all above items and to extraordinary and prior-period items should be disclosed.

10. Certain contingent liabilities, such as the one related to lawsuits, and commitments, such as long-term lease, should be disclosed. (Lawsuits are often not reported until the loss is realized. Although contingent liabilities must be disclosed, the disclosure of commitments is not legally required.)

Two additional comments should be made. First, the effect on income of tax-deductible reserves and nondeductible reserves becomes known to readers when the desirable disclosure concerning valuation of assets and allowances is made. Second, a future forecast is not legally required but is often made available to readers; such a forecast is not checked by independent auditors. International practice differs concerning auditors' responsibility in regard to such forecasts. In the United States auditors would not be encouraged to participate in the preparation of the forecasts, whereas it is regarded as proper in the United Kingdom and West Germany. Japanese CPAs who express views on the point seem to incline toward the European practice.

In the years after World War II, Japanese corporations have been able to balance the merits and demerits of their financial behavior. Western influence, in particular the U.S. Generally Accepted Accounting Principles (GAAP), have been and remain of decisive importance in effecting change. However, an understanding of American practices is not sufficient to understand Japanese practices. In the broadest terms, the Japaneseness of Japanese financial behavior could be viewed as the interaction of four factors, two external and two internal to the company. Each factor is ambivalent in its own right; it works for the better as well as for the worse.

(1) The close government-business relationship is one external factor that remains decisive in regard to financial behavior.

For better:
   Administrative guidance has been and is contributing greatly to further development of corporate financing and disclosure.
   The accounting profession is persistently encouraged.

For worse:

Tax requirements have been and too often remain the basic criteria of accounting practices and financial reporting. They are often unrelated, if not also contradictory, to fair presentation to the shareholder.

(2) Interdependence among companies is the other major external factor.

For better:

Capital has been readily available from related financial institutions.

Subcontracting has been of major help in establishing the international competitiveness of many parent companies, and it also gave the overall economy substantial resilience.

Group support has helped many companies through dire times.

For worse:

Overall, the institutional investor predominates. The investing public plays a minor role, if any.

Subjectivity is the lubricant of most business transactions. It pushes financial reporting into the background, if not out of sight altogether.

At-arm's-length dealings are very difficult to maintain.

(3) Personnel administration is an internal factor determining financial behavior to a major degree.

For better:

The "human relations" emphasis in personnel administration promotes the brand of corporate loyalty that accounts for much of the dynamism of Japanese corporations.

For worse:

Professionalism (in accounting) takes second place to loyalty to one's company.

Responsibility is shared with the result that it is diffused; it may even concentrate on persons and actions bordering on complicity.

Hence, internal control has little objective standing.

(4) Top management and its style are the other internal factor to keep in mind.

For better:

In terms of security and to a meaningful extent in terms of income as well, company executives share the fate of all regular employees of the company.

The long-term view tends to prevail.

For worse:

A proprietary sense colors management's view of the company.

Outside directors could provide a beneficial input, because they are less committed to what is going on in the company and thus more detached in their view. Their small number, however, encourages other directors to promote factional interests.

Directors are often managers and as such are more concerned with operational rather than investigative aspects of financial statements.

External audit, by definition "independent," does not yet square with in-bred executives.

One thing apparently is not about to change in the corporate financial behavior of Japanese corporations. It characterizes both their production and their technology management: they are less concerned with results than with the process or, in a word, growth.

REFERENCES

BIBLIOGRAPHY

Abegglen, James C.
1971 *Business Strategies for Japan*. Tokyo: Sophia/Britannica.
1984 *The Strategy of Japanese Business*. Cambridge, Mass.: Ballinger.

Abegglen, James C., and Rapp, William V.
1970 "Japanese Managerial Behavior and Excessive Competition." *The Developing Economies* 8, no. 4 (December): 427–444.

Abegglen, James C., and Stalk, George, Jr.
1985 *Kaisha: The Japanese Corporation*. New York: Basic Books.

Adams, T. F. M.
1953 *Japanese Securities Markets: A Historical Survey*. Tokyo: Seihei Okuyama.
1964 *A Financial History of Japan*. Tokyo: Research.

Allen, G. C., and Donnithorne, Audrey G.
1954 *Western Enterprise in Far Eastern Economic Development*. London: Allen & Unwin.

American Chamber of Commerce in Japan
1979 *United States' Manufacturing Investment in Japan: A Study*. Tokyo, July.

American Institute of Certified Public Accountants
1973 *Statement on Auditing Standards*. New York.

Anguis, Emmanuel
1983 *Le ressort financier de la croissance des entreprises japonaises*. Bulletin de la Maison Franco-Japonaise, new series 10, nos. 3–4.

Aoki, Masahiko
1987 "The Japanese Firm in Transition." In Yamamura and Yasuba, eds. 1987: 263–288.

Aoki, Masahiko, ed.
1984 *The Economic Analysis of the Japanese Firm*. Amsterdam: North-Holland.

Aoki, Torao
1986 "The National Taxation System." In Shibata 1986: 103–122.

Arai, Akira
1986 "Bond Rating Organizations." *Japan Economic Journal*, November 29, p. 28.

Baldwin, Frank
1973 "The Idioms of Contemporary Japan VI: *Kaishime*." *The Japan Interpreter* 8, no. 3 (Autumn): 396–409.
1974 "The Idioms of Contemporary Japan VII: *Sōkaiya*." *The Japan Interpreter* 8, no. 4 (Winter): 502–509.

Ballon, Robert J.
1969 *The Japanese Employee*. Tokyo: Sophia/Tuttle.
1985a *Salary Administration in Japan: "Regular" Workforce*. Tokyo: Sophia University Institute of Comparative Culture, Business Series No. 100.
1985b *The Business Contract in Japan*. Tokyo: Sophia University Institute of Comparative Culture, Business Series No. 105.
1986 *Labor-Management Relations in Japan*. Tokyo: Sophia University Institute of Comparative Culture, Business Series No. 107.
1988 *Japanese Decision-Making: A Circular Process*. Tokyo: Sophia University Institute of Comparative Culture, Business Series No. 117.

Ballon, Robert J., and Lee, Eugene H., eds.
1972 *Foreign Investment and Japan*. Tokyo: Kodansha International.

Ballon, Robert J.; Tomita, Iwao; and Usami, Hajime
1976 *Financial Reporting in Japan*. Tokyo: Kodansha International.

Bank of Japan
Annual *Economic Statistics*. Tokyo.
1966 *Meiji-ikō Honpō Shuyō Keizai Tōkei* [Basic Economic Statistics from Meiji Onward]. Tokyo.
1973 *Money and Banking in Japan*. London: Macmillan.
1986/10 *Further Relaxation of Financial Conditions and Structural Changes in Corporate Finance*. Tokyo: Special Paper No. 145, October.
1986/11 *Shuyō Kigyō Keiei Bunseki Shōwa 60-nendo* [Management Analysis of Major Enterprises, FY 1985]. Tokyo, November.
1987/3 *Keizai Tōkei Nenpō 1986* [Economic Statistics Annual]. Tokyo, March.
1987 *Comparative Economic and Financial Statistics: Japan and Other Major Countries*. Tokyo.

Bank of International Settlements
1985 *Payment Systems in Eleven Developed Countries*. Basel.

BCG (Boston Consulting Group)
1972a "The Rationalization of the Japanese Motor Vehicle Industry." In Kaplan 1972: 103–136.
1972b "The Expansion of the Japanese Steel Industry." In Kaplan 1972: 137–158.

Bond Underwriters Association
1986 *Kōshasai Nenkan Shōwa 61-nenban* [Bond Annual, 1986]. Tokyo.

Dore, Ronald

1973 *British Factory–Japanese Factory: The Origins of National Diversity in Industrial Relations*. London: Allen & Unwin.

1986 *Flexible Rigidities: Industrial Policy and Structural Adjustment in the Japanese Economy 1970–80*. London: Athlone Press.

1987 *Taking Japan Seriously: A Confucian Perspective on Leading Economic Issues*. London: Athlone Press.

Dotsey, Michael

1986 "Japanese Monetary Policy, a Comparative Analysis." *Economic Review* 72, no. 6 (November/December): 12–24. Richmond: Federal Reserve Bank of Richmond.

Drucker, Peter F.

1974 *Management: Tasks, Responsibilities, Practices*. London: Heinemann.

1975 "Economic Realities and Enterprise Strategy." In Vogel 1975: 228–248.

Economist (London)

1986/6 "Playing *Zaiteku* in the City." June 28.

Elston, C. D.

1981 "The Financing of Japanese Industry." *The Bank of England Quarterly Review*, December.

Emura, Minoru

1953 *Fukushiki Boki Seisei Hattatsu-shi Ron* [Essay on the Origin and Development of Double-Entry Bookkeeping]. Tokyo: Chūō Keizai-sha.

EPA (Economic Planning Agency)

1985 *Economic Survey of Japan 1984/1985*. Tokyo: The Japan Times.

1986 *Economic Survey of Japan 1985/1986*. Tokyo: The Japan Times.

Euromoney (London)

1986/11 "*Zaiteku* Zooms into the Unknown." November, pp. 36–52.

1987/4 *Japan: The Land Where Money Grows*. Supplement.

1987/9 *Japanese Securities Companies*. Supplement.

Federation of Bankers' Associations of Japan

1985 *Payment Systems in Japan*. Tokyo.

1987 *Tegata Kōkan Tōkei Nenpō Shōwa 61-nenban* [Annual Statistics of Clearings, 1986]. Tokyo, May.

Finn, Richard B., ed.

1986 *U.S.-Japan Relations: Learning from Competition. Annual Review, 1985*. New Brunswick: Transaction.

First Boston: Equity Research

1987 "Japanese Corporate Earnings: Zai-tech—A Shot in the Arm to the Bottom Line." Tokyo, July 21.

Focus Japan

1987/7 "Japan's Small and Medium Enterprises Struggle for Life in the Deteriorating Business Environment." *JETRO* (Tokyo) 14, no. 7: 1–2.

Bonds, William P.
1974 *Corporate Bankruptcy in Japan (1964–1974)*. Tokyo: Sophia University Socio-Economic Institute, Bulletin No. 54.

Booz, Allen & Hamilton, Inc.
1987 *Direct Foreign Investment in Japan: The Challenge for Foreign Firms (A Study for the American Chamber of Commerce in Japan and The Council of the European Business Community)*. Tokyo, September.

Bronte, Stephen
1982 *Japanese Finance: Markets and Institutions*. London: Euromoney Publications.

Brown, Robert
1983 "A Lawyer by Any Other Name: Legal Advisors in Japan." In Lincoln and Rosenthal 1983: 201–502.

Campbell, John Creighton
1977 *Contemporary Japanese Budget Process*. Berkeley: University of California Press.

Choi, Frederick D. S., and Hiramatsu Kazuo
1987 *Accounting and Financial Reporting in Japan*. Wokingham: Van Nostrand Reinhold.

Chūō Keizai-sha
1974 *Kaikei Zensho 49-nendo-ban* [Compendium of Accounting, 1974]. Tokyo.

Clark, Rodney
1987 *Venture Capital in Britain, America and Japan*. London: Croom Helm.

Commercial Law Center
1979 *Concerning the Roles of the Legal Departments of Typical Japanese Enter prises*. Tokyo.

Cottrell, Robert
1985 "Before the Fall." *Far Eastern Economic Review* (Hong Kong), August 7.

Crum, M. Colyer, and Meerschwam, David M.
1986 "From Relationship to Price Banking: The Loss of Regulatory Control." McCraw 1986: 261–297.

Davis, Paul A.
1972 *Administrative Guidance in Japan—Legal Considerations*. Tokyo: Sopł University Institute of Comparative Culture, Business Series No. 41.

Dodwell Marketing Consultants
Annual *Industrial Groupings in Japan*. Tokyo.

Doi, Masako
1986 *Mergers and Acquisitions in Japan*. Tokyo: Sophia University M.A. the

Doi, Teruo
1973 *The Anatomy of Dependence*. Tokyo: Kodansha International.

Frank, Isaiah, ed.
1975 *The Japanese Economy in International Perspective*. Baltimore: Johns Hopkins University Press.

FTC (Fair Trade Commission)
1979 *Jigyō Dantai no Katsudō ni Kansuru Dokusen Kinshi-hō-jō no Shishin* [Guidelines Concerning the Activities of Trade Associations under the Antimonopoly Law]. Tokyo. (An English translation of these Guidelines is found in *Law in Japan: An Annual* 12 [1979]: 118–132.)
1983 *Kōsei Torihiki I-inkai Nenji Hōkoku, Shōwa 58-nenban* [Annual Report of the Fair Trade Commission, 1983]. Tokyo.
1983/4 *Sōgō Shōsha no Jigyō Katsudō no Jittai Chōsa* [Survey of the Activities of General Trading Companies]. Tokyo, April.
1983/6 *Kigyō Shūdan no Jittai ni Tsuite* [On the Activities of Enterprise Groups]. Tokyo, June.
1986a *Kōsei Torihiki I-inkai Nenji Hōkoku, Shōwa 61-nenban* [Annual Report of the Fair Trade Commission, 1986]. Tokyo.
1986b *Venchā Kiapitaru ni Kansuru Dokusen Kinshi-hō-jō no Tori-atsukai ni Tsuite* [Concerning the Application of the Antimonopoly Law to Venture Capital]. In *Dokusen Kenshin-hō Kankei Hōrei-shū* [Compendium of Regulations Relating to the Antimonopoly Law]. Tokyo, 266–267.
1986/12 *Kōsoku-yokin no Jittai* [Actual Situation of Compensating Balances]. Tokyo, December.
1987/4 *Kinyū-gyō wo Itonamu Kaisha no Kabushiki Shoyū no Jittai Chōsa ni Tsuite* [About the Survey on the Condition of Shareholding by Financial Institutions]. Tokyo, April 28 (press release).

Gomi, Yuji
1986 *Guide to Japanese Taxes, 1986*. Tokyo: Zaikei Shōhō-sha.

Gregory, Gene
1982 *The Logic of Japanese Enterprise*. Tokyo: Sophia University Institute of Comparative Culture, Bulletin Series No. 92.
1985 *Japanese Electronics Technology: Enterprise and Innovation*. Tokyo: The Japan Times.

Habgood, Anthony
1975 *Debt, Growth and Competitive Position: A Re-examination of Japanese Corporate Financing*. Tokyo: Boston Consulting Group (mimeograph).

Hadley, Eleanor M.
1970 *Antitrust in Japan*. Princeton: Princeton University Press.
1984 "Counterpoint on Business Groupings and Government-Industry Relations in Automobiles." In M. Aoki 1984: 320.

Haley, John Owen
1978 "The Myth of the Reluctant Litigant." *Journal of Japanese Studies* 4, no. 2 (Summer): 359–390.
1986 "Administrative Guidance versus Formal Regulation: Resolving the Paradox of Industrial Policy." In Saxonhouse and Yamamura 1986: 107–128.

Hashidate, Kenji
1976 *Financing Corporations with Convertible Debentures in the U.S.A. and Japan*. Tokyo: Kinokuniya.

Henderson, Dan Fenno
1973 *Foreign Enterprise in Japan: Laws and Policies*. Chapel Hill: University of North Carolina.

Higashi, Chikara
1983 *Japanese Trade Policy Formulation*. New York: Praeger.

Higashi, Chikara, and Lauter, G. Peter
1987 *The Internationalization of the Japanese Economy*. Boston: Kluwer.

Hirschmeier, Johannes
1964 *The Origins of Entrepreneurship in Meiji Japan*. Cambridge: Harvard University Press.

Hirschmeier, Johannes, and Yui, Tsunehiko
1975 *The Development of Japanese Business, 1600–1975*. London: Allen & Unwin.
1981 *The Development of Japanese Business, 1600–1980*. Second ed. London: Allen & Unwin.

Horiguchi, Wataru
1974 "Futto Raito o Abita Kansa-yaku to Atarashii Yaku-wari" [Statutory Auditors in the Limelight and Their New Role]. In Nihonteki Keiei Kenkyūkai 1974: 117–122.

Horne, James
1985 *Japan's Financial Markets: Conflict and Consensus in Policymaking*. Sydney: Allen & Unwin.

Hout, Thomas M.
1974 *Japan's Growth and Corporate Finance*. Boston: Boston Consulting Group (mimeograph).

Ikemoto, Yukio; Tajika, Eiji; and Yui, Yuji
1984 "On the Fiscal Incentives to Investment: The Case of Postwar Japan." *The Developing Economies* 22, no. 4 (December): 372–395.

Inohara, Hideo
1972 *Shukkō: Loan of Personnel in Japanese Industry*. Tokyo: Sophia University Institute of Comparative Culture, Business Series No. 42.

Iwaki, Akinori
1987 "Fund Management: Corporations Zaiteku Their Way Around the Rising Yen." *The Japan Economic Journal, Special Survey: Japanese Management*, September 5, p. 28.

Iyori, Hiroshi
1986 "Antitrust and Industrial Policy in Japan: Competition and Cooperation." In Saxonhouse and Yamamura 1986: 56–82.

Iyori, Hiroshi, and Uesugi, Akinori
1983 *The Antimonopoly Laws of Japan*. New York: Federal Legal Publications.

Japan Economic Federation
1940 *The Capital Market of Japan*. Tokyo, May.

Japan Economic Journal (Tokyo)
1975/2 "MITI Moves to Rescue Yashika After Near 'Hopeless' Situation." February 25, p. 20.
1985/12 "Financial Mart Securitization Rapidly Gaining Ground in Japan." December 28.
1986/5 "Increasing Number of Banks Must Disclose Consolidated Results." May 17.
1986/11 "Bond Rating Organizations." November 29.
1987/3 "Securities Firms to Overhaul Underwriting." March 21.
1987/5 "Land Reform Considered to Ease Price Oppression." May 23.
1987/8 "Analysis: Fragile Castle on Capital Gains." August 1.

Japan Productivity Center
1985 *Practical Handbook of Productivity and Labour Statistics*. Tokyo.

Japan Securities Dealers Association
1962 *Tentō Baibai Meigara no Nedan no Happyō ni Kansuru Kisoku* [Regulation Concerning the Reporting of the Prices of Registered Stocks]. Tokyo.
1987 *Key Statistics in Japanese Securities, 1987*. Tokyo.

Japan Securities Research Institute
1985 *Securities Market in Japan, 1986*. Tokyo.
1987 *Securities Market in Japan, 1988*. Tokyo.

JETRO (Japan External Trade Organization)
1984 *Foreign Companies in Japan*. Tokyo.

JICPA (Japan Institute of Certified Public Accountants)
News. Tokyo.

Johnson, Chalmers
1982 *MITI and the Japanese Miracle: The Growth of Industrial Policy, 1925–1975*. Stanford: Stanford University Press.

Jones, Randall
1987 "Implications of Contrasting U.S. and Japanese Savings Behavior." In Japan Economic Institute, *Report*, no. 17A (May 1).

Kagono, T.; Nonaka, I.; Sakakibara, K.; and Okumura, A.
1985 *Strategic vs. Evolutionary Management: A U.S.-Japan Comparison of Strategy and Organization*. Amsterdam: North-Holland.

Kaisha Shiki-hō [Company Directory]
1987 Spring.

Kaplan, Eugene J.
1972 *Japan—The Government-Business Relationship*. Washington, D.C.: U.S. Department of Commerce, February.

Kawashima, Takeyoshi
1974 "The Legal Consciousness of Contract in Japan." *Law in Japan: An Annual* 7 (1974): 1–21.

Keizai Koho Center
1986 *Japan 1986: An International Comparison.* Tokyo.

Kobayashi, Setsuya
1987 *Contract and Relationship in Japan's Public Sector.* Tokyo: Sophia University Institute of Comparative Culture, Business Series, No. 115.

Kojima, Kiyoshi, and Ozawa, Terutomo
1984 *Japan's General Trading Companies: Merchants of Economic Development.* Paris: OECD, p. 25.

Kono, Toyohiro
1984 *Strategy and Structure of Japanese Enterprises.* London: Macmillan.

Koschmann, J. Victor
1978 "Introduction. Soft Rule and Expressive Protest." In Koschmann, ed. 1978: 1–30.

Koschmann, J. Victor, ed.
1978 *Authority and the Individual in Japan: Citizen Protest in Historical Perspective.* Tokyo: University of Tokyo Press.

Kuboi, Tadashi
1988 *Business Practices and Taxation in Japan.* Tokyo: The Japan Times.

Kuboi, Tadashi, and Paufler, Alexander
1988 *Unternehmung und Besteurung in Japan.* Stuttgart: Poeschel.

Kudo, Hideyuki
1974 "Shagai-jūyaku wa Kyozō ka Jitsuzō ka" [Outside Directors: Illusion or Reality?]. In Nihonteki Keiei Kenkyūkai, ed. 1974: 111.

Lee, Eugene H.
1972 "Business Advisors in Japan." In Ballon and Lee 1972: 57–69.

Lincoln, Edward J., and Rosenthal, Douglas E., chairmen
1983 *Legal Aspects of Doing Business in Japan, 1981.* New York: Practicing Law Institute, 1983.

McCraw, Thomas K., ed.
1986 *America versus Japan.* Boston: Harvard Business School Press.

Minami, Ryoshin
1986 *The Economic Development of Japan: A Quantitative Study.* London: Macmillan.

Ministry of Justice
1982 *Kabushiki-gaisha no Taishaku Taishō-hyō, Son-eki Keisan-sho Eigyō Hōkoku-sho oyobi Fuzoku Meisai-sho no Kansuru Kisoku* [Regulation Concerning the Balance Sheet, Income Statement, and Supplementary Schedules of Stock Corporations]. Tokyo.

MITI (Ministry of International Trade and Industry)
1973 *Chūshō-kigyō Hakusho 1973* [White Paper of Small and Medium Enterprises, 1973]. Tokyo.
1984/10 *White Paper on Small and Medium Enterprises in Japan, 1984.* Tokyo, October.

1985/9 *White Paper on Small and Medium Enterprises in Japan, 1985.* Tokyo, September.

1985a *Sōgō Kei-ei-ryoku Shihyō, Seizō-gyō* [General Characteristics of Management Ability, Manufacturing]. Tokyo.

1985b *Sōgō Kei-ei-ryoku Shihyō, Ko-uri-gyō* [General Characteristics of Management Ability, Retail Industry]. Tokyo.

1986a *White Paper on Small and Medium Enterprises in Japan, 1986.* Tokyo.

1986b *Gaishi-kei Kigyō no Dōkō Dai 18-kai* [Trends of Foreign-Capital Affiliated Firms, 18th Issue]. Tokyo.

1987a *Gaishi-kei Kigyō no Dōkō Dai 19-kai* [Trends of Foreign-Capital Affiliated Firms, 19th Issue]. Tokyo.

1987b *White Paper on Small and Medium Enterprises in Japan, 1987.* Tokyo.

MOF (Ministry of Finance)

1962 *Regulation Concerning Terminology, Form and Method of Preparation of Financial Statements.* Ministerial Ordinance No. 59.

1967 *Renketsu Zaimu-shohyō ni Kansuru Iken-sho* [Opinion Concerning Consolidated Financial Statements]. Tokyo.

1975 *Renketsu Zaimu-shohyō no Seido-ka ni Kansuru Iken-sho* [Opinion on the Systematization of Consolidated Financial Statements]. Tokyo, June 24.

1976 *Renketsu Zaimu-shohyō no Yōgō, Yōshiki oyobi Saku-sei Hōhō ni Kansuru Kisoku* [Regulation Concerning Terminology, Form, and Method of Preparation of Financial Statements]. Tokyo.

MOF Printing Bureau

1974 *Yūka Shōken Hōkoku-sho, Marubeni Kabushiki Kaisha, '74 3* [Securities Report, Marubeni K.K., March 1974]. Tokyo.

1986 *An Outline of Japanese Taxes 1986.* Tokyo.

MOL (Ministry of Labor)

1975 *Sha-nai Yokin Kanri Jisshi Jigyō-jō ni Taisuru Kantoku Shidō Kekka* [Results of the Guidance Given to the Enterprises Where Employees Deposit Savings in the Company]. Tokyo.

1983 *Gaishi-kei Kigyō no Rōshi-kankei-tō Jittai Chōsa Kekka Hōkoku-sho, Dai 3-kai* [Report on the Survey Results of Labor-Management Relations and Others in Foreign-Capital Affiliated Companies, Third Survey]. Tokyo.

1986 *Shanai Yokin no Genjō* [Actual Situation of In-Company Savings]. Tokyo, December.

Monden, Yasuhiro; Shibakawa, Rinya; Takayanagi, Satoru; and Nagao, Teruya

1985 *Innovations in Management: The Japanese Corporation.* Atlanta: Industrial Engineering and Management Press.

Monroe, Wilbur F.

1973 *Japan: Financial Markets and the World Economy.* New York: Praeger.

Murakami, Kiyoshi

1985 *Retirement Benefits and Pension Plans in Japan.* Tokyo: Sophia University Institute of Comparative Culture, Business Series No. 102.

1988 *Retirement Benefits and Pension Plans in Japan.* Tokyo: Sophia University Institute of Comparative Culture, Business Series No. 118.

Nakagawa, Masanao, ed.
1984   *Antimonopoly Legislation of Japan.* Tokyo: Kōsei Torihiki Kyōkai.

Nakamura, Mari
1987   *Japan's Ubiquitous Promissory Note.* Tokyo: Sophia University Institute of Comparative Culture, Business Series No. 113.

Nakatani, Iwao
1984   "The Economic Role of Financial Corporate Grouping." In M. Aoki 1984: 227–258. A rejoinder to this position is given by Hadley 1984: 319–323.
1987   "Japan-U.S. Relations: Asymmetry of Institutional Features as a Source of Trade Frictions." In Patrick and Tachi 1987: 184–195.

Namiki, Kazuo
1984   "Fuwatari no Torihiki Teishi Shobun Seido" [Dishonored Notes and the Suspension of Bank Transactions System]. *Ginkō Business,* June.

Narita, Yoriaki
1968   "Administrative Guidance." *Law in Japan: An Annual* 2: 45–79.

National Tax Administration
1975   *Hōjin Kigyō no Jittai Shōwa 48-nenbun* [Actual Situation of Juridical-Entity Enterprises, Annual 1973]. Tokyo, March.
1977   *Hōjin Kigyō no Jittai Shōwa 50-nenbun* [Actual Situation of Juridical-Entity Enterprises, Annual 1975]. Tokyo, March.
1986   *Hōjin Kigyō no Jittai Shōwa 59-nenbun* [Actual Situation of Juridical-Entity Enterprises, Annual 1984]. Tokyo, March.
1987   *Hōjin Kigyō no Jittai Shōwa 60-nenbun* [Actual Situation of Juridical-Entity Enterprises, Annual 1985]. Tokyo, March.

Nihon Keizai Shinbun
1974/6   "Kansa-yaku Shin-jidai ni Ikigomu" [Statutory Auditors Eager to Start a New Era]. June 21.
1974/12   "Kaisei Shōhō, Mite Minufuri" [Ignored Revision of the Commercial Code]. December 5.
1975/3   "Oyabike Hiritsu 30% Ni" [Oyabike Ratio Down to 30%]. March 2.
1975/3   "Rieki Kakushi ni Kibishii Me" [Severe Look at Hidden Profits]. March 24.
1978   May 29.
1987   March 2.
1987/4   "Misawa to Kabushiki Mochi-ai" [*Mochi-ai* with Misawa]. April 17.
1987/6   "Kabushiki o Tsukatta Jūgyōin Chochiku" [Employee Savings Using Stock]. June 10.
1987/6   "Rieki demo Toppu Mezasu" [Heading for the Top Even in Profits]. June 14.
1987/7   "Kojin Kabunushi 25% Waru" [Individual Shareholding Less than 25%].

Nihonteki Keiei Kenkyūkai
1974   *Kikan Nihon no Keiei Bunka* [Japan's Business Culture Quarterly]. Tokyo: Chūō Keizai-sha, Fall.

Nikkan Kōgyō
1968 "Concentration of Native Capital." Tokyo, June 25.

Nikkei Business
1987 "TOB Sakeru Nihon-gata Kigyō Baishū no Teichaku: Kyūsai-gata kara Hito-gijutsu Katsuyō-gata e" [Japanese-style M&A Taking Root in Order to Avoid TOB: From Remedy-type to Human Resource/Technology Utilization–type]. April 27: 32–42.

Nishikawa, Kojiro
1971 *Nippon Boki-shi Dan* [History of Bookkeeping in Japan]. Tokyo: Dobunkan.

Noda, Yosiyuki
1976 *Introduction to Japanese Law*. Tokyo: University of Tokyo Press.

Nonaka, I., and Okumura, A.
1984 "Comparison of Management in American, Japanese, and European Firms (I)." *Management Japan* 17, no. 1 (Spring): 23–40.

Norbury, Paul, and Bownas, Geoffrey, eds.
1980 *Business in Japan: A Guide to Japanese Practice and Procedure*. London: Macmillan.

OECD (Organisation for Economic Co-operation and Development)
1972 *Monetary Policy in Japan*. Paris, December.
1987 *Revenue Statistics of OECD Member Countries, 1965–1986*. Paris.

Ohkawa, Kazushi, and Rosovsky, Henry
1973 *Japanese Economic Growth-Trend Acceleration in the Twentieth Century*. Stanford: Stanford University Press.

Okimoto, Daniel I.
1986 "Regime Characteristics of Japanese Industrial Policy." In Patrick, ed., 1986: 35–95.

Okita, Yoichi
1975 "Japan's Fiscal Incentive for Exports." In Frank 1975: 207–230.

Okumura, Hiroshi
1982 "The Closed Nature of Japanese Intercorporate Relations." *Japan Echo* 9 no. 3: 53–61.

Okura Zaimu Kyōkai
1974 *An Outline of Japanese Taxes, 1974*. Tokyo.

Patrick, Hugh
1986 "Japanese High Technology Industrial Policy in Comparative Context." In Patrick, ed. 1986: 3–33.

Patrick, Hugh T., ed.
1986 *Japan's High Technology Industries: Lessons and Limitations of Industrial Policy*. Tokyo: University of Tokyo Press.

Patrick, Hugh T., and Rohlen, Thomas P.
1987 "Small-Scale Family Enterprises." In Yamamura and Yasuba, eds. 1987: 331–384.

Patrick, Hugh T., and Tachi, Ryuichiro, eds.
1987 *Japan and the United States Today: Exchange Rates, Macroeconomic Policies, and Financial Market Innovations*. New York: Columbia University, Center on Japanese Economy and Business.

Peck, Merton J.; Levin, Richard C.; and Goto, Akira
1987 "Picking Losers: Public Policy Toward Declining Industries in Japan." *Journal of Japanese Studies* 13, no.1 (Winter 1987): 79–123.

Petach, Susan Kingston
1986 *Corporate Bankrupcty in Japan: Riccar Co., Ltd*. Tokyo: Sophia University Institute of Comparative Culture, Business Series No. 109.

Prindl, Andreas R.
1981 *Japanese Finance: A Guide to Banking in Japan*. Chichester: Wiley.

Roscoe, Bruce
1986 "Scramble for a Ride on the Debt Rollercoaster." *Far Eastern Economic Review* (Hong Kong), September 11, pp. 76–78.

Rukstad, Michael G.
1986 "Fiscal Policy and Business-Government Relations." In McCraw 1986: 299–336.

Sakakibara, Eisuke; Feldman, Robert; and Harada, Yuzo
1982 *The Japanese Financial System in Comparative Perspective*. A study prepared for the use of the Joint Economic Committee, Congress of the United States. Washington, D.C.: U.S. Government Printing Office.

Sakakibara, Eisuke, and Nagao, Yoriyuki
1985 *Study on the Tokyo Capital Markets*. Tokyo: JCFI Policy Study Series No. 2, March.

Sakurai, Kosaku
1986 "Banking." In *Japan Economic Almanac, 1986*: 22–24.

Sarasas, Phra
1940 *Money and Banking in Japan*. London: Heath Cranton.

Sawada, J. Toshio
1968 *Subsequent Conduct and Supervening Events*. Tokyo: University of Tokyo Press.

Saxonhouse, Gary R.
1986 "Industrial Policy and Factor Markets: Biotechnology in Japan and the United States." In Patrick 1986: 97–135.

Saxonhouse, Gary R., and Yamamura, Kozo, eds.
1986 *Law and Trade Issues of the Japanese Economy: American and Japanese Perspectives*. Seattle: University of Washington Press.

SBIC (Small Business Investment Companies)
1987 *Outline of Small Business Investment Companies in Japan.* Tokyo, July.

Schoenberger, Karl
1987 "Japan's Corporate Gadflies Try English." *Asian Wall Street Journal,* June 30.

Schonberger, Richard J.
1982 *Japanese Manufacturing Techniques: Nine Hidden Lessons in Simplicity.* New York: Free Press.

Scott, John
1986 *Capitalist Property and Financial Power: A Comparative Study of Britain, the United States and Japan.* Brighton: Wheatsheaf Books.

Shibakawa, Rinya
1985 "Japanese Financial Management." In Monden, Shibakawa, Takayanagi, and Nagao 1985: 191–203.

Shibata, Tokue, ed.
1986 *Public Finance in Japan.* Tokyo: University of Tokyo Press.

Shimizu, Norihiko
1972 "Financing Foreign Operations." In Ballon and Lee 1972: 211–225.

Shimizu, Ryuei
1986 "Top Management's Decision Making in Japanese Companies." *Keio Business Review,* no. 23: 1–15.

Shōji Hōmu Kenkyūkai
1982 *Kaisha Hōmu-bu* [Corporate Legal Department]. Bessatsu NBL No. 8. Tokyo, May.
1986 *Shōji Hōmu* [Commercial Law Review]. Tokyo, June 30.

Small and Medium Enterprise Agency
1986a *Kigyō Tōsan Chōsa Nenpō, 1986* [Annual Survey of Corporate Bankruptcies, 1986]. Tokyo.
1986b *Survey on Division of Labor in Manufacturing Industries.* Tokyo.

Statistics Bureau, Management and Coordination Agency
1986a *Annual Report on the Unincorporated Enterprise Survey 1985.* Tokyo.
1986b *Japan Statistical Yearbook 1986.* Tokyo.
1987 *Japan Statistical Yearbook 1987.* Tokyo.

Stewart, Brian
1986 *Corporate Insolvency in Japan: Sanko Steamship Co., Ltd.* Tokyo: Sophia University Institute of Comparative Culture, Business Series No. 112.

Supreme Court Secretariate, ed.
1985 *Shihō Tōkei Nenpō Ichi Minji Gyōsei Hen, Shōwa 60-nen* [Annual Report of Judicial Statistics, Volume 1, Civil Cases, 1985]. Tokyo: Hōsō-kai.

Suzuki, Haruo
1970 "Innovation and Integration in Japanese Management." *Journal of the American Chamber of Commerce in Japan.* Tokyo, April 5.

Suzuki, Yoshio
1980 *Money and Banking in Contemporary Japan: The Theoretical Setting and Its Application*. New Haven: Yale University Press.
1986 *Money, Finance, and Macroeconomic Performance in Japan*. New Haven: Yale University Press.

Suzuki, Yoshio, ed.
1987 *The Japanese Financial System*. Oxford: Clarenton.

Takahashi, Ginjiro
1986 "Stock Market." *Japan Economic Almanac*, 1986: 39–41.

Takeuchi, Sumio
1980 "Business and the Law." In Norbury and Bownas 1980: 155–162.

Tanaka, Hideo
1976 *The Japanese Legal System: Introductory Cases and Materials*. Tokyo: University of Tokyo Press.

Tatsuta, Misao
1970 *Securities Regulation in Japan*. Tokyo: University of Tokyo Press.

Teikoku Data Bank
1985 *Konji Keiki Kaifuku Kyokumen ni Okeru Tōsan Tahatsu no Kōzōteki Yō-in Bunseki oyobi Tōsan Jyōhō Hyōka no Arikata ni Kansuru Kinkyū Chōsa* [Structural Factor Analysis of Frequent Bankruptcies and Emergency Survey on the Evaluation of Bankruptcy Information in This Recovery Phase of the Economy]. Tokyo, March.

Teranishi, Juro
1986 "The 'Catch-up' Process, Financial System, and Japan's Rise as a Capital Exporter." *Hitotsubashi Journal of Economics*, vol. 27 (special issue): 133–146.

Tōkei Geppō
1987 "Shin-tenkai: Jōjō Kigyō no Ko-gaisha Setsuritsu Rasshu" [New Development: Mushrooming Subsidiaries of Listed Companies]. Tokyo: Tōyō Keizai, May, pp. 13–25.

Tokyo Stock Exchange
1986a *'86 Fact Book*. Tokyo.
1986b *Shōken Tōkei Nenban, Showa 61-nen* [Annual Securities Statistics, 1986]. Tokyo.
1986c *Monthly Press Release*. Tokyo, January–December.
1987a *Tōshō Yōran—Fact Book 1987*. Tokyo.
1987b *'87 Fact Book*. Tokyo.

Touche Ross & Co.
1986 *Sogo Shosha: Financial Features and Functions. A Guide for the Businessman*. Tokyo.

Tradescope (Tokyo: JETRO)
1987/7 "Evolution of the Japanese Subcontracting System." Vol. 7, no. 7, pp. 22–26.

1987/8 "High Tech Subcontractors in the Tama Area." Vol. 7, no. 8, pp. 19–22.

Troughton, Helen
1986 *Japanese Finance: The Impact of Deregulation.* London: Euromoney Publications.

Tsuji, Kiyoaki
1968 "Decision-Making in the Japanese Government: A Study of *Ringisei.*" In Ward 1968: 457–475.

Tsuji, Kiyoaki, ed.
1980 *Public Administration in Japan.* Tokyo: Tokyo University Press.

Turpin, Dominique V.
1986 *Japan's Small High-Tech Enterprises and Venture Capital.* Tokyo: Sophia University Institute of Comparative Culture, Business Series No. 106.

Tyrni, Ilari
1984 *The Rate of Return, Risk and the Financial Behaviour of the Japanese Industrial Firms.* Helsinki: Finnish Society of Sciences and Letters.

Uno, Kunio
1987 *Japan's Industrial Performance.* Amsterdam: North-Holland.

Upham, Frank K.
1987 *Law and Social Change in Postwar Japan.* Cambridge, Mass.: Harvard University Press.

Vickers da Costa
1986 *Japanese Research: Latent Assets.* London, February.

Viner, Aron
1987 *Inside Japan's Financial Markets.* Tokyo: The Japan Times.

Vogel, Ezra F.
1975 *Modern Japanese Organization and Decision-Making.* Berkeley: University of California Press.

von Mehren, Arthur Taylor, ed.
1963 *Law in Japan: The Legal Order in a Changing Society.* Cambridge, Mass.: Harvard University Press.

Wakō Securities
1974 *Shōken Tōshi* [Securities Investment]. No. 245 (August): 10–15.

Ward, Robert E., ed.
1968 *Political Development in Modern Japan.* Princeton: Princeton University Press.

Watanabe, Takehiko, and Mochizuki, Hiroshi
1986 "Perception Gap Between the U.S. and Japan: Delegation and Sharing of Authority and Responsibility." In Finn 1986: 85–100.

Wheeler, Jimmy W.; Janow, Merit E.; and Pepper, Thomas
1982 *Japanese Industrial Development Policies in the 1980's: Implications for U.S. Trade and Investment.* Croton-on-Hudson: Hudson Institute, October.

Wong, Jesse
1986 "Japanese Firm's Fall Causes Big Losses." *Asian Wall Street Journal*, August 7, pp. 1,5.

Wright, Richard W., and Pauli, Gunter A.
1987 *The Second Wave: Japan's Global Assault on Financial Services.* New York: St. Martin's Press.

Yamamura, Kozo
1974 *A Study of Samurai Income and Entrepreneurship.* Cambridge: Harvard University Press.

Yamamura, Kozo, and Yasuba, Yasukichi, eds.
1987 *The Political Economy of Japan.* Vol. 1, *The Domestic Transformation.* Stanford: Stanford University Press.

Yanaga, Chitoshi
1968 *Big Business in Japanese Politics.* New Haven: Yale University Press.

Yazawa, Jun
1974 "Hōritsu kara Mita Torishimariyaku-kai no Genjō to Kadai" [Actual Situation and Task of the Board of Directors from the Viewpoint of Law]. In Nihonteki Keiei Kenkyūkai 1974: 80–85.

Yeomans, Russell Allen
1986 "Administrative Guidance: A Peregrine View." In *Law in Japan: An Annual* 19: 125–167.

Yoshino, M.Y.
1968 *Japan's Managerial System: Tradition and Innovation.* Cambridge: M.I.T. Press.

Zenkoku Shōken Torihiki-jo
1986 *Kabushiki Bunpu Jōkyō Chōsa Shōwa 60-nendo* [Survey of Stock Distribution, FY 1985]. Tokyo, August.
1987 *Kabushiki Bunpu Jōkyō Chōsa Shōwa 61-nendo* [Survey of Stock Distribution, FY 1986]. Tokyo, August.

GLOSSARY

amakudari: descent from heaven (retired high government officials in private companies)
ao-iro shinkoku-sho: blue form of tax returns (allowing some tax advantages)

betto tsumitate-kin: general reserve (in the balance sheet)
boshū: public offering of new shares
bunsho-ka: archive section (in the corporate structure, where legal matters are handled)

chōki fusai: long-term debt (in the balance sheet)
chūkan shinkoku-sho: interim tax returns
chūshō kigyō: small and medium enterprises
Chūshō Kigyō Tōshi Ikusei K.K. Small Business Investment Company (sponsored by MITI)

dai-kigyō: large corporation (as opposed to *sho-kigyō*, small corporation)
Daini-bu Shijō: Second Section of the Stock Exchange
dōzoku kaisha: family corporation (for tax purposes)

eigyō hōkoku-sho: business report (part of the financial statements according to the Commercial Code)
eigyō jun-eki: net operating income (in the statement of income)

fudō kabu: floating stock; readily marketable shares
fuka-kachi: value added
fukumi shisan: latent assets (of the corporation, in the balance sheet)
funshoku kessan: window dressing (of financial statements)
fusoku: addendum (to a law)
futekisei iken: adverse opinion (of the auditor)
fuzoku meisai-hyō: supporting schedules (part of the financial statements according to the Securities Exchange Law)

fuzoku meisai-sho: supporting schedules (part of the financial statements according to the Commercial Code)

gaibu kansa: external audit (by a certified public accountant)
gaishi-kei kigyō: foreign-capital affiliated company
gappei: merger
genkahō: cost method
genka shōkyaku: depreciation (in the balance sheet and the statement of income)
genkin-yokin: cash and deposit (in the balance sheet)
gentei iken: qualified opinion (by the auditor)
gentei-tsuki tekisei: fair with limitation (qualification of auditor's opinion)
gōmei kaisha: commercial partnership in which liability of the partners is unlimited (form of incorporation)
gōshi kaisha: limited partnership resembling commercial partnership except that it has both general and limited partners (form of incorporation)
gyaku funshoku kessan: window dressing in reverse (of financial statements)
gyōsei shidō: administrative guidance

hai-teku: high technology
hasan: adjudicated bankruptcy
hikiate-kin: allowance; reserve (under liabilities)
hiyō: expenses (in the statement of income)
hōjin: juridical entity
hōjin-zei shinkoku-sho: corporate income tax returns
hōjin-zei tō: corporate income taxes (in the statement of income)
honsha: holding company in prewar *zaibatsu*
Hōsei Shingikai: Legislation Deliberation Board (related to the Ministry of Justice)
hōtei junbi-kin: capital surplus and earned legal reserve (in the balance sheet)
hotoke tsukutte tamashii irezu: an image of the Buddha was made, but it has no soul

ichigō gentei: first-degree qualified opinion (of the auditor, for not conforming to accounting principles)
iken sashi-hikae: disclaimer of opinion (by the auditor)
in-kan: individual seal (in lieu of signature)

jigyōsha dantai: trade association
jiko-kabushiki: treasury stock (in the balance sheet)
jūgyō-in: employee
jūgyō-in azukari-kin: employee deposits (with his company)
juken shihon: authorized capital (in the balance sheet)
junbi-kin: reserve (under retained earnings)

kabunushi sōkai: shareholders' general meeting
kabushiki kaisha: joint stock company (form of incorporation)

Kabushiki Torihiki Jōrei: Stock Exchange Regulation
kaichō: chairman of the board of directors
kaikake-kin: accounts payable (in the balance sheet)
kaishime: collecting shares; cornering a market
kakaku hendō junbi-kin: price fluctuation reserve (in the balance sheet)
kanban: visible record; card (in the context of the just-in-time production system)
kankei-gaisha: related company
kankei-gaisha tōshi: investment in subsidiaries and affiliated companies (in the balance sheet)
Kanpō: *Official Gazette*
kanren-gaisha: affiliated company
kansa: audit
kansa hōjin: audit corporation
kansa-yaku: statutory auditor
kanzai-nin: receiver (in cases of corporate reorganization)
kari-ire-kin: loan (in the balance sheet)
kashi-daore hikiate-kin: allowance for doubtful accounts (in the balance sheet)
Keidanren: Japan Federation of Economic Organizations
keijō rieki: ordinary profit (in the statement of income)
keiretsu: alignment; postwar industrial grouping
keiri-bu: accounting department (in the corporate structure)
keiri-buchō: accounting department manager
Keirishi-hō: Registered Public Accountant Law
kenri: right (legal)
kenri-kin: lump-sum payment on lease or rent
kenshū: inspection (of delivered product)
kesson-gaisha: loss company (for tax purposes)
kifu-kin: donation (in the statement of income)
Kigyō Kaikei Shingikai: Business Accounting Deliberation Board (related to the Ministry of Finance)
kigyō keiretsu: postwar industrial grouping around some major enterprise
Kigyō-zaimu-ka: Corporate Finance Division (Ministry of Finance)
kimatsu teate: seasonal salary allowance, bonus (component of the salary system)
kin-yū keiretsu: postwar industrial grouping around some major bank
Kisai-kai: Bond Flotation Committee
kōbo: public offering of new shares
ko-gaisha: child company (subsidiary)
kōjō zaidan teitō: aggregate mortgage on all facilities of a given factory or plant (in balance sheet)
kōkoku: public notice (of the balance sheet and, for large companies, the statement of income)
kokusaika: internationalization (of Japanese business)
kōnin kaikeishi: certified public accountant (CPA)
Kōnin Kaikeishi-hō: Certified Public Accountant Law
kōri-gashi: loan shark

korogashi: rolling-over of promissory notes
kōsai-hi: entertainment expenses (in the statement of income)
kōsei: corporate reorganization (under court supervision)
kōshinjo: commercial inquiry agency
kōsoku yokin: compensating balance (with banks)
kōsoku yokin-gaku: amount of compensating balance

miharai hiyō: accrued liabilities (in the balance sheet)
mimoto hoshō-sho: letter signed by guarantors (in the context of hiring)
mochi-ai: cross, mutual shareholding
mu-gentei iken: unqualified opinion (of the auditor)

naibu ryūho: internal retention of earnings (in the balance sheet)
nai-fun: internal struggle (in the company)
nai-nai ni sumaseru: to be settled internally
nenkō chingin seido: seniority wage system
nigō gentei: second-degree qualified opinion (of the auditor, for financial statements not being consistent)
nin-i kansa: voluntary audit (as opposed to legally required audit)
nin-i tsumitate-kin: general, voluntary reserves (in the balance sheet)
nottori: management takeover

ōmune tekisei: almost fairly (auditor's opinion)
oyabike: withheld by parent (selective allocation of new shares)
oyabun-kobun: a simulation of father-son or parent-child relationship
oya-gaisha: parent company
oya-ko-gaisha: management takeover

renketsu nogare: transfer of a portion of the shares of a subsidiary (in the consolidation of financial statements)
renketsu zaimu-shohyō: consolidated financial statements
rieki junbi-kin: earned legal reserve (under the Commercial Code)
rieki no shobun matawa sonshitsu no shori ni kansuru gi-an: proposal for disposition of earnings (part of the financial statements according to the Commercial Code)
rieki shobun keiri: accounted for as appropriation of retained earnings (in the balance sheet and proposal of the disposition of earnings)
rishi: interest
rōdō kyōyaku: collective labor agreement

sai-hyōka tsumitate-kin: revaluation surplus account (in the balance sheet)
saiken hozen: loan for preservation of credit (in the context of corporate reorganization)
samurai: warrior-bureaucrat
sangō gentei: third-degree qualified opinion (of the auditor, for disclosure not being in full compliance with laws and regulations)

sekai kigyō: world enterprise (term proposed by *sōgō shōsha* for themselves)

setsu-zei: tax saving (deferral of income tax payment)

sha-ban: company seal (on official documents)

shachō: company president

shadan hōjin: incorporated association

sha-in: company member (as substitute for the term "employee")

shakuchi-ken: leasehold right

shiharai-bi: payment day for supplies

shiharai tegata: notes payable (in the balance sheet)

shihon junbi-kin: capital in excess of par value (in the balance sheet)

shihon-kin: issued, stated capital (in the balance sheet)

Shihon-shijō-ka: Capital Market Division (Ministry of Finance)

Shikin Unyō-bu: Trust Fund Bureau (Ministry of Finance)

shikon shōsai: spirit of the samurai and ability of the merchant

Shingikai: joint deliberation board

shita: below, inferior

shita-uke: subcontracting

shita-uke-gaisha: subcontracting company

Shōken Torihiki-hō: Securities Exchange Law

shōyo hikiate-kin: employee bonus allowance

shū-eki: revenue (in the statement of income)

shūgyō kisoku: rules of employment

shukkō: transfer of personnel

shuryoku ginkō: main bank

shūshin koyō: lifetime employment

sōgō shōsha: general trading company

sōkaiya: general-meeting specialist (in the context of the shareholders' general meeting)

son-eki: income and expenses

son-eki keisansho: income statement (part of the financial statements according to the Commercial Code)

sonkin keiri: accounted for as expense

taishaku taishō-hyō: balance sheet (part of the financial statements according to the Commercial Code)

taishoku-kin: retirement benefit (lump sum, component of the salary system)

taishoku kyūko hikiate-kin: allowance for employee retirement benefit (in the balance sheet)

taitō gappei: merger on equal footing

tana-oroshi shisan: inventories (in the balance sheet)

tanki kari-ire-kin: short-term loan (in the balance sheet)

tasuke-ai: helping each other

tegata: note

tokubetsu rieki: special income (in the statement of income)

tokubetsu shōkyaku: special depreciation (in the balance sheet and the statement of income)

tokushu hōjin: special juridical entity
torihiki: exchange
torihikisho-hō: exchange law
torishimariyaku-kai: board of directors (in the corporate structure)
tōroku kikan: registrar (for all share certificates)
tōsan: business failure (often translated as bankruptcy)
toshi ginkō: city bank
tōshi yūka shōken: investment securities (in the balance sheet)
tsumitate-kin: reserve (under retained earnings)

ue: above; superior
uketori tegata: notes receivable (in the balance sheet)
unten shikin: working capital (in the balance sheet)
uridashi: public offering of issued shares held by major shareholders
urikake-kin: accounts receivable (in the balance sheet)

wakon yōsai: Japanese spirit, Western techniques
waku: quota (of note discount)
warimashi shōkyaku: normal-plus-given-percentage depreciation (in the balance
    sheet and the statement of income)

yaku-in hōshū: remuneration of directors (in the supplementary documentation
    to the financial statements according to the Commercial Code)
yakusoku tegata: promissory note
yobi kabu-ken: reserve share certificate
yūgen kaisha: private corporation (form of incorporation)
yūka shōken hōkoku-sho: annual securities report according to the Securities
    Exchange Law, including financial statements and nonfinancial information
    such as shareholders, outline of business operations, etc.

zaibatsu: prewar form of industrial grouping around a holding company
zaimu-bu: finance department (in the corporate structure)
zaimu-buchō: finance department manager
zaimu shohyō: financial statements (balance sheet, income statement, and pro-
    posal for the disposition of earnings to be approved by the shareholders' meet-
    ing, according to the Commercial Code)
Zaimu Shohyō Kisoku: regulation concerning financial statements according to
    the Securities Exchange Law
zai-teku: financial technology (journalistic term coined in the mid-1980s)
zeirishi: tax agent
Zeirishi-hō: Tax Agent Law

INDEX

Numbers in italics refer to substantive discussions in the text.